UNIVERSITY OF WISCONSIN-MADISON
COLLEGE OF ENGINEERING
OFFICE OF THE DEAN
1415 JOHNSON DRIVE
MADISON, WI 53706-1691

Handbook of Quality Tools:
THE JAPANESE APPROACH

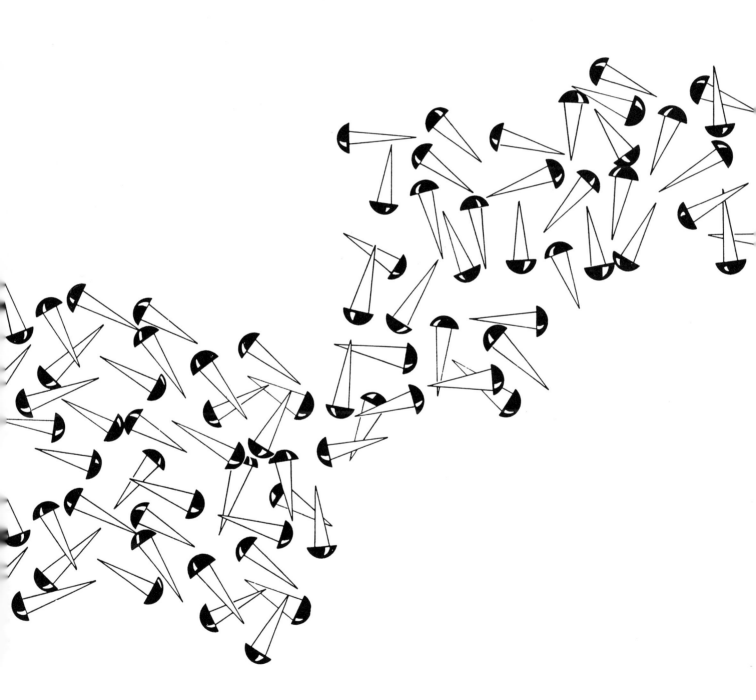

Handbook of Quality Tools

THE JAPANESE APPROACH

Tetsuichi Asaka
General Editor

Kazuo Ozeki
Editor

Publisher's Forward by Norman Bodek,
President, Productivity, Inc.

Productivity Press
Cambridge, Massachusetts
Norwalk, Connecticut

Originally published as *Genbacho no tameno QC Hikkei* copyright © 1988 by Japanese Standards Association, Tokyo.

Editors: Tetsuichi Asaka, Professor Emeritus, Tokyo Univeristy (General Editor); Kazuo Ozeki, Director, Education Department, Nippon Seiko (Editor-in-Chief); Rikio Chiba, Director of QC Promotion Section, Hino Jidosha; Tatsuo Nakamura, General Manager, Seiko Denshi Kogyo

English translation copyright © 1990 by Productivity Press, Inc.

Productivity Press, Inc.
P.O. Box 3007
Cambridge, MA 02140
(617) 497-5146

Library of Congress Catalog Card Number: 89-43211
ISBN: 0-915299-45-3

Book design by Joyce C. Weston
Typeset by Rudra Press, Cambridge, MA
Printed and bound by the Courier Book Companies
Printed in the United States of America

Library of Congress Cataloging-in-Publication Data

Genbacho no tame QC hikkei. English.
    Handbook of quality tools, the Japanese approach/Tetsuichi Asaka, general editor; Kazuo Ozeki, editor.
        p. cm.
    Translation of: Genbacho no tame no QC hikkei.
    ISBN 0-915299-45-3
    1. Quality control — Japan. 2. Production management — Japan.
I. Asaka, Tetsuichi, 1914 -   . II. Ozeki, Kazuo, 1947 -
III. Title.
TS156.G46   1990   658.5'62—dc20

10 9 8 7 6 5 4

Contents

Part II: Tools

Publisher's Foreword

What is Quality? It means delivering products and services that 1) meet customer standards, 2) meet and fulfill customer needs, 3) meet customer expectations, and 4) will meet unanticipated future needs and aspirations. The issue of quality is no longer plus-or-minus 3 percent. It is no longer something the customer "would like to have." It is now expected — 100 percent of the time. Period.

The *Handbook of Quality Tools* comes from Japan. The amazing quality levels in many Japanese plants — measured in parts per million — don't come from running fancy automated equipment. They come from each person in the workplace knowing and applying quality improvement methods, every day.

Every organization that makes and sells products is facing enormous international competition today. In this challenging time, quality is the major key to a successful business. More and more companies are applying the principles of Total Quality Control (TQC), a company-wide strategy for producing the quality customers want in products.

One element of TQC involves managers and staff in planning and quality function deployment. The other major part is involving the work force in the process of improving and standardizing quality. This book provides tools for the people who are the crucial interface between the two parts — the foremen, group leaders, supervisors, QC circle leaders, trainers, quality managers, and many other "quality leaders" charged with turning quality planning into product quality.

In the 1980s, Deming, Juran, Crosby, and other quality gurus gave us the awareness of quality as *the* competitive edge. In 1989, 25,000 applications were mailed out for the Baldrige Prize. The awareness is there now. We need the tools to put it into action.

Quality leaders need skill in leadership and people management as well as in use of the tools needed to produce quality. Part I of the book offers a discussion of the management aspects, including the leadership role, quality function deployment, process control, operating standards, and small group improvement activities.

Part II, "Tools," is seventeen chapters on data collection and quality control methods. These include the seven basic QC tools and five new QC tools. Through step-by-step illustrated examples using sample data, this book provides training in techniques that will enable people in the workplace to participate and make a difference in the quality of their product. Here is a book managers and quality leaders can use to actually do it. Ideal for use with quality methods training courses, it provides guidance and instruction, in simple, concrete language, for a powerful set of tools.

We are pleased to present to you a book originally produced by the Japanese Standards Association, the organization responsible for the Japanese Industrial Standards (JIS), which are an international benchmark for quality control standards. Dr. Asaka, Mr. Ozeki, and their coauthors know their subject and have created a clear and practical presentation so that readers of all levels can learn to use these tools. We hope you will reap the benefits from using it widely throughout your company.

We would like to express our appreciation to Mr. Masao Takeshita of the Japanese Standards Association for his assistance in clarifying the translation. This book was translated by David Cowhig. Karen Jones was project editor, with the assistance of Marianne L'Abbate, Elizabeth Sutherland, Carla Reissman, and Barry Shulak. Elizabeth Sutherland created the index. Thanks to Esme McTighe and David Lennon for production management, to Joyce Weston for the book and cover design, and to the staff of Rudra Press for typesetting and artwork.

Norman Bodek
President
Productivity, Inc.

TQC enables the section head to understand the actual situation in the workplace and then to report it correctly to the department head so that he or she will understand the situation of the department. TQC helps everyone — from the CEO on down — solve the company's problems. Company performance improves as TQC is introduced and promoted throughout the company.

The bottom line is that to solve important problems in the workplace, the section chief must understand what is actually going on in the workplace. This person must know:

1. Is everyone in the workplace concerned with improving quality and making improvements? The following questions will help determine whether this is the case:
   - Is the equipment well maintained?
   - Is the accuracy of the equipment maintained properly to produce the expected quality?
   - Have workers been trained in the skills they need to operate the equipment properly?
   - Is there an operations summary book?
   - Has each person mastered the operations in the summary books?
   - Is there big variation in the quality of work performed by different work groups?
   - Is there variation between work groups in their enthusiasm for their work?
   - Is each employee actively involved in solving problems?
   - Are graphs and control charts used?
   - Is a statistical control method being used?

   The section head must be able to form judgments on many different aspects of plant operations to respond correctly to questions when discussing quality improvement with assistant section managers, staff, and foremen.

2. Should the section head set more ambitious goals for cost reduction?
   - What is done about waste, losses, and irrationalities in the production process?
   - Have the most important sources of waste been identified?
   - Are you trying to cut losses in half instead of eliminating loss?
   - Do the assistant managers, foremen, and team leaders realize the benefits of cutting the defect rate in half? This eliminates material losses and adjustments, increases process capacity, and reduces overtime and holiday work. This considerably reduces overall costs.
   - Have all assistant managers and foremen learned how to apply basic QC methods?
   - Are efforts being made to apply the philosophy and methods of QC at the department head level and below?
   - Study how to apply these methods sensibly in daily management. It is essential to gradually learn the QC way of thinking about problems.
   - Memorizing QC methods is not enough. You must learn QC methods and approaches by applying them in practice.
   - Learning about QC never ends.
3. Are QC methods being applied in the workplace?
   - Is the work approached with an awareness of potential problems? Are problem-solving steps kept in mind when the work is organized?
   - Does everyone participate? Is work organized in a way that encourages everyone's creativity?
   - To accomplish the group's objectives, it is important to read books that are practical and easy to understand and that present lessons that can be applied in the workplace.

It is essential to approach your task with potential problems in mind, using QC methods to solve these problems. If assistant managers, staff, and foremen adapt QC to the needs of the workplace and make the QC approach their own, they will be able to improve the work of the section, to the benefit of the entire company.

Kazuo Ozeki, Rikio Chiba, and Tatsuo Nakamura are highly experienced and accomplished authors who have produced this very useful book. Readers will appreciate the value of this book once they have read it, and understood and mastered the material.

Tetsuichi Asaka
General Editor

Preface

Many books have been published to explain quality control and statistical methods. We have written a book that responds to the desires we hear expressed from time to time for a convenient handbook for foremen.

Foreman who have learned the basic philosophy and methods of QC often find that when the time comes to put QC into practice they have forgotten a formula or the key points of a procedure, or are confused by one issue or another. In these situations, a handbook that can answer most of their questions is very useful. This is the sort of book you want to have at your side to consult rapidly when a problem arises.

This book was primarily intended for the manufacturing sector, and particularly for field work in the construction and transportation industries. It was written and edited with shop floor leadership in mind — supervisors in the line departments, assistant managers in the manufacturing and field sectors, foremen, team leaders, and other group leaders. The content is derived from materials presented in the Quality Control Seminar for Foremen taught by Tokyo University Professor Emeritus Tetsuichi Asaka. This course, sponsored by the Japanese Standards Association, has been held continuously since 1962. The scope of the materials has been broadened somewhat with the introduction of new methods.

The book has two main parts, Part I (Management) and Part II (Tools). The Management section summarizes essential material on the role of the foreman, how to carry out improvements, process control, standardizing operations, leadership, group activities, and so on. The Tools section summarizes the "seven QC tools" (graphs, Pareto diagrams, cause-and-effect diagrams, check sheets, histograms, control charts, and scatter diagrams) as well as five of the "seven new QC tools," useful strategy methods on the floor or in the field (affinity diagrams, relations diagrams, systematic diagrams, matrix diagrams, and arrow diagrams). The layout of the Tools section — procedures and formulas on the left, examples on the right — is designed to make the material easier to understand.

As a lecturer in the Quality Control Seminar for Foremen, I had the benefit of guidance from two experts at practical work in the field, Rikio Chiba and Tatsuo Nakamura. From the first drafts of this book to several late-night conferences during its final revisions, we have striven to create a book at once rich in content and compact in format.

At the end of this book you will find the 35-year history of quality control in Japan, a chronology, and slogans for quality control months. The different slogans through the years tell the story of quality control in Japan. We stress that changes in the international and economic environments have created a strong demand for new technology, the development of new products, and guarantees of high quality and high reliability. The motto of TQC can be summed up as "Quality comes first." We will be pleased if this book contributes in some small way to making work on the floor or in the field better and to improving company organization.

We want to express our deep gratitude to Professor Tetsuichi Asaka for his work as General Editor. This book, which took three years from planning to publication, was published with the perseverance and energy of Mitsugi Izumi, director of the Publications Department of the Japanese Standards Association, as well as of Masao Takeshita and Yoshiko Mike, also of the Publications Department. To all these people we express our sincere thanks.

For the editors and authors
Kazuo Ozeki

I

Management

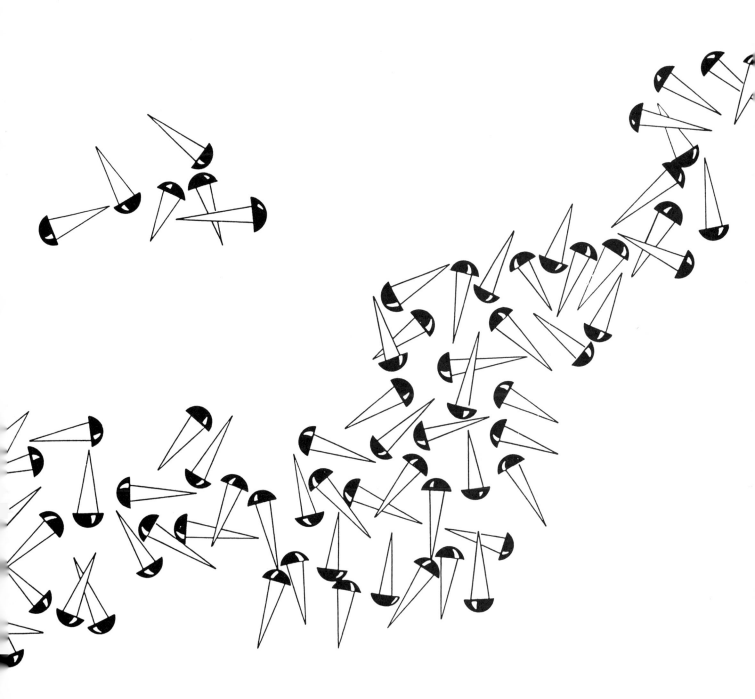

Essentials of Quality Control

Japanese Industrial Standard JIS Z 8101-1981, "Glossary of Terms Used in Quality Control," defines quality control (QC) as a system of techniques for economically producing goods and services that meet the customer's requirements.*

To effectively implement quality control there must be collaboration among all phases of the business activities, including market surveys, research and development, product planning and design, design of the manufacturing process, purchasing, subcontracting, manufacturing, inspection, sales, and customer service, as well as financial, personnel, and educational activities. Every person in the company must be involved, from top management to supervisors and production workers. This comprehensive implementation of quality control is called company-wide quality control (CWQC) or total quality control (TQC).

From SQC to TQC

Statistical quality control (SQC) is a branch of quality control based on statistical methods. It was introduced in Japan after World War II by U.S. quality experts Dr. W.E. Deming and Dr. J.M. Juran. As SQC caught on and became more popular, Japanese companies incorporated it into a wider range of activities and developed it further. They created systems in which exclusive responsibility for quality control was taken from management and staff and replaced with company-wide, comprehensive TQC programs in which every employee had a role.

---

* The JIS definitions in this section are from original Japanese (translated) quoted in the original edition of this book, rather than from the English version of JIS Z 8101-1981. — Ed.

QC circle programs, begun in Japan in 1962 as operator-run quality improvement activities, originally stressed the role of top management. The introduction of reliability technology into technical departments renewed the effort to build a quality assurance system that started in the new-product development stage. This brought about the organization of a cooperative system involving everyone from management to operators; integrating the technical, executive, and manufacturing divisions. This grew into the organized company-wide TQC activities in use today.

What Is Quality?

Japanese Industrial Standard JIS Z 8101-1981 defines quality as the totality of the characteristics or performance that can be used to determine whether or not a product or service fulfills its intended application. A remark that accompanies the definition states that when determining whether a product or service fulfills its application, the effect of that product or service on society must also be considered.

A second remark defines quality characteristics, the elements of which quality is composed. The quality characteristics of a fluorescent lamp, for example, include power consumption, diameter, length, shape and measurements of the base, start-up time, lumen maintenance, strength of adhesion to base, color of light source, and external appearance.

Design Quality Goals and Manufacturing Quality

Design quality goals (also known as "quality goals") are the quality objectives set for the process of manufacturing a designed product. Manufacturing quality (also known as "quality results") measures how well manufactured products fulfill the design quality goals. Standard values for quality characteristics are provided in product specifications. Blueprints show specifically what is meant by a "good product." Manufacturing quality shows to what extent the resulting product meets the goals of design quality. Although manufacturing quality must be improved by managing the manufacturing process, design quality must also be adjusted to meet customer requirements. No matter how high the quality result of a product, quality control objectives have not been met if the product does not fill essential customer requirements.

Quality Reliability

Product quality is evaluated on the basis of whether or not the product carries out its intended functions. The extent to which a product or service meets the requirements of the user is called its fitness for use. Product quality is not merely the proper performance of its functions at the time of shipment or at the time of purchase, but rather its continued, trouble-free operation in a specified environment beyond a specified period of time. The degree of stability over time of the system, machines, components, and so on, is called reliability. The probability that a function will continue to be performed is the reliability factor. Quality assurance depends on maintaining the reliability of these functions.

Quality and the Effect of the Product on Society

With mass production and mass consumption come an increase in products' effects on society. Pollution, waste, and the need to recycle resources have made quality problems an increasingly important part of a company's responsibilities to society. Product safety must be ensured to prevent accidents caused by defective products. The manufacturer and retailer of a product are responsible for "product liability" — damages for injuries users or third parties suffer from defective products. Businesses must prevent these injuries.

Consumer-oriented Quality

A business should be consumer-oriented in its efforts to create and then satisfy demand. Even if a company sets a goal of improving consumer safety and quality of life and understands consumers' quality requirements, its products still must meet these requirements or it will not be able to sell its products. Business must change its fundamental philosophy from getting products out the door to making products that will get into the market.

After quality, consumers tend to look for variety. Since the market demands ever higher levels of quality, businesses must always be developing new products. Of course, this means adjusting to technical advances and higher quality standards as they develop new products.

Quality of Services

We can compare the "hard" quality of products with the "soft" quality of services. Both hard and soft qualities are intended to satisfy certain functions. The quality of many types of services is a proper object of quality control. These include direct product servicing and customer education to prevent the misuse or willful abuse of a product, as well as services provided by service businesses such as information communications, distribution, and so on.

Companies today are learning to use the concept of "quality of work" to express the capabilities and roles of the executive, personnel, computer, and other nonproduction sections. Better management plans and organized activities aimed at making companies more prosperous are continually being developed.

What Is Management?

The Management Cycle: PDCA

Management in the broad sense is planning and implementing controls for organized activities to meet company objectives in a rational and efficient manner. Quality control boils down to a four-step cycle known as PDCA:

1. *Plan:* Determine your goals and make a plan to achieve those goals.
2. *Do:* Implement your plan.
3. *Check:* Evaluate the results of your plan.
4. *Action:* Take the necessary action.

Figure 1-1 shows the PDCA management cycle. The four procedures shown in the circle are the "management cycle." Performing this cycle is sometimes called "going around the PDCA circle" or "doing PDCA." (See Chapter 4 for more about this cycle.)

Figure 1-1: **Management Cycle**

Reality-based Management

The reality-based management methods of quality control are characteristics of modern scientific management: grasping the situation through data that reflects reality, examining relationships between cause and effect, analyzing processes using statistical methods, using data to evaluate the effectiveness of improvements, as well as using data to evaluate the effectiveness of maintenance management.

Gathering data that enables you accurately and objectively to grasp facts related to your company's goals is an important part of making sound business decisions. Accordingly, the manager must accurately report information on the situation, design and revise plans based on the facts, rapidly take appropriate action, and improve the organization of data reporting on items that need to be controlled.

Maintenance Management and Making Improvements

Maintenance management, at its current stage of technical development, aims at determining the cause of the defect(s) and devising measures for preventing recurrences, as well as making on-the-spot emergency repairs. When a defect occurs, recurrence prevention measures reduce the extent of the damage and help maintain a stable state.

Once a goal for achieving a higher level of quality has been set, incremental improvements are made in the current condition by solving problems one by one. A satisfactorily stable condition means no problems can be discovered and no worthwhile improvements can be made in the condition of the product — optimal conditions have been achieved. Bear in mind that even if your improvements take a great deal of effort, neglecting to standardize the maintenance management for your improvements and preventing its deterioration will lead you to lose everything you have gained.

Technical progress in maintenance management has its own cycle that must be followed: maintenance management —> improvements —> maintenance management —> improvements, and so on. See Figure 1-2.

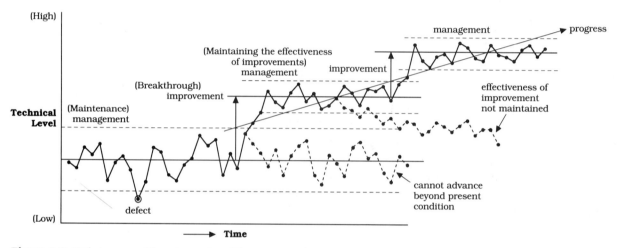

Figure 1-2: **Maintenance Management and Improvements**

Addressing the Root Cause of the Problem

"Putting your finger on the problem" is one of the basic imperatives of quality control. You can carry out a repair procedure that eliminates the current phenomenon, even if you do not know its cause. It is more advantageous however, to determine the root cause of the problem and to carry out a repair strategy that eliminates it.

Although you can prevent the recurrence of one problem, it is also important to discuss how its causes create rejects and defects in similar products and processes. This can prevent the appearance of defects that have not yet manifested themselves. In particular, when a long run of positive results has been obtained, you should determine what set of conditions produced these excellent results. Your investigation will help you with improvements you can make in similar products or processes.

Design surveys during product development are used to anticipate similar problems and defects and to devise methods for preventing them. The problem can be taken back to the planning stage in the department from which it originated. The design and plans for the product are examined and the reliability of product quality is improved.

Promoting Company-wide Quality Control

Successful promotion of quality control in a company requires the participation of everyone, from the CEO to hourly workers. If QC is to be effective, all departments must participate, including executive, research and development, planning, production technology, purchasing, inspection, management, and personnel. Total quality control (TQC) is a quality control program that organizes all company personnel and all company departments in the quality control effort. Quality assurance should be implemented at each stage. Every department should improve its management and operations for TQC to be promoted properly company-wide. This means that at each step in the process, from information, surveys, research and development, planning, design and prototyping, preparation for manufacturing, purchasing, subcontracting, manufacturing, inspection, transportation, and storage all the way to service, a change in outlook based on integrated quality assurance guidelines for quality of "things" and quality of "work" is essential.

Moreover, functions related to quality control (such as quality evaluation, reliability testing, quality surveys, standardization, equipment management, instrumentation management, cost management, production schedule control, education and training, product liability prevention, QC system surveys, and management of operators' small-group improvement activities) are managed as separate functions. Promotion of QC activities should reflect company-wide collaboration and cooperation among the departments required to achieve the overall goal.

References

"Japanese Industrial Standard JIS Z 8101-1981: Glossary of Terms Used in Quality Control." Japanese Standards Association.

Quality Control Fundamentals: Seminar Text for Responsible Persons for Promotion of Industrial Standardization and Quality Control. Japanese Standards Association, 1984.

2

The Role of
the Foreman

What Is a Foreman?

Manufacturing products is the central function of a
company that manufactures, sells, and services products
in response to the demand of the marketplace. Manufacturing is the source of the company's profits.

The foreman is the person on the front line of manufacturing who directs and supervises employees. In the
broader sense, a foreman may also be the front-line
person who directs and supervises employees in a distribution, sales, or services company. The title of this role
may be foreman, supervisor, group leader, factory manager, director, section head, shopkeeper, chief, or another
designation, depending on the type of business and
occupational category. Although many of the methods
presented here can be applied in service or office settings,
this book is concerned mainly with the foreman as the
front-line supervisor in a workplace where a product is
manufactured.

Basic Duties of the Foreman

The basic duties of the foreman are to direct and supervise employees on the front line of production so that the
plans and goals of the company will be achieved. Thus the
foreman, using materials and machinery, directs and
supervises employees to achieve the quality (Q), cost (C),
delivery (D), and goals and plans for the product. The
foreman performs the duties of managing and training
employees, improving work procedures, collaborating
with colleagues, and assisting superiors. (See Figure 2-1.)

Quality is composed of characteristics. If the quality of
a component or product is unsatisfactory, the product
may be referred to as bad, not made to specification, or

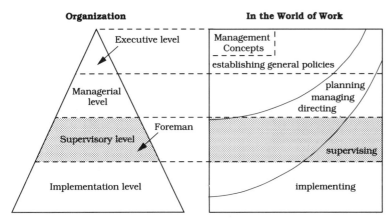

Figure 2-1: **Role of the Foreman**

defective. The quality of products mass-produced in lot quantities is evaluated using mean values and standard deviations, or defect rate and number of defects in a given lot quantity. These concepts are explained in more detail in Chapters 16 through 18.

Cost is the expense of manufacturing one component or product. Achieving the target cost goal is important given today's intense price competition. Increasing costs of losses due to claims processing and disposal of defective products reduce profits.

Delivery, a "secondary process," is the time limit for sending and delivering a product to the customer. Management wants to ensure timely deliveries because of market competition. Moreover, late delivery often coincides with quality problems, which can lead to claims. Handling delay results in loss of customer confidence and higher costs.

Thus, Q, C, and D are production targets based on customer requirements for components and products. Considered as management items, they are actually a single objective with three rhythms. Managers must know how to harmonize Q, C, and D.

Managing Work

1. Design a plan
   - Use 5W1H to make a plan:
     WHAT (subject)
     WHY (objective)
     WHEN (date and time)
     WHO (person)
     WHERE (place)
     HOW (method)
   - Understand the actual situation thoroughly to plan more effectively. It is important to practice "management at the source" every day. The foreman goes to the source to understand conditions better at the source, and then makes the proper decision at the source. He or she uses the seven tools of quality control to help understand the situation thoroughly, clearly identify the objective, and design a plan suitable for achieving that objective.
2. Consider talents and needs when allocating personnel
   - Choose people and allocate tasks based on knowledge, skills, attitudes, abilities, and human relations.
   - People's interest in and concern about their work, particularly their enthusiasm, is an important factor to consider when assigning tasks.
3. Give clear directions
   - Carry out every detail of the 5W1H plan.
   - Use instruction manuals, production planning and preparation manuals, work standards manuals, and other written materials as much as possible to minimize errors.
   - Make sure directives are repeated and properly understood.
4. Make necessary adjustments
   - Make adjustments with your managers to achieve the plan (for example, improving the quality of the components' preprocessing, strictly observing delivery times, making sure that the project stays within the budget, etc.).
5. Make inspections to ensure quality
   - Inspect the quality of workmanship based on product specifications and samples.

- Confirm that the cost and product quantities specified in objectives and instructions are being achieved.
- Check the current fulfillment status of the daily plan.

6. Think about the next plan
- On the basis of inspection results, determine if there are problems in the layout of the workplace or in methods for determining standards. Draw up a list of problems to be solved.
- When considering the fulfillment status of an inadequate plan, attack the root of the problem.

The Concerns of the Foreman

The foreman must treat the workplace as a family unit, and must sometimes be as stern or as gentle as a parent. An important part of a foreman's job is showing the workers he or she cares about the situation and is working hard to improve it.

1. Always inspect the workplace properly. Strive to discover problems and to make improvements.*
2. Understand the capabilities of your employees. Guide and train them to the full extent of their abilties.*
3. Be broad-minded. Use your discrimination and make correct judgments.*
4. Establish good human relations and strive to make the atmosphere as conducive to efficient work as possible.
5. Have an affectionate attitude toward your employees and demonstrate your concern for them.
6. Understand your work thoroughly and strive to become outstanding in all its technical aspects.
7. Pass on what you have learned to your employees.
8. Lead by taking the initiative and setting an example.
9. Use your authority to carry out what you want to achieve.
10. Encourage employees to work autonomously and creatively and to make improvements.

---

* Tetsuichi Asaka, *Fundamentals of TQC* (Japanese Standards Association, 1983), 111.

MANAGEMENT POINTS FOR THE FOREMAN

The foreman instructs and supervises employees to ensure that the work will be carried out smoothly and according to plan, and that no problems or difficulties will arise. He or she is especially concerned with improvement activities that will save time and fulfill targets for higher volume and lower expenses. The foreman should concentrate on the management of daily work and increasing the effectiveness of improvement activities.

Management Philosophy Guidelines

- Carry out completely the work standards, the established procedure, and the work plan.
- Pick out the positive points as well as the problems in the work and operations of employees.
- Discover problems by looking for deviation of actual values from the plan or target values.
- Clarify the measurement of the six basic management elements (Quality, Cost, Delivery, Productivity, Safety, Morale) to grasp problems.
- Find the cause of problems and make improvements.
- Focus on managing the elements of the causal system — materials, machinery and equipment, methods, and operators — and make improvements there.
- Compare your targets with those of other workplaces and other companies to raise them and then make improvements.

Measurement of the Six Management Elements

- *Quality* (Q): Factors that affect the rate of production of products and components; the defect rate for different processes; the number of defects that occur during different operations; vibration in work platforms or machinery; as well as noise, temperature, humidity, and litter in the workplace.
- *Cost* (C): The success rate for meeting targets for cost reduction on individual components, and the difference between the workplace budget and actual expenses.

- *Delivery* (D): Deliveries within the established delivery period and changes in the inventory of individual components at the workplace.
- *Productivity* (P): The number of units produced daily per person and the value of hourly production.
- *Safety* (S): The number of accidents that occur, the length of continuous accident-free operation, the number of "near-misses," the number of days lost due to injury, and the number of pollution prevention warnings with respect to the workplace.
- *Morale* (M): Absentee rate, the diligence of each employee, and the number of improvements suggested per individual.

POSITIVE HUMAN RELATIONS IN THE WORKPLACE

Everything Depends on Working Together

Everyone in the workplace should perform their tasks cheerfully, feel positive about their fellow workers, and take the initiative in performing their tasks. A workplace that does this will have high Q, C, D results. Foremen should have this kind of workplace in mind.

A foreman should treat people as individuals, however, each with a unique perspective. If individual differences are overlooked, conflicts arising from disagreements among the employees or between the foreman and employees will make it impossible to create a productive workplace.

The foreman should understand that successful work depends on the establishment of positive human relations. Positive human relations do not arise naturally; the foreman must work at creating and maintaining them.

Points for Building Positive Human Relations

1. The foreman should strive to earn the trust of employees. Respecting the humanity of each individual is fundamental.
   - Act fairly.
   - Keep your promises.
   - Do not deceive people.

- Act courteously.
- Let your hair down with the workers now and then.
2. Strive to understand the personalities of your employees.
   - Be concerned about your employees.
   - Call workers by their names.
   - Share activities with them (parties, sports, etc.).
3. Talk with your subordinates. Keep communications open.
   - Encourage them when they fail or are disheartened.
   - Listen to them when they are angry or dissatisfied.
   - Give suggestions in conversation when difficulties arise.
   - Praise openly when praise should be given and criticize when criticism is appropriate.
   - Explain clearly what you expect.
   - Discuss with employees what improvements should be made.
   - Discuss your own experiences.
   - Follow up on the results of conversations with subordinates.

RESPONDING TO CHANGE

Japan is going through great changes as it moves toward the twenty-first century. The privatization of the national telephone and railroad companies, tax reform, education reform, and industrial restructuring have transformed the business environment. Companies in the United States are likewise challenged by deregulation of major industries and new technologies. A foreman who ignores these changes cannot lead effectively. Changes in industrial structure and the effect of internationalization have completely altered occupational categories within companies. If the foreman cannot reorganize and reassign employees to different tasks, and change his or her own thinking and that of the workers, the company will not be able to respond to these changes. Essential points for responding to changes are:

1. Understand well the great changes that are taking place in the world.

- Be acquainted with changes in politics, economics, and society. *Examples:* Tokyo is becoming the financial capital of the world; advances by the developing countries have made it impossible for Japan to compete with them for some products on the basis of cost (TVs, radios, watches, etc.).
- Be acquainted with management measures adopted to adjust to these changes. *Example:* Business policy, business strategy, statements of the CEO, and so on.
- Be aware of changes in daily life. *Examples:* Examine trendy shopping areas for products and styles; watch television programs for young people.

2. Understand the effect of these changes on your workplace and respond to them.
   - Understand company policies such as changes in working conditions, transfers, and the merit system. *Example:* Changing from the seniority system to evaluating personnel on the basis of merit; transfers from the manufacturing department to the executive department.
   - First change your own thinking and behavior. *Examples:* get to work earlier; master the word processor and the personal computer.
   - Exchange views with colleagues and people in other workplaces. *Examples:* hold a foreman's study group every Monday evening; talk with section heads and foremen from other companies.

3. Learn new technologies and new skills in response to changes in the job.
   - Be aware of changes in the way the work is done. *Examples:* A semiconductor plant adds a night shift; as the assembly process shifts from manual to robot assembly, the process is controlled from a control board.
   - Be aware of changes in processing methods with the introduction of new materials. *Examples:* With the switch from aluminum to plastics, processing methods changed from die cast processing to extrusion molding; as the composition of components changes from copper to plastics, welding is replaced by adhesive bonds.

CHANGING THE WORKPLACE CULTURE

A workplace develops its own distinctive behavior and work patterns over the years. The actions and attitudes of operators, leaders, or supervisors when a problem arises; the reaction of employees to a difficult assignment; and particularly the daily work attitudes and courtesies express the unique behavior patterns of a workplace. These patterns are often called the "workplace culture" or "organizational culture." Foremen must not neglect this workplace culture that is essential to achieving the targets of Q, C, and D. The workplace culture can make the difference between a lack of cooperation for common goals and employees bending over backward to meet a delivery schedule.

The Need for Reform

As corporate competition becomes more intense, sales, productivity, and other objectives have been raised. Foremen have increasing responsibility for attaining these objectives. These problems must be handled by a small group of people who understand various aspects of the situation. The results must be evaluated rigorously.

As companies carry out management policies developed in response to changes in the business environment or in relationships with competitors, a workplace culture once considered positive can become an obstacle. For example, a company that has emphasized human relations without rationalizing how it does the work will not be able to discover root causes of its problems and prevent their recurrence. Over time, this situation will make a company uncompetitive. Accordingly, a foreman who neglects the balance of the workplace culture is not fulfilling his or her responsibilities.

Workplace Culture Reform Points

Workplace culture reform points are solutions to problems in the way employees approach the work. Consider the following:

1. Customs are changed by changing organizations and systems. An example is evaluating people by merit and not promoting them according to seniority.

2. Find the root causes of problems that arise in the workplace. By solving the root cause, a problematic aspect of a specific custom can be changed.

3. When a foreman decides to reform the workplace culture, the problem should be attacked vigorously. Use the Workplace Culture Analysis Sheet in Figure 2-2 to understand the situation and decide which changes you want to make.

4. Many workplace customs are formed by the foreman's own philosophy and actions. The foreman should look at points 2 and 3 and decide if there are any problems for which he or she is responsible. If so, it is important that the foreman change his or her philosophy and actions to enlighten the workers and improve the workplace.

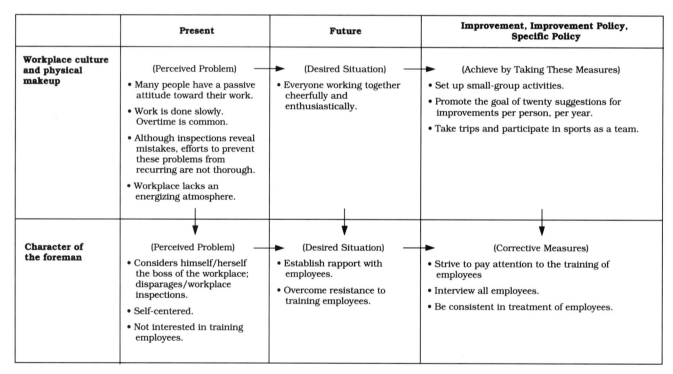

	Present	**Future**	**Improvement, Improvement Policy, Specific Policy**
Workplace culture and physical makeup	(Perceived Problem) • Many people have a passive attitude toward their work. • Work is done slowly. Overtime is common. • Although inspections reveal mistakes, efforts to prevent these problems from recurring are not thorough. • Workplace lacks an energizing atmosphere.	(Desired Situation) • Everyone working together cheerfully and enthusiastically.	(Achieve by Taking These Measures) • Set up small-group activities. • Promote the goal of twenty suggestions for improvements per person, per year. • Take trips and participate in sports as a team.
Character of the foreman	(Perceived Problem) • Considers himself/herself the boss of the workplace; disparages/workplace inspections. • Self-centered. • Not interested in training employees.	(Desired Situation) • Establish rapport with employees. • Overcome resistance to training employees.	(Corrective Measures) • Strive to pay attention to the training of employees • Interview all employees. • Be consistent in treatment of employees.

Figure 2-2: **Workplace Culture Analysis Sheet (Example)**

The appropriate procedure to adopt will depend on the foreman's judgment of the situation. Strong determination and leadership are essential to the reform of the workplace culture.

Education and Training

The foreman, while striving to improve his or her own understanding and technical level, should carry out a plan for training the workers as well. Elements of such a plan include:

1. Replacing old with new technology and skills, in accordance with company policy when beginning a new activity.
2. Upgrading the level of workers' knowledge and skills to achieve high Q, C, and D objectives.
3. Stimulating employees' desire and requests for education and training programs by harnessing their interest in advancement, promotion, and improved standard of living.

On-the-job training (OJT), off-the-job training, and independent study are the basic methods of education and training. From the standpoint of personnel training, there should be a lifetime training program and objectives for each individual. The achievement of these objectives depends on a planned job rotation system and creating an atmosphere favorable to education.* The foreman could encourage employees to achieve specific goals, for example, obtaining national certification in existing technologies and skills used widely in the industry.

OJT (On-the-job training): Training employees through their work is the most effective and most important training method. The foreman is always responsible for training his or her employees in a planned manner. The essentials of OJT are:

---

* Although not universally accepted in the United States, job rotation and cross-training are the norm in many Japanese factories. — Ed.

1. Strive to find ways to perform duties and work that need to be done.
2. Help workers reach their independent study goals.
3. If workers are learning off the job, assign tasks related to what they are learning.
4. Take the initiative in showing employees how the work is to be done.
5. Strive to create opportunities for employees to join study groups, participate in meetings, and take business trips.
6. See that employees have successful experiences. If they sometimes fail, see that they understand what they can learn from the failure.

Off-the-job training: Employees spend this time away from their duties, entirely devoted to group study and training.   During off-the-job training, employees are stimulated by their contact with people from other workplaces and companies. This experience strongly motivates them to pursue independent study.

The education department of the company can help the foreman develop an education plan for workers. It also presents lectures and workshops by outside experts in workplace subjects.

Independent study: Many opportunities exist today for independent study and self-improvement. These include books, magazines, videocassettes, audiotapes, and correspondence courses on work-related subjects. Conferences and study groups involving people from outside the company stimulate independent study.

BOOSTING CREATIVITY AND THE DESIRE TO IMPROVE

Work is necessary, of course, to make a living; however, creative work is essential to making life worth living. This kind of work needs dedicated people. Transforming the everyday mechanical grind of work into self-directed, creative work makes life worth living and work worth doing. Doing this kind of work makes people feel they are growing as human beings.

The foreman's methods and coaching play an important role in motivating employees to work autonomously and make improvements in their own work.

1. Bringing an improvement theme into the business plan
   - The daily activities plan focuses on the improvement theme.
   - The foreman sets the theme for workplace improvement proposal activities.
   - The foreman passes problems along to QC team leaders for the team to work on.
2. Working toward the company improvement proposal objective
   - Select an improvement proposal objective that the workplace can achieve.
   - Graph the number of suggestions offered by each person to spur friendly competition.
   - Give awards to encourage workers, such as prizes for the best proposal and for the most proposals.
3. Fostering and supporting QC circles
   - Get everyone in the QC circle involved in the improvement theme rather than trying to solve the problem by yourself.
   - By helping each other understand the problem better, everyone will get a feeling of having accomplished something.
   - Someone who has presented a theme at a QC circle conference will take up the next improvement with greater enthusiasm.
   - Stimulate the QC circle through exchanges with QC circles in other companies and in other departments.
   - The foreman should encourage the QC circle by participating in and working with it to solve a problem and offering his or her views to the group.

Quality Assurance On-site

Japanese Industrial Standard JIS Z 8101-1981 defines quality assurance as systematic activities undertaken by manufacturers to assure that the quality of a product completely satisfies the requirements of the consumer. The foreman can understand and implement this definition of quality assurance in the following manner:

1. What degree of quality does the consumer demand? The kinds of quality and standards demanded by consumers vary over time. The foreman must understand what these quality characteristics are to ensure quality in the workplace and meet these changing quality requirements.
2. Once the foreman has clarified what quality characteristics should be ensured in the workplace, he or she should reflect and work on specific steps to ensure this quality.
3. The foreman should determine what degree of quality must be ensured and the units, such as ppm (parts per million) and percentage, in which the defect rate is to be expressed.
4. The foreman should determine the quality assurance problem spots in the workplace. He or she should create a quality assurance organization that carries out improvement activities so that the causes of problems can be rooted out to prevent recurrences.

BUILDING QUALITY CHARACTERISTICS INTO THE WORKPLACE

The process of *quality deployment* (also called quality function deployment, or QFD) defines the functions of planning, development, design, and manufacturing of a product to satisfy the quality requirements of customers. Quality deployment is generally charted using a two-dimensional diagram, with customer quality requirements on the vertical axis and the quality characteristics needed to satisfy the customer quality requirements on the horizontal axis. A sample quality deployment chart for automotive lamp bulbs is presented in Figure 2-3.

The company's technical department defines the relationship between existing technology and the management methods needed to develop the quality characteristics the customers require. The foreman can do the following things to help assure that the necessary quality characteristics are achieved:

1. Manage by selecting the important quality characteristics shown on the quality deployment chart. The foreman should enter the important quality characteristics, by process, in the QC process chart that determine the items to be managed. He or she should

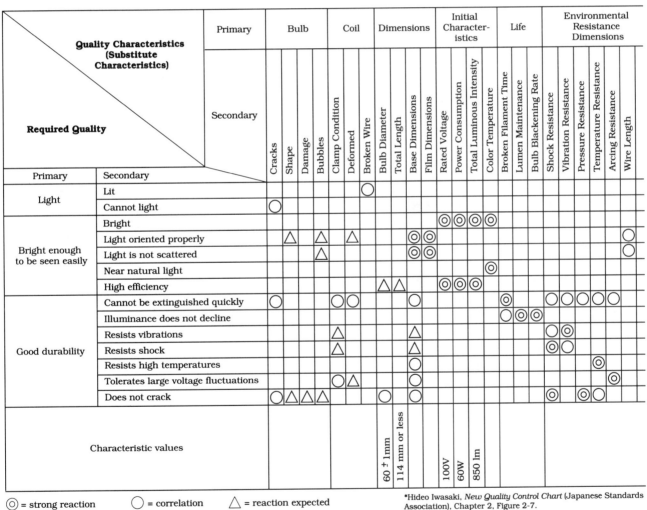

◎ = strong reaction   ○ = correlation   △ = reaction expected

*Hideo Iwasaki, *New Quality Control Chart* (Japanese Standards Association), Chapter 2, Figure 2-7.

Figure 2-3: **Quality Deployment Chart (Example)***

specify the work methods and management methods in work standards and other manuals (see Figure 2-4).

2. When a claim related to a quality characteristic arises, the foreman should examine the management methods related to that quality characteristic and strive to improve them.

3. The foreman should be energetic in improving quality characteristics and in changing management methods to achieve that goal. This will help keep the company responsive over time to changes in customer emphasis on different quality requirements.

4. If no quality deployment chart exists, the foreman should strive to define the relationship between the causes of the quality characteristics the customers require and the management points of the workplace.

5. The foreman should work with the foremen of preceding and following processes to build in quality characteristics based on data.

FUNDAMENTALS OF QUALITY ASSURANCE

Make Quality Your Top Priority

Putting quality first is fundamental to the long-term survival of a company. Companies that neglect quality assurance in favor of delivering a product first in a competitive market later discover defects and suffer for it in the long run. Many companies have failed for this reason.

Built-in Quality

It should be understood that inspections do not create quality; quality is built in during the manufacturing process. Foremen need to create improvement targets to build quality into the manufacturing process. The foreman might set the target at 133% or more of the current process capability, and then work with employees to create and implement a quality improvement plan.

Problems Are Opportunities to Improve the Quality Assurance System

Foremen should see claims and quality problems as opportunities to improve organization and attitudes and

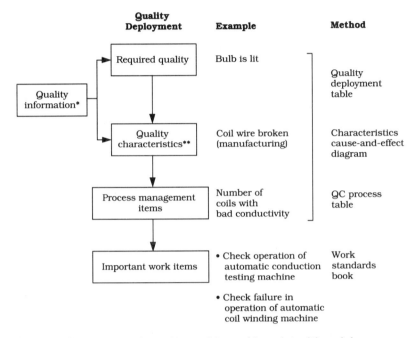

* Quality information consists of the problems and desires of the market and the workplace.

** Quality characteristics can be precisely broken down into several different functions including development, design, manufacturing, and inspection.

Figure 2-4: **The Quality Deployment Concept**

to make reforms. The fundamental principle of QC is to identify the root cause of a problem so it will not recur. If the foreman does not search for the root cause and strive to prevent the recurrence of the problem, his or her work becomes haphazard. Thoroughly search for the root cause. Most problems can be classified as follows:

1. Problems related to worker skills or attitudes
   • Pure mistake
   • Not following the operating procedure
   • Skills not yet adequate
   • Concern for quality not strong enough
2. Problems related to the workplace quality assurance system
   • The quality characteristic to be assured is not well defined
   • Operating standards incomplete
   • Management points unclear

- Casual about lot quality assurance methods
- QC process chart not yet complete
3. Lack of motivation to solve the foreman's problem
   - No desire to delve deeply into the problem and solve it
   - Foreman's leadership in setting improvement goals and in making improvements is inadequate
4. Problems in the workplace culture
   - Never delving deeply into problems
   - Blaming the workplace custom
5. Problems originating in another department
   - Design error
   - Error in determining customer specifications

If you solve problems in a haphazard manner, you might mistake a problem to be a recurring worker error when the true cause is the daily training and quality control education you are providing to the workers. Try to create an atmosphere that motivates everyone to want to build quality into their products.

A supervisor should look for the root cause of any problem that occurs, consider if he or she, not others, is causing the problem, and implement the basic policies needed to correct it.

QUALITY ASSURANCE CHECKPOINTS

1. Motivating for quality consciousness
   - Are the philosophy and general policies of the company and of top management easy to understand and have they been thoroughly implemented?
   - Have you made your employees aware of the damages the company suffers due to defective products on the market and customer claims (loss of customer confidence, loss of brand image, and so on)?
   - Have you provided concrete examples for your employees showing the importance of quality as a shortcut to lower costs, higher customer confidence, and a greater sense of achievement in working?
   - Have you helped your employees to understand the role product quality plays in their work?

2. Objectives and planning
   - Are workplace quality targets such as the defect rate, ppm, and the process capability index clear?
   - Did you make the QC improvement theme clear?
   - Did you give each individual instructions for his or her part in the plan for carrying out the improvement themes that will achieve these targets?
   - Are the plans related to these targets and improvement themes clear?

3. Education
   - Are you improving your chances for achieving the goals and plans through education, exchanges with other companies, and participation in events outside the company?
   - Have you explained the functions that make the product useful to the market and the current extent of the product's use on the market?
   - If a problem arises, do you take charge, give proper instructions for solving the problem, and direct the improvement activities?

4. Practical work and its improvement
   - Do you thoroughly carry out tasks related to the quality characteristics?
   - Have you used a handbook summarizing work procedures to teach your employees how to do their jobs?
   - Have you taught workers how to use machines, instruments, and tools, and to make inspections and adjustments?
   - Do you check to see if the work methods are performed properly?
   - Do you encourage your workers to upgrade their technical knowledge and skills?

5. Problem solving and QC circles
   - When claims or accidents occur, do you guide your workers in solving the problem?
   - When on-the-spot emergency repairs must be made, do you go on to find the root cause of the problem to make sure it doesn't recur?
   - Do you direct the QC circle and the project team to work together to solve a problem?

- Do you use effective and rational problem-solving methods, such as the seven QC tools?
- If improvements and reforms are needed in organization, systems, or standards to prevent a problem from recurring, do you work with the people involved to take the necessary actions?
- Do you consider carefully whether your workplace culture is the problem and take appropriate measures to change the situation?

PREVENTING PROBLEMS FROM RECURRING

If machinery is operated improperly, many defective parts will be made. This will raise the number of customer claims. How should the foreman respond to this type of problem? In carrying out the quality assurance program, the foreman should view these incidents as an opportunity to make improvements and his or her goal as preventing the problem from recurring.

1. Establish rules for reporting abnormalities and for contacting people
   - If a defect is discovered in the workplace, the supervisor should be informed first.
   - Do not conceal defects when making reports and contacting people.
   - The foreman is responsible for taking the appropriate measures for defects discovered in his or her workplace.
   - Take up far-ranging problems with managers and related departments.
2. Emergency measures
   - Recover and replace defective parts.
   - If machinery is hazardous, tell employees not to use the equipment.
3. Temporary repairs
   - Determine which abnormalities you can solve with resources right there in the workplace.
   - Make changes in the materials used, the operating procedure, the personnel, and machinery and equipment according to the determined or suspected cause so that the problem is not compounded.

4. Permanent measures to prevent recurrences
  - Search for the root cause of the abnormality.
  - Take measures appropriate to the cause of the abnormality. If the abnormality cannot be solved in the workplace, seek help from related departments.
  - Plan improvements to strike at the true causes and problems. Check their effectiveness to prevent the problem from recurring.

References

Asaka, Tetsuichi. *Fundamentals of TQC.* 111. Japanese Standards Association, 1983.

Iwasaki, Hideo. *New Quality Control Chart,* Chapter 2, Figure 2-7. Japanese Standards Association.

Noda, Takashi. *Foreman (Occupational Responsibilities).* Management Institute, 1976.

PHP Institute, ed. *Winning the Trust of Your Superiors and Your Subordinates.* PHP Institute, 1983.

3

How to Implement Improvements

Understanding the Problem

Generally, *policy* specifies what should be done and the necessary plans. An *objective* expresses quantitatively a result that should be achieved. Departments organize their activities to carry out policies and achieve objectives. People become aware of what their own department and workplace should be doing and of their own responsibilities. They learn to recognize problems by comparing the situation with the policy and objectives. The basic seven-step procedure for making improvements is shown in Figure 3-1.

CHECKLISTS FOR PROBLEM IDENTIFICATION

Parameters for Evaluating Successful Work: QCDPSM

1. Is Quality a problem?
2. Is Cost a problem?
3. Is Delivery a problem?
4. Is Productivity a problem?
5. Is Safety a problem?
6. Is Morale a problem?

The Four Factors of Production: 4M

1. Is there a problem with materials?
2. Is there a problem with machinery or equipment?
3. Is there a problem with a man or woman?
4. Is there a problem with the method?

The "Big Three" Problems

1. Is there waste?
2. Are there irregularities?
3. Is the requirement unreasonable?

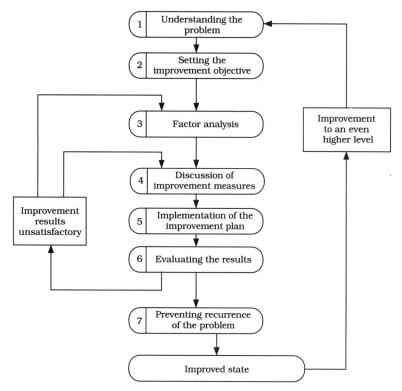

Figure 3-1: **Improvement Procedure**

UNDERSTANDING THE SITUATION THROUGH DATA

Assessing the damage: How much damage does the problem cause? You should know the cost of the damage to understand how serious the problem is. You also need this information to evaluate the effectiveness of the improvement.

Understanding subsequent processes: Is meshing this process with preceding and subsequent processes a problem? "Subsequent processing is the customer's responsibility" is the view often expressed. This "over-the-wall" approach—passing on work-in-process with no concern for problems caused for later processing—will make a company uncompetitive. To create products that serve its market, a company must eliminate the ignorance of its employees about the subsequent processes.

Applying statistical methods: Draw *histograms* to understand the data distributions (see Chapter 14). Use the histogram to determine whether the average value of the data is consistent with the specified and target values and to watch for deviation from those values.

Use a time series of line graphs or a *control chart* to understand changes in the data distribution (see Chapters 10 and 18). These graphs and charts show changes, patterns, and peculiarities in the data. In particular, by examining the *stratification* of the data relating to the problem, you can localize the problem if there is a difference between levels (see Chapter 15).

Identifying key focus areas: Key focus points are aspects of problems that are considered particularly important and are given special attention. Limited resources such as personnel, capital, and time should not be used haphazardly. These resources are focused on specific areas where they will be used most efficiently. *Pareto analysis* is one effective method for identifying key focus points (see Chapter 11).

Setting Improvement Objectives

Establish Specific Numerical Objectives
1. What: the item or characteristic evaluated
2. To what extent: the target value to be reached
3. When: delivery date, date of completion

Set Achievable Targets
Set a high but achievable target that will encourage people to rise to a challenge, but keep in mind the results of previous improvements, present capabilities, the difficulty of the problem, and the delivery date. In the first stage, the improvement activity target should not be set too high. Results are better if the target is realistically achievable. Improvement activities are run cyclically. The

target is higher each time to stimulate greater effort and to achieve better understanding of what can be done.

Develop Objectives in Accordance with the Business Policy

While autonomous goal-setting and the satisfaction of achieving the goals are important, these goals should be set within the larger framework of company policy and correspond to the role and capabilities of the department and the workplace. The bottom line is that these autonomously set goals should help meet overall company objectives. Getting management's consent for these goals and making agreements with related workplaces is essential.

Factor Analysis

Arrange Factors Using Cause-and-effect Diagrams

A *cause-and-effect diagram* describes an unsatisfactory condition or phenomenon and helps examine why that problem arises by systematically arranging the factors of major, medium, and minor importance in a "why" cause-and-effect diagram.

A "how" cause-and-effect chart does not explain the cause of a phenomenon. The purpose of the "how" chart is problem solving. This approach analyzes the desired solution to determine the best way to reach it and permanently eliminate the problem. Determining the root cause of the problem is the main purpose. Figure 3-2 compares these two types of charts.

Examine Data on the Influence of the Factor

1. *Examine data obtained earlier.* When condition factors change, compare data recorded earlier with current data to determine how these changes have affected quality characteristics.
2. *Rework data collection and arrangement to serve the objective of your investigation.* If previous data cannot be analyzed because the conditions under which it

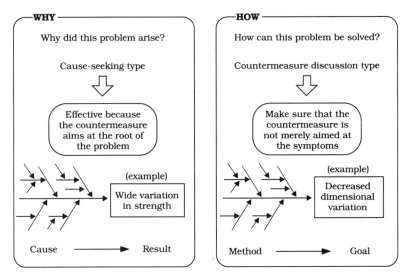

Figure 3-2: "Why" and "How" Cause-and-effect Diagrams

was collected are not completely known, revise the method of collecting data. Arrange the data so that the relationship between different strata of the data can be studied. Systematically record and analyze the data.

3. *Deliberately obtain experimental data when condition factors change.* Run new experiments to examine the effects of condition factors. Intentionally extend the range of the experiments beyond the range of the factors and analyze the data. Follow an experiment planning method to design experiments and analyze data efficiently.

Measured and Counted (Numerical) Factors*

When working with counted (numerical) factors, stratify the data and check for inconsistencies between different strata. For example, stratify data on machinery, materials, or other products by manufacturer or by some other breakdown such as 5MET:

---

* See Chapter 9 for more on the distinction between these two types of data. — Ed.

- Material
- Machine
- Man or woman
- Method
- Measurement
- Environment
- Time

Draw histograms and control charts to find differences between manufacturers on the basis of the distribution of the average values or the defect rate.

When working with measured factors, check for a relationship between each measured factor and the effect it is being compared with. For example: draw a scatter diagram comparing the purity of the material with the yield of the product to determine whether the two distributions are correlated. (See Figure 3-3.)

Pay Attention to Changes and Abnormalities Appearing in Data Collected Over Time

1. *Periodic changes:* What factor is responsible for the time intervals?
2. *Sudden abnormality:* What factor is responsible for the sudden change?
3. *Scattered abnormalities:* When does the problem always occur?
4. *Chronic defect:* What is the most important factor?

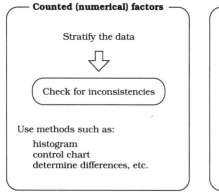
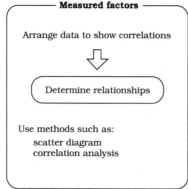

Figure 3-3: **Counted and Measured Factors**

DISCUSSING IMPROVEMENT THEMES

Basic Preparations

1. Reexamine the goals and targets.
2. Stimulate the untapped potential for creating new ideas, fostering individual creativity, and drawing strength from thorough knowledge.
3. Be fair, unbiased, and flexible in your thinking.
4. Strive every day to broaden your knowledge and experience.

Make an Ideal Proposal

At the outset, you should refuse to be bound by present constraints of the situation. Instead, develop an ideal proposal for achieving the final goal. Then think of a series of remedial steps that will bring you closer to that goal. Carry out primary and secondary measures in steps to make sure they are reliable. Initially, you can use model cases that are restricted to a limited area. As the effectiveness of these cases is demonstrated experimentally, their range of applicability can be extended gradually.

Alternate Improvement Measures

More than one measure is adopted to achieve the goal. Many second and third proposals, as well as substitute proposals, can be considered. Review the advantages, disadvantages and constraints of each proposal before selecting the best.

Brainstorming to Generate Ideas

Bringing together a group of people to freely suggest and develop new ideas based on the comments of others in the group can result in better proposals. These meetings should be governed by four basic principles:

1. *No criticism:* All ideas should be accepted for discussion without judgment.
2. *No constraints:* The present situation and common sense should not be a constraint; wild ideas and startling opinions should also be expressed.
3. *Build on other people's ideas:* Taking off from, extending, or expanding on someone else's idea should be welcome.

4. *Encourage participation:* People should be encouraged to speak out often. The more ideas suggested, the higher the quality of the ideas developed.

Idea Development Checklist

Use the "idea generation checklist," based on principles developed by A.F. Osborn, to come up with ideas for new proposals:

- Elimination: What will happen if something is eliminated?
- Reversal: What will happen if something is reversed?
- Normal and abnormal: Is something an abnormality or does it occur all the time?
- Constant and variable: What will happen if only the changing item is treated as an exception?
- Enlargement and reduction: What will happen if something is enlarged or reduced?
- Linking and separating: What will happen if some things are joined or taken apart?
- Concentration and dispersion: What will happen if some things are concentrated or dispersed?
- Addition and removal: What will happen if something is added or removed?
- Replacement and substitution: What will happen if you use something in another setting or substitute something else?
- Differences and similarities: Is there a method to easily separate different things? Is there a method to group similar things?
- Changing the sequence: What will happen if a different assembly procedure is used?
- Parallel and sequential: Can two or more things be done at the same time? Must they be done sequentially?

Use 5W1H to Draw Up Your Implementation Plan

Use 5W1H to clearly define the division of labor and the daily organization of work and to implement the improvement plan as a group:

- What
- Why

- When
- Who
- Where
- How

Implementing the Improvement Plan

Developing Understanding and Consensus

Most people, even if they understand the improvement plan intellectually, will oppose changes in the status quo. You must explain the intent and content of the improvements to the people involved to win their hearts as well as their minds.

Doing Trial Runs of New Arrangements for Thorough Preparation

Aim at success and avoiding false steps from the outset. Compare each step and aspect of the new arrangement with the original configuration. Sweep away doubts by experimentally demonstrating the effectiveness of the new arrangement. Review it using the 5W1H system with the people concerned. Prepare the implementation carefully, focusing on each detail.

Using Data for Validating Effectiveness

Select certain quality characteristics and causal factors as criteria for evaluating the effectiveness of improvements. Continue to obtain data on these points until you are certain the effectiveness of the improvements is maintained.

Responding to Unexpected Problems

Encountering an unexpected problem while you are carrying out a plan creates confusion. A solution that works for one process may affect other processes and other departments. You should resolve this type of conflict as rapidly as possible. It is essential, however, to work quickly and diligently, with the help of people in other affected departments, to revise the plan and eliminate such conflicts in a way that works for all concerned.

Evaluating the Results of Improvements

Evaluation Standard: The Initial Improvement Objective

Using the characteristic items determined at the improvement objective-setting stage, gather performance data and compare data from before and after the improvement. Then express graphically and numerically to what extent it was possible to meet the target value you set.

Consider Tangible and Intangible Influences and Effects

The characteristics of quality, prices, delivery date, productivity, safety, and employee enthusiasm and involvement are related to one another. Other characteristics can also have beneficial effects as well as negative effects. Intangible, unmeasurable effects should be evaluated as well as tangible ones. For example, activities to reduce fatigue, improve skills and abilities, or strengthen participation have a positive effect.

Thank Departments That Assist You

When you have finally reached your target, everyone is filled with the joy of success, team spirit, and self-confidence. Do not forget at this time to save a sincere thanks for other departments that helped you achieve your goal.

Take Up a New Challenge

Do not be discouraged if the measures you took to make improvements are not as successful as you had hoped. Reflect on shortcomings and take up a new challenge. Modify your improvement plan. Revise your analysis of the cause of the problem and consider your improvement measures from a new standpoint.

Making Improvements Permanent

Upgrading Improved Equipment and Tools

During the maintenance management stage, the results of improvement are consolidated and made permanent. Most improved machines that have been tested and mistake-proofed can be further upgraded by expanding their range of applications either across the board or in pilot projects.

Work Methods and Standardization

Make work changes permanent by standardizing procedures and methods through these vehicles:

1. *Structure:* Determine operating standards such as work sequence, division of labor, methods, systems, and so on.
2. *Mechanism:* Provide mechanisms in the correct places to perform maintenance management by checking for a problem and sounding an alarm if an error is detected.
3. *Discipline:* Stick to procedures already decided to ensure reliability. Have operations requiring skilled labor done by a skilled worker.

Reflect on Improvement Activities

1. Can other products in the same category or similar processes benefit from tested improvements?
2. Are you neglecting remaining problems?
3. Are new problems hidden behind the improvement results?
4. Should you revise your approach to the way an improvement is implemented?

Report Your Improvement Activities in a "QC Story"

Summarize the development and results of your improvement activity in a visual display called a "QC story." The plot of the QC story is built around the steps in the development of the improvement method. The basic structure of a QC story is:

1. Theme
2. Outline of process
3. Reason for selecting the theme
4. Understanding the situation
5. Setting the target
6. Factor analysis
7. Measure
8. Effect
9. Standardizing the improvement
10. Remaining problems and future plans

References

Ozeki, Kazuo, *QC Introductory Series 2: Promotion of Management and Improvement.* Japanese Standards Association, 1983.

4

Process Control

The term *control* has various meanings, including to supervise, govern, regulate, or restrain. The *control* in *quality control* means defining the objective of the job, developing and carrying out a plan to meet that objective, and checking to determine if the anticipated results are achieved. If the anticipated results are not achieved, modifications are made in the work procedure to fulfill the plan.

The word *management* describes many different functions, encompassing policy management, human resources management, and safety control, as well as component control and management of materials, equipment, and daily schedules.

MANAGEMENT PROCEDURE

The management cycle comprises the four steps of plan, do, check, and action.

- *Plan (P): devise a plan.* Define your objective and determine the conditions and methods required to achieve your objective. Describe clearly the goals and policies needed to achieve the objective at this stage. Express a specific objective numerically. Determine the procedures and conditions for the means and methods you will use to achieve the objective.
- *Do (D): execute the plan.* Create the conditions and perform the necessary teaching and training to execute the plan. Make sure everyone thoroughly understands the objectives and the plan. Teach workers the procedures and skills they need to fulfill the plan and thoroughly understand the job. Then perform the work according to these procedures.
- *Check (C): check the results.* Check to determine whether work is progressing according to the plan and whether the expected results are obtained. Check for performance of the set procedures, changes in conditions, or

abnormalities that may appear. As often as possible, compare the results of the work with the objectives.

- *Action (A): take the necessary action.* If your checkup reveals that the work is not being performed according to plan or that results are not what was anticipated, devise measures for appropriate action.

If a check detects an abnormality — that is, if the actual value differs from the target value — then search for the cause of the abnormality to prevent its recurrence. Sometimes you may need to retrain workers and revise procedures. Make sure these changes are reflected and more fully developed in the next plan.

GOING AROUND THE PDCA CIRCLE

The four-step procedure shown in Figure 4-1 is often referred to as *PDCA*. Repeatedly going through this management cycle is known as "going around the PDCA circle."

These procedures not only ensure that the quality of the manufactured goods meets expectations, but they also ensure that the anticipated price and delivery date are fulfilled. Sometimes our preoccupation with current concerns makes us unable to achieve optimal results. By going around the PDCA circle, we can improve our working methods and obtain the desired results. Repeated use of PDCA makes it possible to improve the quality of the work, the work methods, and the results. This concept can be seen in the ascending spiral of Figure 4-2.

Manufacturing Process Management

The four primary factors of material, machine, employees, and method, as well as power, energy, safety, and the work environment, must be utilized effectively if the manufacturing workplace is to achieve its goals of quality, cost, and delivery. Figure 4-3 shows how these factors must be managed effectively to achieve the three goals.

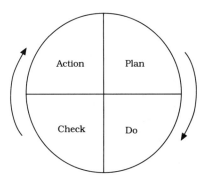

Figure 4-1: **Management Cycle**

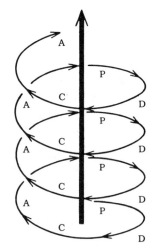

Figure 4-2: **Ascending Spiral**

MATERIAL MANAGEMENT

If you are managing items such as raw materials, processed products from subcontractors, and purchased components, you should review the following points.

1. *Prevent mixture of different materials:* Check to make certain that the goods placed in inventory match their stock tickets. Store each material in a separate area so they will not be mixed together.
2. *Distinguish lots clearly from one another:* Clearly labeling lots and storing them separately is important. If problems during the manufacturing process are traced back to materials, then the process that produced the lot should be examined to take appropriate remedial action.
3. *First in, first out:* First in, first out is a basic principle of materials management. Arrange materials this way to prevent deterioration, deformation, and problems associated with losing information about older goods. This smoothes the flow of entering inventory, storage, and shipment.

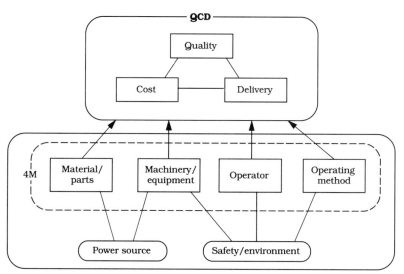

* Kazuo Ozeki, *QC Introductory Series 2: Promotion of Management and Improvement* (Japanese Standards Association, 1983), 62.

Figure 4-3: **Relationship Between Manufacturing Process and Product***

MANAGEMENT OF MACHINERY AND EQUIPMENT

Pay special attention to the following points of machinery and equipment management, including tools and instrumentation:

1. *Daily inspection:* Daily inspection, cleaning, lubrication, and adjustment is necessary to obtain top performance from machinery and equipment. Use an inspection and checkout worksheet to ensure a thorough inspection. Take action if you find an abnormality.

2. *Periodic inspection:* Inspect periodically and replace worn out parts. If necessary, disassemble the equipment and perform preventive maintenance to complement daily maintenance inspections.

3. *Planned maintenance:* Wear in rotating machine parts and in tools reduces their accuracy. Perform planned reconditioning and replacement after a standard number of processing operations or on a predetermined replacement schedule. Keep records on the performance, inspections, adjustments, and so on, of each part. You must use a precision test tag to keep close track of instrumentation accuracy.

OPERATOR MANAGEMENT

No matter how efficient the materials, machinery, and equipment may be, you cannot produce high-quality products if the operators in the workplace are not motivated and skilled.

Motivating Operators

Worker initiative and motivation will decline if the human dignity of operators is ignored. Management cannot rely on orders and authority to boost productivity, stop waste in processing, and eliminate operator mistakes during the manufacturing process. There are four basic conditions for creating a workplace that motivates operators to perform their work well:

1. Operators clearly understand the significance and objective of their work.
2. Authority is delegated so that operators are responsible for performing the work.
3. The efforts and achievements of workers are recognized.
4. People come to work expecting to perform to high standards (especially important).

Skill Evaluation and Education and Training

Operators must be able to perform many different jobs because of the rapid increase in the variety of products and the number of different articles. For the foreman to evaluate the skills of each operator and prepare people to perform various tasks, planned and diversified operator training and education program is needed.

Job design methods permit operators to improve their skills as they carry out their tasks. These methods include job enrichment, job enhancement, and job rotation.

1. *Job enrichment:* The content of the operator's job is enriched by giving him or her responsibility not only for performing the operation, but for related tasks ranging from designing the operation to product quality inspection.
2. *Job enhancement:* The scope of the job is expanded by teaching the employee how to operate other equipment and machinery so that he or she can assume responsibility for earlier and later processes.
3. *Job rotation:* Operators periodically exchange jobs with other operators. This reduces boredom and makes it easier to train operators in a variety of skills.

MANAGING OPERATING METHODS

Operating standards and operating summary books describe the procedures and essential points for manufacturing quality products. These books are effective only if the procedures and points described therein are followed.

1. *Accurately describe procedures and important points in operating standards and operating summary books.* The operating standards book describes the operating conditions (the equipment, machinery, or tools used) and basic operating procedures. The operating summary depicts the essentials of the operation.

2. *Check to see that the procedure is performed properly.* It is important that operators personally check their performance as described in the operating standards and operating summary books. Depending on the workplace, the foreman may also check the process with an inspection and validation check sheet.

3. *Clearly indicate methods for finding and resolving abnormalities.* Clearly describe methods for discovering abnormalities in the machinery and materials used in the process, and in the parts being assembled or processed. Specify methods for resolving a problem once an abnormality has been discovered.

4. *Revise and update operating standards and operating summary books.* Improvements in process that result from investigations into the causes of abnormalities should be incorporated into the operating standards and operating summary books. Revising these books is essential.

MANAGING SAFETY, POWER, AND ENERGY

Workplace safety is an important part of workplace management. The work environment strongly influences product quality. Power and energy management are also important in this era of resource and energy conservation.

Preventing accidents and disasters takes more than safety and warning devices on equipment, respecting safety standards and safety rules, and displaying safety warning posters. An organized "safety first" campaign involving everyone from the executives to the operators should make all employees more aware of the importance of health and safety.

Power and energy, although intangible, must be managed in the workplace as essential resources for production. Management should strive to use resources and energy effectively, while eliminating waste of oil, gas, electric power, water, and so on.

Process Control Standards

The two most important elements of manufacturing process control are checking the results and taking action if abnormalities appear. To ensure that all the products made in a continuous process meet standards for quality, you should understand the relationship between your process and the preceding and following processes. In addition to understanding the relationship between quality characteristics (results) and production conditions (causes), you should establish control points at important stages in the process to confirm product quality and production conditions. These are necessary to keep the process operating normally.

Control points are generally used as control standards for a process presented on a large chart. The name of this chart varies from company to company, but it is often called a QC process table, QC process diagram, process control table, or process control diagram (see Table 4-1).

DEFINING THE CONTROL POINTS

Control points are classified as control items or inspection items depending on how the checks are performed.*

$$\text{Control points} \begin{cases} \text{control item (checking results)} \\ \text{inspection item (checking cause)} \end{cases}$$

Control Items

Control items are sometimes called the resulting quality characteristics of the product. The check is whether the quality of the product produced by the process meets the quality target or standard. If a defect occurs, this item is used to treat the process that caused the defect.

---

* S. Miura, N. Kano, Y. Tsuda, and Y. Ohashi, eds., *TQC Terminology Dictionary* (Japanese Standards Association, 1985).

Product Name	Product A	Process Name	Overcoat	**Product A Overcoat QC Process Chart**		
Specifications	ESU—245 Type	**Order Date**	21 May 1986			
Product Number	2413	**Date of Manufacture**	1 June 1986			

	Process				Control Point						
Process Procedure	Flowchart			Process Name	Inspection Item (check cause)				Control Item (check result)		
Component or Material	Material Process	Preparatory Process	Main Process	Contents of Process	5M Factor	Rank	Constraints	Conditions	Rank	Control Point (Inspection Item)	Abnormality Criteria
Tanpo printing finished keytop				Storage							
				Top surface wiped off	Method	C	Impregnation				
				(Dirt and impurities wiped off keytops)	Method	C	Change base coat				
					Method	A	Wiping method		B	Waste thread not well attached	According to control chart
				Air jet attached	Equipment	A	Air pressure				
				(Impurities completely removed from keytop surface)	Equipment	C	Application of alcohol		A	Waste thread not well attached	According to control chart
				Masking	Tool	C	Mask hole diameter	Outer diameter of keytop +0.1 mm -0			
UV paint				Storage	Material	B	Paint viscosity	0.6 ± 0.4 poise			
					Material	C	Storage period	within 3 months			
					Material	C	Storage place	30°C or less			
Xylidine				Storage	Material	B	Viscosity	0.4 ± 0.2 poise			
					Material	C	Storage period	within 3 months			
					Material	C	Storage place	30°C or less			
				Paint viscosity adjustment	Method	AA	mixing ratio 4:1 weight ratio 2:1				
				(for smooth coating)	Method	B	place in material mixer	Five minutes or more			
					Method	C	place in container		AA	Viscosity	Sinking time 9 ± 1 second
									C	Weight	5 ± 0.1 kg

Revision History	Symbol	Date	Reason for Revision	Supvr.	Check
	△1	· ·			
	△2	· ·			
	△3	· ·			

* Tadayoshi Ohoka, "Actual Applications of Quality Deployment in the Development of New Products (5), Using QC Process Tables," *Standardization and Quality Control*, 39(8): 85.]

Table 4-1: **Sample QC Process Chart (Process Control Diagram)***

Accepted		Agreement				Execution				Control No. FOC—001
Factory Director	Quality Control	Technology	Production Technology	Merchandise Purchasing		Director of Manufacturing Section	Inspection Stamp	Person in Charge		
SS	FB	NM	TK	KG		HT	MN			

Management Method

Sampling Measurement Method				Control Materials		Person Responsible for Control (C) and Action (A)					Action After Check	Related Standard No.	
Frequency	Sampling Method	Measurement Method (instrument)	Person in Charge	Control Chart	Check Sheet	Section Head	Chief Clerk	Group Leader	Prep Leader	Fore- man			
												Directions No. OC-01	
Every 10 units	Fixed interval sampling	Visual	Operator					A		C			
Twice daily	9 a.m., 1 p.m.	Pressure gauge	Operator		OS-02			A	C			Directions No. OC-02	
Every 10 units	Fixed interval sampling	Visual	Operator		OS-11								
Every three months	According to instructions	Slide calipers	Reserve	OS-21					C			Instruction No. OC-03	
Each container	Top 1/3	Viscosity meter	Reserve	OS-12				A	C		Disposal of the material	Material specifications 433K-ST-1501	
" "	All		"	OS-12				A	C				
" "	All		"					A	C				
Each container	Top 1/3	Viscosity meter	Reserve					A	C		Disposal of the material	Material specifications 433K-ST-1502	
" "	All		"					A	C				
" "	All		"					A	C				
										C	Disposal of liquid mixture	Instruction No. OC-04	
										C		Viscosity measurement method 433K-SU-2400	
Every mixture	Top 1/3	Stopwatch	Reserve	X̄ - R		A		C		C		OC-01	
"	All	Scale	"		OS-12								

Symbol	Date	Reason for Revision	Supvr.	Check
▵4	· ·			
▵5	· ·			
▵6	· ·			

Inspection Items

In addition to checking the quality characteristics of the end product and taking action on the cause of an abnormality, you should also check the production conditions. Correcting bad production conditions before a problem arises will keep the production process in good operating condition. Inspection items include causal system items, such as materials, equipment and machinery, and methods that affect the end product of the process.

SELECTING CONTROL POINTS

Control items are selected to check whether the dimensions, hardness, yield, or defect rate of the end product of a process meets the preset target or standards. Inspection items are causal system elements such as materials, equipment and machinery, tools, processing conditions, and processing methods that are checked to determine their influence on the quality characteristics of the product. Table 4-2 shows examples of control and inspection items.

Control Item	Inspection Item
Lens does not adhere properly	Hardness of bond, amount of bond applied to surface, jig tightness, drying temperature, drying time, plate hole diameter
Spot weld strength	Input voltage and current, air pressure, quality and thickness of materials used in parts, welding methods
Pin external diameter	Material hardness, chuck tightening torque, bit feeding speed, work rotation speed

Table 4-2: Control and Inspection Items (Examples)

DETERMINING THE MANAGEMENT METHOD

Once the control and inspection items have been determined, you can decide how the process should be controlled and what management methods should be used. The control level, sampling, measurements, control records, abnormality handling, and the person responsible for controlling the process should all be discussed.

1. *Control level:* You must determine the control points in the technical standards shown in plans and specifications. Then set control levels and control limits for inspection items that fully satisfy manufacturing standards. If you are using a control chart to control a process, draw the median line and the control limits clearly (see Chapter 18).

2. *Sampling:* Decide what to sample, the size of the sample, the frequency of sampling, the sampling method, and the person to do the sampling.

3. *Measurements:* Decide who is to measure, the place where measurements will be made, the measuring instruments, the measurement method, and the data recording method.

4. *Control records:* Decide the recording method for detecting abnormalities, using check sheets, graphs, control diagrams, and process capacity diagrams. Then investigate the cause of the abnormality.

5. *Abnormality handling:* Determine methods for judging if abnormalities are present, for taking action, and for contacting people when abnormalities occur.

6. *Process control manager:* Choose the appropriate person to run a system that checks the control points and the inspection items, to take action when an abnormality appears, and to report on abnormalities and follow through.

Managing the Workplace

A QC process table systematically arranges and specifies the control points that reflect product quality. The foreman, in addition to maintaining the QC process table, should manage the following control indices as part of his or her management of the entire process:

- *Quality (Q):* Non-adjusted ratio, process defect rate, process capability, etc.
- *Cost (C):* Materials cost, labor cost, expenses, etc.

- *Quantity and Date (D):* Utilization rate, delivery date, fulfillment rate, daily delivery delay rate, etc.
- *Productivity (P):* Quantity produced per unit time, number of times each unit handled by a worker, etc.
- *Safety (S):* Number of accidents, number of consecutive days without an accident, etc.
- *Morale (M):* Absentee rate, number of improvement proposals submitted, etc.

The foreman faces many difficulties in managing the workplace. He or she must work hard to foster a better workplace and improve results. The foreman should keep the following points in mind to accomplish these goals.

SORTING AND SELECTION IN THE WORKPLACE

Good housekeeping practices is an important foundation of the improvement process. Contaminated materials and defective products appear more often in workplaces that do not carry out a program of sorting and selecting.*

Sorting is separating clearly what is needed from what is not needed and disposing of what is not needed. The presence of unnecessary objects increases the time it takes to get the necessary objects, and makes it more likely that the wrong object will be taken or the necessary object will not be found.

Selecting is deciding on a place where needed objects can be found quickly. You have to search for an object if a place is not designated, if the location number is not marked clearly, or if the object is not in the designated place. Some guidelines to use in sorting and selecting follow:

1. Separate objects used daily from other objects.
2. Store objects not used daily in inventory.
3. Place objects used frequently in places where they can be obtained quickly.

---

* Sorting and selecting are two main elements of 4S, a set of industrial housekeeping principles widely used in Japan, though uniquely expressed and defined at each company. The other main elements are cleaning and maintaining cleanliness throughout the workday. Some companies add discipline or adherence as a fifth principle. — Ed.

4. Indicate the place where an object is stored and clearly write the information on the object itself.

5. Clearly indicate and teach a method for returning objects to their proper places.

MANAGEMENT BY VISUAL CONTROL

If you do not fully understand the condition of the workplace, you will not notice problems and will not be able to make improvements. Visual control management is a method for making workplace problems stand out. Here are a few examples:

1. *Production control display:* A display board shows the difference between the anticipated and the actual cumulative production. This method informs the foreman and operators if the process is behind schedule and expedites the work. (See Figure 4-4.)

2. *Process abnormality display:* This system informs the foremen and concerned operators on preceding and following processes when a process abnormality occurs. When a problem requires an operator to slow down the process in his or her own area, that person presses an emergency contact switch that turns on a red light and sounds an alarm. (See Figure 4-5.)

3. *Inventory management using multicolored displays:* An inventory management method using yellow, green, and red on the parts shelves to signal if inventories are too low, just right, or too high can prevent shortages and excessive numbers of parts. See Figure 4-6 for an example.

4. *Tool control board:* If the tools needed to recondition equipment or to set up a die change are not available, production will be delayed. The tool control board is useful for storing frequently used tools. Figure 4-7 is an example.

5. *Skill evaluation table:* The foreman must correctly evaluate operator's skills and then develop an educational and training plan to improve those skills. The skill evaluation chart enables the foreman to find at a glance the skill levels of different operators for working on various processes. See Figure 4-8 for an example.

Figure 4-4: **Production Control Display**

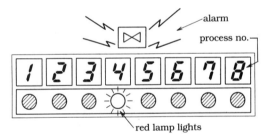

Figure 4-5: **Process Abnormality Display**

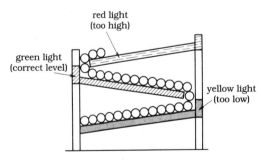

Figure 4-6: **Color Display for Inventory Management**

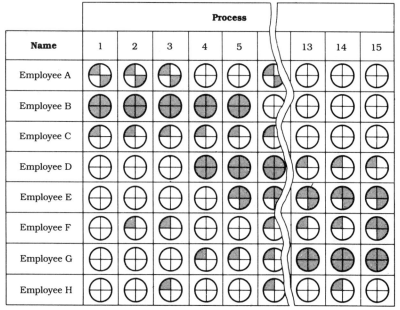

Name	Process								
	1	2	3	4	5		13	14	15
Employee A									
Employee B									
Employee C									
Employee D									
Employee E									
Employee F									
Employee G									
Employee H									

1: Processing   2: Planning   3: Measurement and judgment   4: Directions

Figure 4-8: **Skill Evaluation Table**

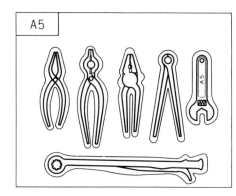

Figure 4-7: **Tool Control Board**

FOSTERING QUALITY CONSCIOUSNESS

The workmanship of goods produced in the workplace is affected by the attitude of each worker. A poor attitude can result in scratched products from mishandling parts as well as assembly errors, such as using a mismatched or defective part. Operators should be devoted to their job and committed to quality.

When a shortcoming appears in the workplace, the foreman should examine the training given to workers. He or she should strive to foster the quality consciousness of operators through a program of daily education and training.

FACT-BASED DECISION MAKING

Management based on facts is called fact control. Judgments are made not just on experience and intuition but on the basis of data. Some things in the workplace cause defects and delay delivery. Moreover, machine break-downs can also stop a production line. If you examine these facts closely, you will be able to discover the cause of the problem and carry out measures to resolve it. Examining the facts, analyzing data, and making correct judgments are important. If you examine the workplace and the work and analyze data, you will discover new facts and causes that escaped you earlier.

MISTAKE-PROOFING DEVICES*

The last workplace problem we will consider is operator mistakes, including not catching machine mistakes. Few workers want to make errors, but it is human nature to forget things, even after thorough training and education. Using mistake-proofing devices and *poka-yoke* procedures against mistakes and oversights is an effective approach to this problem.*

Mistake-proofing methods can be divided into two types: alarms and controls. Alarm devices light a red lamp, sound a buzzer, or flash an alarm light if a mistake is detected. Control devices interrupt the work by releasing a clamp, stopping a machine, or halting a conveyor if a mistake occurs so that a defect does not move on to the next process.

CREATING A COMFORTABLE, COOPERATIVE WORKPLACE

Daily inspection and preventive maintenance have become more important as workplaces have turned to increased mechanization and automation to boost productivity. Reliance on automation increases the risk of large losses from process abnormalities and machine stoppages. People must master process control techniques and equipment repair and maintenance technologies. Today's workplace has become much more knowledge

---

* For more discussion of mistake-proofing systems, see Shigeo Shingo, *Zero Quality Control: Source Inspection and the Poka-Yoke System* (Productivity Press, 1986) and *Poka-Yoke: Improving Product Quality by Preventing Defects* (Productivity Press, 1989). — Ed.

intensive than the traditional factory. Employees must be able to respond to these changes by improving their capabilities.

To create a lively and enthusiastic workplace, each person needs to:

- develop his or her ability and help each other in this development
- take full advantage of capabilities of others in the workplace
- accept the challenge of unlimited possibilities

Foremen should think about giving their employees work they will want to do and improving the abilities of each worker. The foreman and employees can thus work together to respond to the changes in the workplace.

RESPONDING TO FUTURE AUTOMATION

Many factories today are using automation to support continuous production processes. A number of plants have adopted flexible manufacturing systems that can produce many different kinds of products in response to the greater variety in product specifications.

Automation does not always lead to higher productivity, however. Complaints like "We automated but it didn't reduce our labor requirements," "Automation increased the amount of work," or "Automation caused frequent production line stops" are sometimes heard. Thoroughly analyzing the process and the work before moving to factory automation is the best prevention for these pitfalls.

Workplace operations include processing, assembly, inspection, transportation, and storage of finished goods. Inspection, transportation, and inventory storage do not add value. Automation is moving forward because it can eliminate useless transportation and accumulation in inventory of finished goods. Understand the work situation and avoid automating useless operations.

References

Ishikawa, Kaoru, and Kozo Koura. *Quality Control Guidelines*. Tax Accounting Association, 1980.

Management Technology Pocket Dictionary Editorial Committee, ed. *Management Technology Pocket Dictionary*. JUSE Press Ltd., 1984.

Matsuda, Kameda. *New Workplace QC Reader 19: Production Management in the Workplace*. JUSE Press Ltd., 1985.

Miura, S., N. Kano, Y. Tsuda, and Y. Ohashi, eds. *TQC Terminology Dictionary*. Japanese Standards Association, 1985.

New Quality Control Handbook Editorial Committee. "New Quality Control Handbook." Japanese Standards Association, 1987.

Ohoka, Tadayoshi. "Actual Applications of Quality Deployment in the Development of New Products (5), Using QC Process Tables." *Standardization and Quality Control*, 39 (8): 85.

Ozeki, Kazuo. *QC Introductory Series 2: Promotion of Management and Improvement*. 62. Japanese Standards Association, 1983.

5

Standardizing Operations

Operation Standardization Objectives

The standardization of operations serves five essential purposes in the workplace:

1. *Maintaining and improving quality.* Standardization reduces deviations in the 4M causal system (materials, machinery, men/women, and methods), and stabilizes the process to assure quality and reliability.
2. *Reducing costs.* Standardization reduces costs and boosts operating efficiency by simplifying and reducing the number and varieties of materials and components to cut inventories.
3. *Improving efficiency.* Standards reduce mistakes and boost efficiency by integrating and making appropriate rules for work procedures, processes, and methods.
4. *Maintaining safe and healthy working conditions.* Adherence to equipment operating, maintenance, and work standards helps prevent accidents, ensure health and safety, protect the environment, and prevent pollution.
5. *Communicating information reliably.* Specification books store and transmit the technological intellectual property of the company. They should clearly describe the product quality and performance required and give directions for performing work according to standards.

Basic Standardization Terminology*

Company standardization is the organized behavior of a factory or other organization that establishes appropriate

---

* The JIS definitions in this section are from original Japanese (translated) quoted in the original edition of this book, rather than from the English version of JIS Z 8101 -1981. — Ed.

standards for materials, components, and products and uses these standards to efficiently carry out company activities such as purchasing, manufacturing, inspecting, managing, and so on.

A *standard* is a decision concerning materials, performance, capability, arrangements, conditions, actions, methods, procedures, formalities, responsibilities, duties, authority, philosophies, concepts, and so on, agreed upon by people involved to legitimately obtain mutual advantage or benefit through consolidation and simplification.

Standardization is the organized activity of setting and implementing standards.

A *technical standard* is an agreed document established mainly with respect to technical matters related directly or indirectly to an article or service among those specified in the definition of standard.

Regulations are operation standards based on agreements about items related to the contents of the work, procedures, processes, and methods.*

A *specification* is a specific agreed-upon requirement covering the shape, structure, dimension, composition, capability, precision, performance, method of manufacture, or testing relating to materials, products, tools, or equipments.

Work Standards for a Company Standardization System

Classification by Nature of the Specification

1. *Quality standard:* A specified standard related to the structure, material, dimensions, characteristics, or other aspect of the product quality.
2. *Methods standard:* An established standard concerning methods and formalities related to design, production, operations, experiments, business matters, and so on.

---

* Miura, Shin, ed., *A Dictionary of Total Quality Control Terms* (Japanese Standards Association, 1985), 96.

3. *Basic standard:* Specified standards related to basic items such as terminology and symbols, specifications, and units of measurement.

Classification by Subject

1. *Company rules:* Basic rules relating to company organization and activities. Example: articles of incorporation, work regulations, organization regulations, regulations on the division of duties, job definition rules, and so on.
2. *Business standards:* Rules relating to the organization of important tasks so that company activities will proceed smoothly and uniformly. Example: Standard management regulations, quality control regulations, equipment control regulations, purchasing control regulations, and so on.
3. *Technical standards:* Set quantitative technical standards for materials, components, and products, as well as for performance, specifications, arrangement, procedures, methods, and so on, involved in their design, manufacture, and testing. Example: Product specifications, material specifications, design standards, packaging standards, and so on.

Classification by Area of Company Activities

These standards vary according to the nature of the industry, company size, organizational structure, and system of manufacturing. Figure 5-1 presents an array of these various kinds of standards.

Operation Standards

According to JIS Z 8101-1981 ("Glossary of Terms Used in Quality Control") operation standards are standards that have been set relating to operating conditions, operating methods, management methods, materials used, equipment used, and other important items.*

---

* JIS Z 8101-1981 uses the term *process specification* for this definition. The *Dictionary of Total Quality Control Terms* (Japanese Standards Association, 1985) gives both terms as English equivalents of the Japanese expression. — Ed.

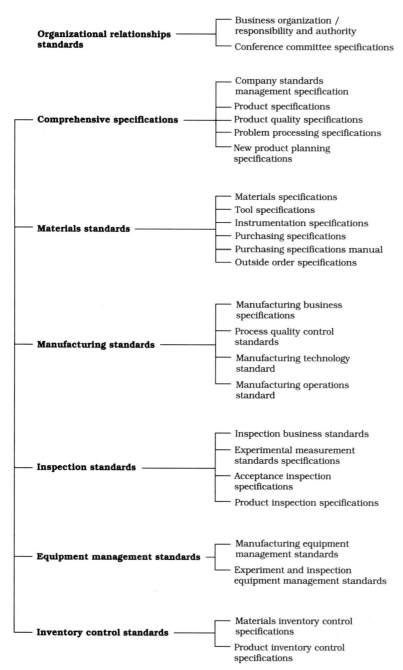

Figure 5-1: **Standards Classified by Company Activities**

The objective of operation standards is to make clear the fundamentals of management of such factors as quality, cost, delivery, productivity, and safety and thus maintain quality, improve operation efficiency, and ensure safety.

Conditions for Operation Standards

Determine how to attack the most important conditions involved in achieving your goal. Decide what you want to do and how to master the most important causal factors affecting your goal. If, in your efforts to achieve your objective, you focus on factors that do not affect your objective and do not master the critical factors, you will not get to the crux of the problem. Important conditions include:

- *Realistic technical standards:* It is useless to make regulations that cannot be followed because they are beyond the accuracy or capabilities of current equipment or machinery, or are not suited to workplace conditions. Practical reforms that can improve process capacity depend not just on automation and skilled labor, but also on standards that are practical from the material, quantitative, and time standpoints.

- *Specific technical standards:* People understand things in different ways. Use figures, diagrams, tables, drawings, and photographs to describe procedures step by step. For example, do not state the procedure as "dry well." Instead, make a clear explanation: "Today, maintain a temperature of 65°C ± 3°C for 10 minutes ± 1 minute." When using a dryer that can fulfill these conditions without requiring workers to measure time and temperature, you can write a simpler yet still specific rule: "Move the dial to *high* on the temperature scale, set the timer to 10 minutes, and switch it on."

- *Focus on safety:* Dangerous methods are not acceptable, even if they are optimal from the quality and efficiency standpoints. Determine what methods are too dangerous and clearly state the necessary safety warnings. Although it is essential to provide protection equipment and safety warning devices, you must have regulations for using emergency equipment, if necessary.

- *Coordination of related standards and specifications:* Make thorough checks to ensure that new general and technical standards conform to those used previously and that they do not conflict with those for related processes. Troubles often arise when improvements are made to only one part of a system. Failure to harmonize standards shows insufficient cooperation with related departments and with people responsible for preceding and following processes. You should discuss the close coordination of standards with all people involved.
- *A simple system for managing modifications:* For standards to be followed, they must be workable standards. Problem-solving measures and many minor improvements should be incorporated diligently into the record of the standard. It is essential to manage operating standards so that they can be easily revised when improvements are made.

The term *operation standard* encompasses the content of the technical standard or specification as well as issues about writing, issuing, and revising technical specifications. It is used in many different ways, according to the product as well as the size and organization of the factory. Managing technical specifications involves making specifications appropriate to their purpose, putting them in an accessible format, and managing the contents of the specifications themselves.

Some general purpose equipment and machinery make products that have many different quality specifications. By changing dies, tools, and settings such as temperature and revolutions per minute, these machines can be used flexibly to respond to the increasing variety of products required by customers. In this situation, two types of manuals should be used for operation standards — an operation manual and a separate instruction sheet for each type of product (see Figure 5-2).

Operation Manuals for Each Process

Write an operation manual for each machine and piece of equipment used in each process, based principally on the techniques involved in the technical standards relating to each process. You should describe the organization of

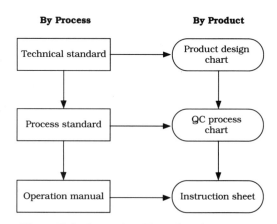

Figure 5-2: **Operation Manual and Instruction Sheet**

machinery and equipment and the process standards that determine the conditions set for the process. In addition to planning, machine operation, adjustment, and maintenance methods, the operation manual should include a conditions and settings chart and specification values in the appendix.

The operation manual should be used as an education and training manual rather than as a text. Operations instructors should each have a copy to show to operators as they direct and train them. As the trained operators acquire the skill needed for the job, they will not need to refer frequently to the operation manual during the course of daily work. The manual should be kept in the workplace, however, for reference when the need arises. Figure 5-3 shows the layout of an operation manual page.

Instruction Sheets for Each Product

Instruction sheets contain the important points of a processing operation performed by a certain machine on a particular product. They are issued according to product numbers and displayed in the workplace while that particular product is being made. The sheet includes information on processing conditions, such as die and tool specifications; settings such as temperature, rotational frequency, and oil pressure; quality characteristic targets such as precision of measurements and surface hardness; and inspection methods in tables and diagrams. Particularly important safety and quality notes are also indicated.

Instruction sheets summarize important instructions and quantitative information on the organization of the manufacturing process for each product. They are based on product design diagrams for each product, on the QC process table that determines the control method for each process, and on condition settings from the instruction manual mentioned above. A card format instruction sheet is shown in Figure 5-4.

After acquiring skills in the training course and from the instruction manual, operators consult the instruction sheets, summarizing the main points of their work, to perform their work correctly and efficiently. Instruction manuals are sometimes called summary or proce-

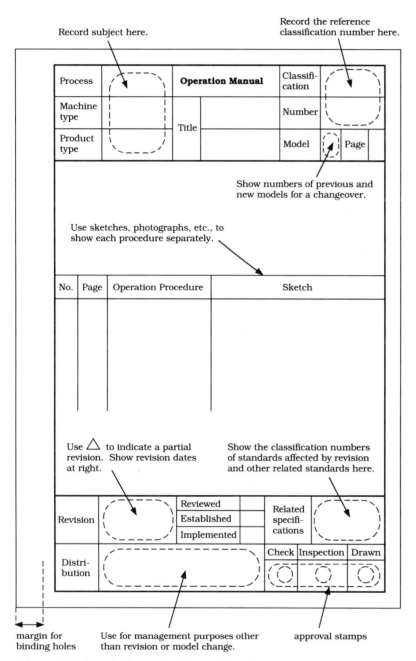

Record subject here.

Record the reference classification number here.

Show numbers of previous and new models for a changeover.

Use sketches, photographs, etc., to show each procedure separately.

Use △ to indicate a partial revision. Show revision dates at right.

Show the classification numbers of standards affected by revision and other related standards here.

margin for binding holes

Use for management purposes other than revision or model change.

approval stamps

Figure 5-3: **Sample Operation Manual Page Format**

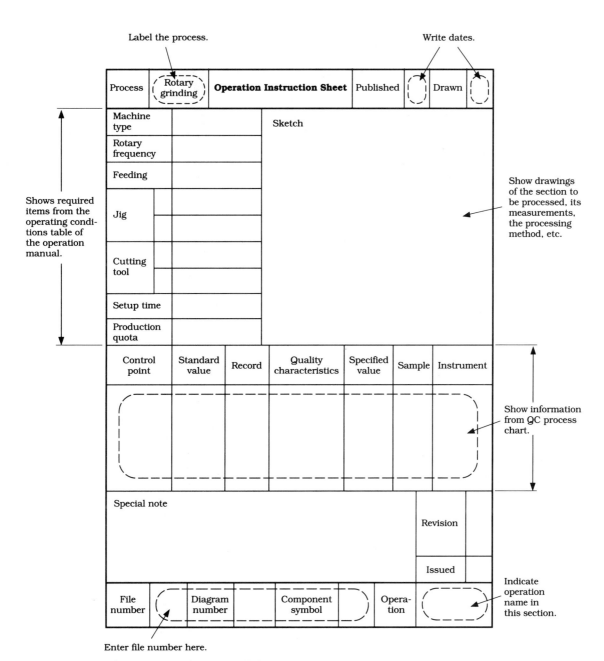

Label the process.

Write dates.

Shows required items from the operating conditions table of the operation manual.

Show drawings of the section to be processed, its measurements, the processing method, etc.

Show information from QC process chart.

Indicate operation name in this section.

Enter file number here.

Figure 5-4: **Sample Instruction Sheet Format**

dure books, and instruction sheets may be called instruction tables or diagram books. However you refer to them, take care not to confuse the two and let the workplace terminology become ambiguous.

To ensure rapid and detailed revisions, the operation manual and instruction sheet editor should delegate responsibility for preparing them to the supervisor or manager who is responsible for the workplace. This arrangement will make the standards and specifications for process and technical standards already discussed workable. Maintenance management should be performed under dynamic standards.

The ongoing technical revolution is gradually transforming the form of operation standards. This is particularly true of numerically controlled (NC) machinery in which the operating standard is a program tape. Systems control using mechatronics is changing operation standards as robots, factory automation, and other forms of automation are developed. The medium for conveying information from one human being to another is changing from paper to color CRT display. Necessary instructions and warnings are moving on-line through control panel keyboards. Whatever form standards take in the future, remember the fundamentals of operating systems and develop your management systems in response to technological developments.

References

"Japanese Industrial Standard JIS Z 8101-1981: Glossary of Terms Used in Quality Control." Japanese Standards Association.

Japanese Standards Association. "Standardization." *JIS Handbook.* Japanese Standards Association, 1986.

Miura, Shin, ed. *A Dictionary of Total Quality Control Terms.* Japanese Standards Association, 1985.

Ozeki, Kazuo, *QC Introductory Series 2: Promotion of Management and Improvement.* Japanese Standards Association, 1983.

6

Leadership

The Leadership of the Foreman

The leadership of the foreman is the method by which he or she communicates goals and tasks to subordinates to obtain their cooperation and creative engagement in the task. It is not acquired simply through education and is not merely a matter of giving orders. If the foreman is to win the trust and enthusiastic cooperation of workers, he or she needs to acquire knowledge and experience through earnest effort and a certain level of achievement. A supervisor must also be able to influence employees through example and leadership.

Guidelines of Exercising Leadership

One of the foreman's primary responsibilities is arousing the employees' enthusiasm through leadership. Some guidelines follow.

A Leader Nourishes Dreams

The leader should have a dream for the work, the workplace, or the project. This is not simply a daydream; it is more like a vision. This vision should inspire the enthusiasm and help actualize the potential of members or workers to reach a goal. This dream takes time, intelligence, and everyone's cooperation. Asking superiors and related departments for help is especially important.

Understand People Better

A leader who doesn't understand human psychology is not qualified to lead. A leader who unconsciously hurts the feelings of employees will not last long. If you do not understand the ins and outs of human psychology, you will not win people's hearts or lead them well, no matter how good your intentions.

Especially today, with the increasing diversity of human values, you must understand that people have different philosophies and desires. Simply offering more money (for example, adjusting compensation or bonus) or higher status does not necessarily motivate people. Leadership requires management based on human feelings to complement management based on logic.

Delegate

Delegating authority is an essential part of inspiring enthusiasm in people. Delegating authority involves clarifying the objectives and conditions, and then giving employees and team members the authority to use the methods they see fit to meet the objective.

Delegating authority takes courage on the part of the leader — he or she is responsible for the consequences. The foreman should therefore think very carefully about the employees who will be entrusted with the job. He or she should keep several alternative plans in reserve. Otherwise he or she can only accept the workers' evaluation of the solution and will not be able to develop a better conclusion or give improved instructions. Delegating authority gives the foreman a chance to operate on a higher level; he or she has the time to step back and investigate problems from a different perspective. Discussing difficulties with workers and giving them advice is most important. Exercise strong personal direction only in emergencies.

A leader must judge whether or not to delegate a certain task. The maturity of the workers, in part, will determine whether a task can be completely or only partially delegated. A leader must be able to objectively assess the workers' abilities and reserve the decision of delegating if he or she cannot assume responsibility for the results.

Strive to Build Character

Employees will not follow a leader who does not possess, at least to some extent, enthusiasm, knowledge, skill, and accurate judgment. As a leader moves up the hierarchy, character becomes increasingly important. Although many factors are responsible for character formation, personal growth within an organization is a strong ingredient. Strive to become an excellent leader.

Train and Educate Your Employees

Just as iron is forged in heat, new and young workers are strengthened by training and practical experience in the workplace. The foreman should be aware of training opportunities offered by the corporate staff or by various line departments for practical workshops or on-the-job training.

Establish challenging goals to encourage workers to realize their full potential. This will give them a feeling of accomplishment and the experience of success once they have reached their goal. You should praise employees when they reach their goals. Criticism for laziness and inappropriate behavior is also important.

Checklists for Exercising Leadership

To help you develop your leadership abilities, here are several checklists gathered from a number of sources on leadership.

Ten Skills for Leadership*

1. Ability to adjust to the situation
   - Hard work, rather than any special qualification, makes a leader.
   - There is no one leadership style that is best in all circumstances.
   - Be firm yet accessible at work, easy-going after hours.
2. Ability to understand people
   - First impressions are often wrong.
   - Understand different types of people. Do not be reserved.
   - Try to understand other people by putting yourself in their place.

---

* Jun Matsumoto, *The Leadership.* (Japan Management Instruction Center, 1987).

3. Ability to direct and educate
   - Build on the strong points of workers.
   - Strive to become the director of a group of professionals.
   - Give praise and criticism at appropriate times.
4. Ability to raise morale
   - Arouse and boost your employees' enthusiasm for their task.
   - Boost the workers' desire to perform with the "three fundamentals"—encouragement, concern, and spontaneity.
   - Praise employees who are interested in their work. Speak candidly with those who are not trying to improve.
   - Try to find the causes of dissatisfaction among workers and resolve the problem.
5. Ability to motivate people
   - Learn some background about a person before your first interview with him or her.
   - Look at things from the other person's perspective rather than reacting quickly from your own point of view.
   - Do not focus on your improvement goal at the expense of the big picture, the workplace culture.
6. Ability to deal with people
   - Strive to learn how to handle difficult people.
   - Learn from all people.
   - Notice good points in other people.
7. Political ability
   - Develop your ability to exercise political power through understanding of yourself and others.
   - Use your strong points to attack weak counter-arguments that could block your progress.
   - Understand each other's desires to balance advantages and disadvantages in a compromise.
8. Ability to control
   - If you strive to be a leader who pleases employees, you will not be in control.
   - A leader should carefully diffuse challenges from workers.
   - A leader must act firmly in emergency situations.

9. Ability to master a group
    • Learn what workers expect as a group and strive to accomplish it.
    • Be aware of the actions of informal as well as formal groups.
    • Be sensitive to changes in the group's interest in its work.
10. Ability to understand the ambitions of others
    • Put yourself in another's place to understand that person better.
    • Express your views gently so that employees will be more likely to accept them.
    • Allow information to flow to you from the workers.

Ten Ways to Alienate Your Employees*

1. Scold the workers
    • Criticize someone in front of others.
    • Always find fault with employees' work.
    • Call attention only to problems and defects (ignore good work).
2. Abdicate the leader's role
    • Neither criticize nor give praise.
    • Show no concern about the results of work. Don't react to anything.
    • Do no more that what is expected.
3. Assign tasks inappropriately
    • Assign work to employees without regard for their abilities.
    • Force people to do certain tasks.
    • Do not tell people the purpose of a job when directing them how to do it.
4. Do not accept workers' opinions
    • Do not give employees an opportunity to express their opinions.
    • Listen but do not accept workers' opinions.
    • Never explain why you accept or reject someone's suggestion.

---

* Masumasa Imaizumi, ed., "QC Points Anthology," *The Workplace QC Reader* (JUSE Press Ltd., 1967), 59.

5. Show poor leadership
   - Deal with issues emotionally and irrationally.
   - Always stick to the rules (be a bureaucrat).
   - Don't show ambition.
6. Act unfairly
   - Favor a particular employee.
   - Decide salary increases unfairly.
   - Openly show affection or dislike for certain workers.
7. Fail to train and guide employees
   - Offer no advice about how to do the work.
   - Keep all knowledge to yourself and do not teach the workers.
   - Use ineffective teaching methods.
8. Do not plan properly
   - Change policies often.
   - Do not show plans to employees.
   - Change directions you have given in the middle of the job.
9. Do not accept responsibility
   - Shift responsibility to employees.
10. Do not define responsibilities and authority
    - Delegate responsibility but not authority.

Four Functions of Leadership

1. *Asking:* The leader interacts directly with employees on the job, showing them how to boost productivity.
   - Does the leader ask employees to persevere until the goal is achieved?
   - Does the leader ask employees to execute a plan faithfully once it has been decided upon?
   - Does the leader ask employees to find problems in the present situation and improve their work methods?
   - Does the leader check whether employees' work meets strict quality standards?
   - Does the leader ask workers to cut wasted and lost production?
2. *Sympathetic:* The leader is concerned with workers' feelings and behavior in the workplace.
   - Does the leader think the opinions and feelings of workers are important?

- Does the leader get together with employees to discuss problems when they arise?
- Does the leader control his or her feelings when employees make mistakes?
- Does the leader know the strong and weak points of his or her employees?
- Does the leader try to build teamwork?

3. *Mutual understanding:* The leader makes employees' work meaningful and important by providing necessary information and knowledge as the work progresses. This builds mutual understanding.
   - Does the leader keep workers informed of the company's philosophy and policies at all levels?
   - Does the leader pass on information and news of the activities of other departments?
   - Does the leader explain why policies and plans are being changed to obtain employee assent?
   - Does the leader describe long-term projects for the workplace?

4. *Reliability:* A workplace supervisor who is not a natural leader should be asked to consent to the following to fulfill the role of leader:
   - Are the leader's decisions and judgments trusted by other workers?
   - Does the leader make judgments and decisions quickly?
   - Does the leader handle worker's problems fairly?
   - Does the leader carry out plans that have been decided upon?
   - Does the leader offer his or her own new proposals while trying to solve a problem?

References

Imaizumi, Masumasa, ed. "QC Points Anthology." *The Workplace QC Reader* 59. JUSE Press Ltd., 1967.

Matsumoto, Jun. *The Leadership.* Japan Management Instruction Center, 1987.

7

Small Group Activities

The gathering together of people from the same workplace to participate in some activity with a common goal is called small group activity. Small group activities are valuable because:

1. People have different ways of thinking and different approaches. A small group can foster a creative atmosphere that will benefit from these differences.
2. New concepts can be created during intense discussions of how to discover and solve problems.
3. The cooperation of group members makes it possible to bring the collective capabilities of the group into play—the synergy effect.

The quality control (QC) circle (also known as a quality circle or a quality team) is one type of group activity seen frequently. Self-managing teams and zero defects circles are other examples.

What Is a QC Circle?

"*QC circles* are small groups from the same workplace, that operate autonomously and carry out quality control activities. The members of these small groups learn on their own and teach one another as part of a company-wide quality control movement. The circles use QC methods to involve the entire work force in continuously improving the management of the workplace."*

QC circle activities were inspired by the late Professor Kaoru Ishikawa's suggestion to "build a group around the foreman in which operators and all personnel can participate." The quality circle, a Japanese invention, has been

---

* QC Circle Center, ed., *QC Circle Summary* (JUSE Press Ltd., 1970), 1, 2, 15, 33.

extremely successful. Today companies in the United States and many European and Asian countries are using this group improvement approach. The quality circle movement has expanded beyond manufacturing to fields such as the construction industry, the service industry, and financial service companies.

BASIC QUALITY CIRCLE CONCEPTS*

1. Contribute to the improvement of company organization. Once people working on the front line have begun acting autonomously through QC circles, they help create a strong organization with better management and improvements in the workplace. The QC circles promote company growth by improving the structure of the company as a whole.

2. Respect human nature and create a lively workplace. We must move away from the premodern management style that emphasized efficiency exclusively and ignored the humanity of the workers. Improve human relations in the workplace by respecting the will, autonomy, and humanity of the workers and stimulating their creativity. This results in a lively, motivating workplace.

3. Realize human capabilities and draw on unlimited potential. Through self-study and cooperation, QC circle activities gradually raise employees' capabilities. The workers learn to do what they couldn't do before.

Preparing for QC Circle Activities**

1. *Self-study.* In self-study, individuals strive to realize their potential by developing their abilities in a new area that they feel they need to work on. The foreman should be a resource and guide for the self-study efforts of QC circle members.

---

* QC Circle Center, ed., *QC Circle Summary* (JUSE Press Ltd., 1970), 1, 2, 15, 33.
** Ibid.

2. *Respect for autonomy.* QC circle activities respect autonomy. The effectiveness of these groups is closely related to the stimulation autonomy gives to the activities.

3. *Group activity.* QC circle activities are carried out by a group of fellow workers from the same workplace who share the same goal. The best ideas of each QC circle member stimulate and advance the circle's activities.

4. *Total participation.* In workplaces where QC circles are established, everyone is a member of a QC circle and participates in QC conferences. Everyone has something to contribute. Each member helps the QC circle by contributing his or her thoughts and statements.

5. *Applying QC methods.* QC circles autonomously discover problems, analyze the causes, and then perform management improvement activities designed to prevent the problems from recurring. These groups do not rely only on experience and intuition, they study and apply QC methods to gather data, analyze it, and use the information to make valid judgments and take appropriate action.

6. *Tying activities closely to the workplace.* Since QC circle activities take place within the company, they cannot operate independently of the workplace. QC circle activities may break to make presentations at outside QC conferences, but otherwise they proceed continuously.

7. *Keeping QC circles active over the long term.* QC circle activities are one facet of a company-wide quality control program. Managers and production workers must cooperate to keep QC circles active and vigorous over the long term.

8. *A place for mutual education.* The cooperation of the entire work force can make QC activities lively. The members of a QC circle can upgrade their skills and knowledge by teaching one another. This mutual education provides group members with new perspectives and teaches them new methods for carrying out their work.

9. *Thinking through improvement proposals.* Not all suggested schemes are truly creative proposals. People need to study problems and think carefully to propose intelligent suggestions. Members need to learn how to change their viewpoints and ways of thinking.

10. *Quality, problem, and improvement awareness.* QC circles should always be concerned with improving quality, discovering the causes of workplace problems, and finding better ways to accomplish goals. The foreman has the essential role of encouraging the QC circles by explaining plans clearly, stimulating their activities, and supporting them.

Introducing QC Circle Activities

If QC circles are properly introduced into a company, they will develop rapidly. Often the first step is to expose workers and managers to group improvement activities at QC circle conferences and QC circle exchange meetings.* However, companies that try to introduce QC circles in every workplace simultaneously usually find that QC circles established as a result of a top management order do not last long. The best approach is to begin by making workplaces autonomous.

Although several methods for starting QC circle activities are presented below, there is no one best method. Adapt the ideas below to the unique needs of your company.

Methods for Initiating QC Circle Activities

- *Attend a QC circle conference to hear QC case presentations from other companies.* In Japan, foremen, workers, and management representatives promoting QC circle activities attend a conference sponsored by the national QC circle headquarters or by a branch office to hear the experiences of other companies. QC conferences may include presentations by various QC circles

---

* QC Circle Center, ed., *Fundamentals of QC Circle Activity Management* (JUSE Press Ltd., 1971), 114, 116, 117.

as well as talks by professors, consultants, and other promoters of QC circles, discussion groups, and factory tours.

- *Visit a plant that incorporates QC circle activities and learn how QC circles were introduced.* Listen to stories about methods for introducing QC circles and examples of its implementation, difficulties, and failures. This will help you understand what QC circles are and what are the proper methods for introducing and promoting QC circles.

- *Read books and magazines about QC circle program management.* Learn about managing QC circle programs and activities through books and articles written by people with experience. Many books are available about QC circles; select simple books to start with.

- *Hold a workplace meeting and discuss starting QC circles with your employees.* Discuss how to start QC circles with the people who will be in the first QC circle. Rely on advice and cooperation from your superiors. Talk with people in the QC promotion department and rely on their support for management methods.

- *Hold a start-up meeting to establish a QC circle in your own workplace and discuss how to select a theme.* First, the leader creates a group of between six and eight people. Important workplace matters such as equipment arrangement, safety, compliance with operation standards, and so on, are discussed. The group draws up an implementation plan, consisting of surveying the current situation, setting goals, analyzing causes, taking measures to resolve the problem, confirming the effectiveness of the solution, and ensuring that the problem does not recur.

- *The QC circle begins work on the selected theme in parallel with its studies.* Start QC circle activities by taking up the theme you have selected. Gain experience with methods for solving problems, applying QC methods, conducting a circle meeting, and cooperatively delegating responsibility for action steps.

- *Discuss experience gained from QC circle activities and how to proceed in the future.* The people involved reflect on theme selection, problem-solving procedures, effectiveness of meetings, and relations with managers based on their experience in the circle. They also discuss how the circle should conduct itself in future activities.

Promoting QC Circle Activities

Once a QC circle program has been established in a company, the next step is to ensure that it will survive as a continuing, autonomous activity. There are instances in which QC circles have been successful after several failures, but it is easier to plan well and not have to overcome the inertia of failure. Here we present a model for planning QC circle promotion activities. You will want to adapt this or design your own to meet the needs of your workplace.

Step 1: Organizing a QC Circle of Employees from the Same Workplace

A QC circle is a small group of people from the same workplace who autonomously perform quality control activities. Leaders and QC circle members from the same workplace are basically organized as shown in Figure 7-1. The QC circle should have no more than ten members. If the circle group has too many members, divide it into mini-circles, as shown in Figure 7-2.

Step 2: Choosing a Leader

When QC circles are introduced, the leader's enthusiasm can make a great difference in the success of the group. The foreman often serves as the group leader at the start. Once the activities are well underway and the members' abilities have been demonstrated, a leader is selected from among the members of the group.

Step 3: Registering the QC Circle

Although the QC circle is an autonomous activity, it will become inactive and eventually die if it is neglected. The company's QC circle promotion office should establish a registration system as it organizes QC circles. Setting up a registration system will help the QC circle promotion office keep track of QC circle activities. Table 7-1 shows

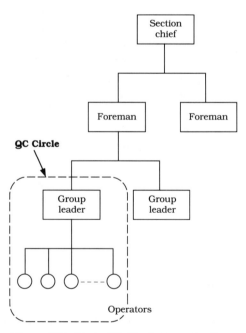

Figure 7-1: **Basic QC Circle Organization**

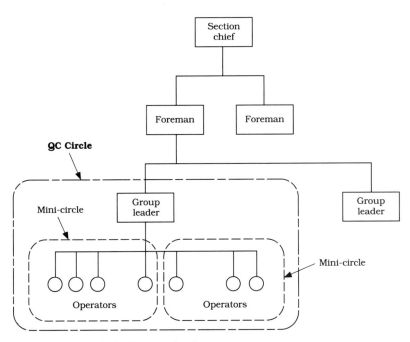

Figure 7-2: **Mini-circle Organization**

a sample company QC circle registration form. QC circles in Japan can register nationally with the QC Circle Center (part of the Japan Science and Technology Federation).*

Step 4: Drawing Up an Annual Activities Plan for Growth in the Number of Circles

Soon after QC circles are introduced in the company, organize group study on topics such as how to conduct a QC circle, how to improve presentations to management, learning QC methods, and problem-solving methods. Next, present more specific study topics such as organizing and arranging the workplace, reducing costs, improving productivity, and increasing the machine utilization ratio. Set goals for the circles, such as increasing the number of themes completed each year or winning various company-wide awards for quality improvement.

---

* In the United States, organizations such as the Association for Quality and Participation (AQP) track national membership in quality circles and foster team-based improvement efforts. — Ed.

Annual QC Circle Registered Membership										
Circle Name	Registration Number					Name of Circle Leader			Plant Dept. Section	
No.	Name	Male	Female	Part-time	Age	Years continuously employed	Years in this circle	Occupation	QC Circle educational background (course name and date)	Notes
1										
2										
3										

*Katsukichi Ishihara, *Collection of Checklists and Worksheets for QC Circle Activities* JUSE Press Ltd., 1982), 29, 85, 87, 88.

Table 7-1: **QC Circle Registered Member Chart***

Once the circle has chosen a theme and set a goal, the leader solicits the opinions of circle members on the steps involved in achieving the goal. To develop a plan, the group discusses matters such as scheduling and assigning authority and responsibility.

Step 5: Selecting a Theme Based on the Circle's Experience in Improvement Activities

If you select a difficult theme to start with, the QC circle will not be successful. Choosing a small problem that the circle can solve fairly quickly will build confidence within the circle and move its activities forward. Theme selection should pass through the following stages:

1. Hold a meeting in which the group studies how to run a QC circle and learns simple QC methods to obtain a basic understanding of how a QC circle works. A study of the Seven QC Tools (see Part II) is a good place to start.
2. Consider workplace problems such as organization, arrangement, and safety.

3. Consider problems of processing, assembly, and common errors that occur in the workplace.

4. Consider workplace problems such as improper assembly, defective parts, and delays in delivery.

Step 6: Performing Data Analysis to Solve Problems

Members of quality circles can get a feeling of accomplishment and work toward personal growth as they solve problems. Problem-solving methods are presented in Chapter 3.

Step 7: Evaluating QC Circle Activities

The QC circle as a group should occasionally check on its own activities and results and evaluate correctly the positive and negative aspects. There are two main types of evaluation:

• Checking the results of circle activities. Compare the target values you hoped to achieve in the QC activity plan with the actual values achieved. Table 7-2 gives an example of these evaluation items.

• Checking the way QC circle activities are performed. The sample checklists in Tables 7-3 and 7-4 give methods for checking theme selection, the way activities are carried out, applications of QC techniques, member motivation, and so on.

Quality	Number of claims, product defect rate, number of processing mistakes, strength of product, number of assembly line adjustments, product precision.
Cost	Cost reduction rate, labor reduction rate, materials retained, cost of mistakes, reduction rate of original units, etc.
Delivery date	Number of delivery delays, number of days delivery delayed, number of misdirected deliveries or deliveries of the wrong goods, number of wrong products or defective products, the number of instances when an insufficient quantity or too large a quantity of the product was delivered, etc.
Safety and the environment	Number of disasters, number of accidents, number of environmental improvement cases, number of cases in which items were not arranged properly or were not in the proper order, number of cases in which operations that create worker fatigue were improved, etc.
Morale	Attendance rate, number of proposals, number of suggestions for improving the workplace, meeting attendance, number of case presentations made, etc.
Management	Number of cases when work was performed to prevent a problem from recurring, number of standards set, number of control points set, number of control charts made, number of check sheets made, etc.

Table 7-2: **Sample Activity Evaluation Items**

Evaluation Item	Summary of Evaluation			Points
1. Theme selection (20 points)	1) Did all the circle members discuss the theme thoroughly? 2) Did the circle understand the background and drawbacks of the theme? 3) Did the circle stress the effectiveness of the theme?			20 10 0
2. Number of people participating (20 points)	1) Did the circle members participate actively in the theme? 2) Was it always possible to assist work stations whenever they asked for help? 3) Did the involved work stations enthusiastically provide assistance?			20 10 0
3. Was the theme suitably implemented? (40 points)	Evaluation Items	Evaluation Summary	Evaluation Points	
	1. Achieving objective of the activity (10 points)	1) Can the initial objective be fully accomplished? 2) Is the method for achieving the objective appropriate?	10 5 0	40 30 20 10 0
	2. Analysis (10 points)	1) Has the circle thoroughly grasped previous data? 2) Has the circle thoroughly thought out its method of analysis? 3) Did the group apply QC methods well to its analysis?	10 5 0	
	3. QC circle activities (5 points)	1) Was there effective teamwork? 2) Was there enthusiastic cooperation?	5 3 0	
	4. Check (5 points)	1) Were all the results checked? 2) Was the problem clarified while checks were performed?	5 3 0	
	5. Standardization (10 points)	1) Was a system set in place to establish ongoing management of the problem?	10 5 0	
4. Applicability of the management technology (10 points)	1) Was analysis performed using appropriate methods at each step? 2) Were QC and IE methods used well? 3) How were special methods used?			10 5 0
5. Satisfaction of superiors (10 points)	1) Did a superior examine the results thoroughly? 2) Did a superior examine the QC circle activity thoroughly? 3) Is the supervisor satisfied with the organizational methods of the QC circle leader?			10 5 0

*QC Circle Center, ed., *Fundamentals of QC Circle Activity Management* (JUSE Press Ltd., 1971), 114, 116, 117.

Table 7-3: **Sample Self-evaluation Checklist for QC Circle Activities***

Observation Point	Evaluation				Observation Point	Evaluation		
	Good	Average	Bad			Good	Average	Bad
1. Workplace environment 1) Can you create a cheerful workplace environment? 2) Can you improve on existing technology? 3) Can you improve the defect rate, the pace of production, and efficiency? 4) Can you improve attendance? 5) Are there safety problems?					**6. Developing a problem-solving plan** 1) Did all circle members discuss the plan? 2) Is it possible to implement your plan? 3) Have all circle members been assigned a function? 4) Are methods applied properly? 5) Is teamwork needed to solve problems?			
2. Members' will to work 1) Do the members want to participate in QC circle activities? 2) Are QC circle activities explained so that the members will understand them? 3) Do the members strive to improve their own capabilities? 4) Are the members becoming more aware of problems? 5) Is education thorough?					**7. Checking results to avoid recurrence** 1) Is the activity carried out according to plan? 2) Are the results evaluated correctly? 3) Is the proposed improvement approved by the relevant person? 4) Is the improvement made a standard? 5) Are the members thoroughly informed of the improvement point?			
3. Carrying out circle activities 1) Are the QC circles carried out autonomously? 2) Is the QC circle leader effective? 3) Is there harmony within the group? 4) Does the group get suitable guidance from superiors and staff? 5) Is the discussion of the theme carried out according to plan?					**8. Arranging the results** 1) Does the report of results tell a QC story? 2) Are the results evaluated correctly? 3) Are the results reported to superiors? 4) Are there opportunities for the circle to present its results at a meeting of QC circles? 5) Does one particular person tend to present the results at the meeting of QC circles?			
4. QC circle meetings 1) Do meetings begin on time? 2) Are some members absent or late? 3) Do all members participate actively in discussions? 4) Do all members help the meeting move along? 5) Do all members carry out the decision of the meeting?					**9. Moving to new themes** 1) Do the members have confidence and a fighting spirit? 2) Do the members understand the problems in the previous theme? 3) Are problems solved in the operation of the QC circle? 4) Can members tell that the circle is making progress? 5) Are the new members trained well?			
5. Theme selection 1) Are themes selected autonomously by the circle? 2) Does the theme help superiors achieve their policy goals? 3) Does the theme selected correspond to the abilities of the members? 4) Is the objective clear? 5) Have relations with other departments been considered?					**10. Reviewing the activity** 1) Did the circle use its meeting time effectively? 2) Is the circle able to make use of morning or evening meetings or idle time? 3) Did the circle present reports at large QC circles conferences inside and outside the company? 4) Are the members kept informed of the related activities of other QC circles? 5) Did the circle come up with its proposal spontaneously?			

Reviewing the period during which we worked on this theme, what did we think was positive?	Total (A)		
	Factor		
What would we like to see from superiors and staff?	Total (B)		
	Total points		

*QC Circle Center, ed., *Fundamentals of QC Circle Activity Management* (JUSE Press Ltd., 1971), 114, 116, 117.

Table 7-4: **Sample Self-evaluation Checklist for QC Circle Activities***

Step 8: Presenting the Results

The presentation of results is an integral part of QC circle activities. With each opportunity to present its results at a conference, the circle summarizes its experience up to that time. This experience helps the circle understand its successes and setbacks and move into higher levels of improvement activities. Some guidelines for QC circle presentations:

1. Think about how to present the material. Although the material is the same, different presentations will make different impressions on the audience. Use aids such as wall maps, overhead transparencies, and slides. Objects for the audience to examine are very useful.
2. Everyone should participate in planning the presentation. The presentation is the product of all the QC circle members. Accordingly, all members of the circle should discuss the contents of the report and preparations for the presentation.
3. Rehearse the presentation. Find ways to improve the length of the presentation, the volume of the speaker's voice, the speaker's approach, and the contents of the presentation. Everyone should work together and suggest improvements to produce an effective presentation.

Step 9: Reviewing the Past Year's Activities

QC circle activities are carried out continuously in the workplace. As soon as one improvement theme has been concluded and the circle's experience with that theme has been reviewed, a new theme is selected. QC circles in many companies complete between two and five themes annually.

Throughout the year, the QC circle assesses the value of its role in the company quality control program, using checklists such as the one shown in Table 7-5. The members of the QC circle, together with their superiors, review the way the circle has carried out its activities and the results it has obtained. They then consider plans for the next year's QC circle activities.

Item	Subject	Evaluation Points
1. Number of themes registered (20 points)	1) Number of themes the circle is able to take up every year. (_____ cases) 2) Are records of the activities arranged and preserved? (_____ cases) 3) Were any themes abandoned? (_____ cases)	20 10 0
2. Effectiveness (20 points)	1) Was it possible to check for concrete results? • Defect rate: _____ % → _____ % • Effective value: $ _____ 2) Was the desired effect achieved? • (Objective achieved: _____ %) 3) Are the incidental effects well understood?	20 10 0
3. Cooperative system (20 points)	1) Did the circle members actively participate? • Number of times meetings lasted longer than 30 minutes. Times: _____ Time Extension: _____ • Participation rate during meetings: _____ % • Number of circle meeting reports: _____ 2) Was the division of labor among members suitable for the themes chosen? Were the themes arranged so that all members could participate? 3) Could cooperation be obtained from management and related workplaces?	20 10 0
4. Number of reports given inside and outside the company (20 points)	1) Number of reports given at company QC circle conferences. • Dept. meeting Number of participants: — Number of reports: — • Plant conferences Number of participants: — Number of reports: — • Company conferences Number of participants: — Number of reports: — 2) Number of occasions on which reports were given at QC circle conferences outside the company • Number of cases: _____	20 10 0
5. Degree of management satisfaction (20 points)	1) Does the management thoroughly evaluate the results and effectiveness of the year's activities? • Activity reports to supervisor: _____ reports _____ projects begun 2) Did the supervisor feel the circle organized its activities well? • Level of autonomy: _____ %	20 10 0
(Review of QC circle activities)	Total evaluation points — QC circle	100 points / points
	Total evaluation points — Supervisor	100 points / points

*Katsukichi Ishihara, *Collection of Checklists and Worksheets for QC Circle Activities.* (JUSE Press Ltd., 1982), 29, 85, 87, 88.

Table 7-5: **QC Circle Activity Annual Checklist***

The QC Circle Promotion Organization

Although QC circle activity is autonomous, a circle program will run into obstacles that block progress if the company neglects it. To guide and support the QC circles, a company must create an organization that promotes them as part of a company-wide quality control program. The next sections discuss various aspects of a QC circle promotion organization. Figure 7-3 shows a checklist for the topics of this discussion.

Appointing Someone to Be Responsible for QC Circle Promotion

In a company with a company-wide quality control program, there are often many well-qualified candidates for the head of the QC circle promotion office. The factory

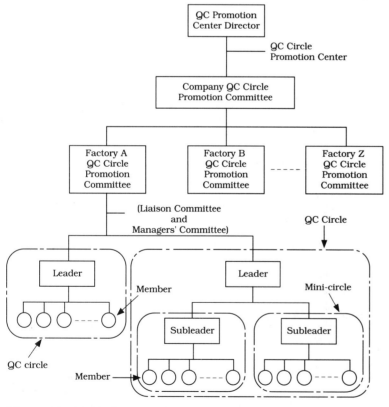

Figure 7-3: **QC Circle Promotion Organization**

managers and department heads determine the managerial functions for the QC circle promotion office at the factory and departmental levels.

Setting Up a QC Circle Promotion Office

Setting up a QC circle promotion center within the company QC office is convenient, but the QC office should not promote QC circles to the exclusion of promoting all quality control activities throughout the company. If necessary, decentralize — establish a QC circle promotion center within each factory and designate a person responsible for QC circle promotion within each department.

Setting Up a QC Circle Promotion Committee

Many companies, realizing that QC circle activities are autonomous, have set up QC circle promotion committees in each factory or each department. Composed of section heads, foremen, and QC circle leaders chosen from each factory or department, these committees have made QC circles more effective. The company QC circle promotion committee is often composed of representatives from the QC circle promotion committees of each factory or department.

Setting Up Liaison Committees

As the managerial plan for the QC circles progresses and the QC circles become more autonomous—operating according to the ideas of the QC circle representatives— it is helpful for foremen with experience on QC circle promotion committees and QC circle leaders to set up liaison committees and managers' committees to guide and support the QC circles.

Managing QC Circle Promotion

Annual QC Circle Promotion Policy and Promotion Plan

QC circle promotion policy and promotion planning are central to QC circle activities. The QC circle promotion center and the company QC circle promotion committee both review the QC circle activities of the previous year, funda-mental QC circle concepts, and company policy as they set a QC circle promotion policy and plan for the coming year. Once this policy and plan has been accepted by the head of the QC circle office, it is sent to the circles in the name of the company QC circle promotion commit-tee.

Registration of QC Circles within the Company

The QC circle promotion center should establish a regis-tration system once the circles are organized. Although QC circles are autonomous, they are likely to fail if neglected. Once a QC circle has been organized, register the group right away so that the QC circle promotion center will be aware of it. This registration enables the QC circle promotion center and the promotion committees to keep track of the situation in each workplace in the company and to assist the QC circles there.

QC Circle Meetings

Meetings are an important part of QC circle activities. The circle can discuss the topic of the meeting, provide infor-mation, and facilitate the mutual enlightenment of its members. To promote QC circle activities, everyone should attend and have the opportunity to speak and participate.

1. *Frequency of meetings.* Many different meeting sched-ules are used. Some examples are a five-minute morning meeting every day; a weekly thirty-minute meeting during the Wednesday lunch break; or fifteen minutes at 3 p.m. on the first and third Thursdays of the month, plus an hour after work on the first and third Mondays of the month. Set your own schedule according to your workplace situation. Meetings should last no longer than an hour.
2. *When to hold meetings.* Although meetings are some-times held after work, the recent trend is to hold them on company time. If there are two shifts, hold a meeting just before work. If you hold meetings after

company hours, you should consider any inconvenience this might cause parents or night school students. Finding a meeting time that suits your workplace is essential.

3. *Spacing meetings.* Meeting frequency often depends on the theme the circle has selected, but many QC circles have two monthly meetings. Some circles, depending on the progress of their activity, shorten the interval between meetings and reduce the length of each meeting. You must rely on your own intuition to discover the relationship between meeting interval and meeting length; however, it's generally desirable to shorten the meetings and hold them more often.

4. *Compensation for meetings not held on company time.* Although QC circle activities are autonomous activities, many companies compensate personnel for time spent at meetings related to their work (other than for study). Some companies ask workers to participate at least partly on their own time.

QC Circle Activities Reporting System

QC circles, once they have decided on an improvement theme, should register it with the company's QC circle promotion center. When they have completed their theme, they should issue a simple report on their work. The report should include complete instructions on the technique for preventing the problem from recurring, standardization, and daily management methods.

QC Circle Education and Training

Educating groups of workers in training courses is important but on-the-job training and education is essential. Training from supervisors and experienced leaders in the following areas is particularly important to the development of QC circles:

- fundamentals of quality control
- basic concepts and management of QC circles
- problem-solving procedures
- applying QC methods

QC Circle Activity Evaluation

QC circle evaluation plays an important part in invigorating autonomous QC circle activities and in fostering the continuity of QC circles. These evaluation methods are:

1. QC circle self-evaluation (see Tables 7-3 and 7-4).
2. Supervisor or QC circle promotion committee evaluation of the QC circle (see Tables 7-6 and 7-7).
3. Comprehensive evaluation (see Table 7-8).

Exchanges with Other QC Circles

QC circle leaders and members visit other workplaces and factories in and outside their company to discuss QC circle experiences. Touring different workplaces is an extremely effective method for QC circles to learn from one another.

QC Circle Conferences

Reporting the experiences of the QC circle to a company-wide QC circle conference when a project has been completed promotes QC circle activities. See the checklists in Tables 7-7 and 7-9. The company can take advantage of QC circle conferences sponsored through the activities of various organizations outside the company.*

Awards and Recognition

An award system is an important factor in strengthening and ensuring the continuity of QC circle activities. Among the award schemes devised by various companies are:

1. Evaluate and present awards for each QC circle activity.
2. Evaluate QC circles' progress annually or semi-annually and present awards.
3. Sponsor QC circle conferences, evaluate the presentations, and present awards.

---

* Western organizations holding such meetings include the Association for Quality and Participation (AQP). —Ed.

Evaluation Items	Evaluation Summary	Evaluation Points
1. Character-istics of the activity	1) Did you clarify the circumstances under which the problem arose? 2) Did you make your discussion of difficulties, failures, or successes easy to understand? 3) Did you strive for a creative activity? 4) Did your circle give its best effort? 5) Did you consider the continuity and strengthening of the group in carrying out the activity?	5 3 1
2. Planning	1) Does the circle understand the policies and goals of its superiors and then autonomously and spontaneously devise a plan? 2) Is a consensus for the activity plan developed among the members? Are the members well educated about the plan? 3) Do you check on the progress of the plan? 4) Do you make the long-term plan clear? 5) Do you understand the present problem and consider it in your future plans?	5 3 1
3. Activity implementa-tion methods	1) Do you select a theme suitable for your group? 2) Did you apply data and QC methods? 3) Does cooperation and division of labor among members work out well? 4) Does the work of the circle develop with direction and assistance of superiors and staff? 5) Do the members cheerfully and willingly participate in circle activities?	5 3 1
4. Practice and results of activities	1) Do the members understand the nature of the QC circle and encourage its autonomous and spontaneous development? 2) Has the awareness of problems, quality, and improvements increased? 3) Has the willingness of circle members to study on their own and to take courses to improve their capabilities increased? 4) Do you strive to create a cheerful, lively workplace? 5) Does the circle present tangible as well as intangible results?	5 3 1
5. Methods for making presenta-tions	1) Does your circle increase the effectiveness of its talk by giving an enthusiastic, cheerful presentation? 2) The presentation has a focus — the workplace; is your presentation a QC story? 3) Do you strive to reach your listeners? 4) Do you try to use original presentation methods? 5) Do you make your main points within the time allotted?	5 3 1

*Katsukichi Ishihara, *Collection of Checklists and Worksheets for QC Circle Activities.* (JUSE Press Ltd., 1982), 29, 85, 87, 88.

Table 7-6:** **QC Circle Activity Checklist (for Reporting Activities)

Evaluation Items	Evaluation Summary	Evaluation Points
1. Theme selection method (10 points)	• Did you understand the situation well and analyze it thoroughly to select your theme? • Did the circle choose a theme in which everyone can participate? • Is there a clear relationship between the theme and management policy? • Are the theme's characteristic values clear?	10 5 0
2. Implementation of the activity and its degree of difficulty (20 points)	• Do the leader and members join in one autonomous circle to attack the essentials of the problem? • Is there creative thinking in the circle members' opinions? • Are circle meetings enthusiastic? • Are the circle steps (PDCA) carried out properly? • Is the circle's ability to carry out its activities continually strengthened?	20 10 0
3. Application of QC methods (10 points)	• Do you consider simple as well as complex QC methods and use them effectively? • Do you fully understand the QC methods you use? • Do you use cause-and-effect diagrams, Pareto diagrams, histograms, and control charts effectively? • Do you avoid errors by using control charts appropriately?	10 5 0
4. Action countermeasure (10 points)	• Is the countermeasure related to the cause of the abnormality? • Do you check the effectiveness of the various actions and countermeasures? • Do you rely on other departments when appropriate? • Is the circle capable of implementing the countermeasures to prevent the problem from recurring?	10 5 0
5. Effectiveness (10 points)	• Was the objective affected in the way desired? • Did you correctly evaluate tangible and intangible effects? • Did you evaluate the financial value of tangible effects? • Did you go beyond merely evaluating the effectiveness of the improvement?	10 5 0
6. Preventing the problem from recurring (10 points)	• Did you standardize whatever will prevent the problem from recurring? • Do you know how effective your efforts are? • Have you standardized similar work as well? • Was the countermeasure added to the standard, or was the standard revised?	10 5 0
7. Review and future planning (10 points)	• Did you look for problems as you made the review? • Are problems definitely specified? • Are future plans clearly defined? • Does the group persevere when the problem has not been solved and discuss the problem simply and from a broad perspective?	10 5 0
8. Perfecting the presentation (20 points)	• Was the presentation easy to understand? • Was the presentation well organized? • Do you use wall charts and exhibits well? • Did you respond to questions about your report in the allotted time?	20 10 0

*Katsukichi Ishihara, *Collection of Checklists and Worksheets for QC Circle Activities.* (JUSE Press Ltd., 1982), 29, 85, 87, 88.

Table 7-7: **QC Circle Conference Presentation Checklist***

Evaluation Items	Evaluation Summary	Evaluation Points
1. Can you organize and register a QC circle?	• Did all the people concerned join the QC circle? • Did you obtain the consent of your superior and register with the QC circle promotion office? • Do you have an organization table and registration form and revise when appropriate?	5 3 1
2. Is the activity plan of the QC circle clear?	• Do you make periodic and monthly activity plans? • Do you obtain guidance and approval from supervisors? • Are you able to check on the progress of the group?	5 3 1
3. What is the activity of the QC circle?	• Is the activity of the group in keeping with company policy? • Are most of the group's activities autonomous, or is the group directed by a supervisor? • Do you ask for your supervisor's help with your activities?	5 3 1
4. How are QC circle activities guided and supported?	• How did the superior guide QC circle activities? • How did the QC circle leader guide and teach the members of the circle? • How did the staff support the QC circle?	5 3 1
5. Was the method for selecting the theme appropriate?	• Was the theme chosen in keeping with company policy? • Was a suitable theme for QC circle activity chosen? • How did the supervisor guide the circle?	5 3 1
6. How was the theme carried out?	• Did all the circle members carry out the theme enthusiastically? • Is the activity moving along like a QC story? • Do you check if the activity is progressing according to the activity plan?	5 3 1
7. How are QC circle meetings conducted?	• Are meetings held regularly? • Do all members participate in and speak up at meetings? • Was attention paid to the way meetings are conducted?	5 3 1
8. Does the QC circle use QC methods effectively?	• Do you understand QC methods well? • Do you strive to use QC methods well? • Do you pay attention to using even simple methods well?	5 3 1
9. Can you confirm the effectiveness of the activity results?	• Do you confirm the effectiveness of activity results periodically? • How do you determine the effectiveness of activity results? • How many examples of effective activities do you have?	5 3 1
10. Do you consolidate the results of your activity by changing procedures so that the problem will not recur, and do you review the results of the activity?	• Do you revise standards books, summary books, control charts, etc.? • Do you revise related work so that similar problems will not occur? • Do you set the direction of future activities?	5 3 1

Table 7-8: **QC Circle Activities Global Evaluation Checklist**

Item	Topic	Evaluation Points	Presenting Circle			
			(1)	(2)	(3)	(10)
1. Theme selection method	• Is the reason for picking a particular theme clear? • Is the theme suitable for the group? • Is the theme related to the management's plans? • Were the opinions of circle members considered in the theme selection?	10				
2. Circle activities	• Did all the members participate in the creation and autonomous implementation of the execution plan? • Were circle meetings enthusiastic? (Were plans made for the participation of each member by assigning tasks, etc.?) • Was the activity carried out with the direction and support of superiors and staff? • Was the activity carried out with originality? • Were efforts made to improve the capabilities of circle members through self-study and by learning from one another? • Is the future direction of activities suitable?	30				
3. Problem-solving methods	• Is the method for determining the objective suitable (target value, date)? • Are you using an appropriate method for attacking a problem and eliminating the cause? • Did you discover the cause and handle it properly? • Did you find a measure for eliminating the problem? • Does the activity help you attain the objective? • Have you formulated a method for consolidating your results so that the problem will not recur?	20				
4. Application of QC methods	• Do you use data related to the objective effectively? • Do you make your plans hierarchically? • Do you understand the QC methods well and use them properly? • Do you use the QC methods creatively?	20				
5. Presentation methods	• Is the presentation suitable, enthusiastic, and persuasive? • Is the presentation easy to understand? Are the main points emphasized? • Are difficulties and failures described modestly in the talk? • Is the method of presentation original? • Is time budgeted appropriately in the presentation?	20				
Total		**100**				
Rank						
Notes						

Table 7-9: **QC Circle Conference Presentation Checklist**

Leadership Roles in the QC Circle Program

For QC circle activities to develop successfully, the foreman must understand QC circle fundamentals and guide, support, and cooperate with the QC circle.

The Role of the Manager

1. The manager should understand the nature of QC circle activities, develop a departmental plan in line with the policies of his or her own managers, and orient the activities of the QC circle.
2. The manager should thoroughly understand the significance of QC circle activities, adjust them to the operation of the organization, and support them.
3. It is important to create an atmosphere favoring the autonomous and spontaneous activities of the QC circle. Allow the QC circle to play a leading role.
4. Although the manager does not directly participate in the activities of the QC circle, he or she serves as an active adviser to the QC circle for selecting a theme, drawing up an activity plan, applying QC methods, running the QC circle, and so on.

The Role of the Foreman

1. The foreman should devise a basic plan for QC circle activities based on an understanding of the fundamental concepts and purpose of the QC circle.
2. The foreman should motivate the QC circle and support and train the circle leader to invigorate QC circle activities.
3. The foreman should understand the conditions under which the QC circle is operating, and create an environment in which the group can successfully pursue appropriate action in those conditions.
4. The foreman should plan QC circle activity report meetings, circle exchanges, and other communication activities. He or she should help circle members teach one another.

The Role of the Team Leader

1. The leader calls QC circle meetings. The QC circle meeting is an important QC circle activity for discussion and strategic action. The leader should plan the meeting carefully so that it will be effective in achieving its purpose.

2. The leader should organize a mutual assistance program for the members. Everyone should participate, speak, and play a part in this program.

3. The leader should foster cooperative relationships among the members of the group. Create teamwork by considering the feelings of each member of the team — circle members naturally will have differing points of view.

4. The leader should direct the members of the group. This requires the leader to study so that he or she can instruct and share information with the other members. The leader should strive to teach all members of the group to improve their capabilities while the circle works on its theme.

5. The leader should train an assistant to replace the leader after a suitable period of time. After a long period of leading a QC circle, he or she may get into a rut; a new outlook can revitalize the group.

References

Ishihara, Katsukichi. *Collection of Checklists and Worksheets for QC Circle Activities.* 29, 85, 87, 88. JUSE Press Ltd., 1982.

Management Technology Pocket Dictionary Editorial Committee, ed. *Management Technology Pocket Dictionary.* JUSE Press, 1984.

Miura, S., N. Kano, Y. Tsuda, and Y. Ohashi, eds. *TQC Terminology Dictionary.* Japanese Standards Association, 1985.

QC Circle Center, ed. *Fundamentals of QC Circle Activity Management.* 114, 116, 117. JUSE Press Ltd., 1971.

QC Circle Center, ed. *QC Circle Summary.* 1, 2, 15, 33. JUSE Press Ltd., 1970.

II
Tools

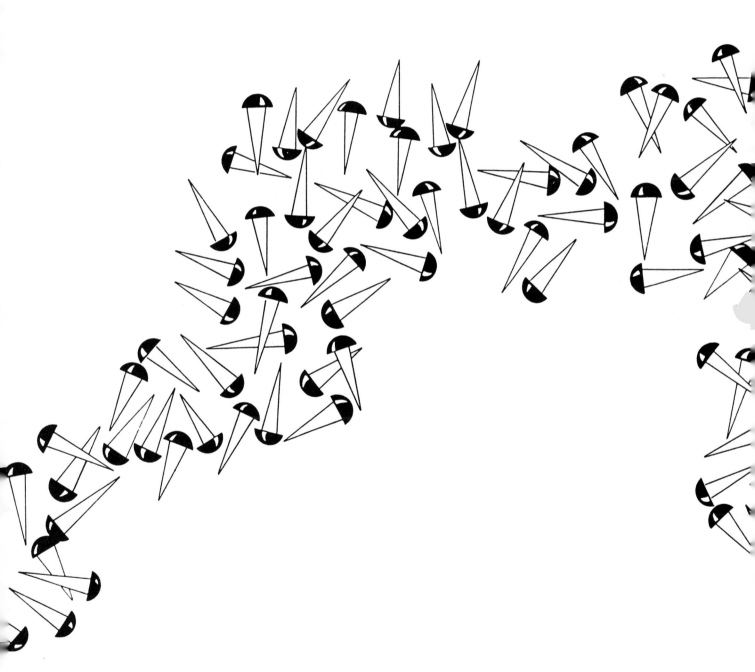

8

Applying Methods

Use a Method Suited to Your Objectives

The appropriate QC method should be selected and implemented properly to solve problems and make lasting improvements. Use the seven steps listed below to determine the cause of a problem and what must be done to resolve it. This systematic approach will help you select the method best suited to solve the problem and properly apply that method.

1. Grasp the problem.
2. Set the improvement objective.
3. Analyze the cause.
4. Discuss the improvement proposal.
5. Implement the improvement plan.
6. Evaluate the results of the improvement.
7. Make sure that the problem will not recur.

This section of the book introduces the use of the "Seven QC Tools"— graphs, Pareto diagrams, cause-and-effect diagrams, checksheets, histograms, control charts, and scatter diagrams. It also includes instruction on using five of the "Seven New QC Tools," a helpful set of planning techniques that includes affinity diagrams, relations diagrams, systematic diagrams, matrix diagrams, and arrow diagrams. Table 8-1 indicates the stages in which each of these twelve tools is most useful.

Fundamentals of Applying QC Methods

1. **Clearly understand your objective.** The first priority is to understand the actual situation, to define the problem clearly and to understand clearly the goals and objectives of the improvement.
2. **Use data that reflects the actual situation.** Knowing the origin of the data you are using is essential if you are to make objective judgments based on the actual situation. You must have objective data to evaluate

Improvement Step	Application or Objectives	Graph	Pareto diagram	Cause-and-effect diagram	Check sheet	Histogram	Control chart	Scatter diagram	Affinity diagram	Relations diagram	Systematic diagram	Matrix diagram	Arrow diagram
1. Understand the problem	Understand the actual situation								◎				
	Determine the problems		○	○	○				◎	○		○	
	Look at the scattering of the data					◎		○					
	Look at variations over time	◎					○						
	Stratify and compare data	◎			○	◎							
	Discuss the relative importance of various problems		◎							○	○	◎	
2. Set the improvement target	Discuss the difficulty of problems		◎								○		
	Evaluate the importance of problems		◎								○		
	Estimate the effectiveness of the improvement	○	○				○						
3. Factor analysis	Determine the factors involved		○	◎						◎	◎	○	
	Select the most important factors		◎	○	○					○	○	◎	
	Stratify and investigate the factors	○		○		◎	○			○			
	Look for relationships among factors			○				◎		○	◎	◎	
	Check the time series relationship among factors	○					◎						
4. Discuss the improvement measure	Generate and arrange ideas				◎						◎		
	Consider the improvement measure									○	○		
	Evaluate the improvement proposal		○		○						○	○	
	Examine the improvement results	○	○				○				○	○	
	Make an implementation plan												◎
5. Implementation of the improvement plan	Implement the improvement plan				◎								○
	Gather post-improvement data	○			○	○	○	○					
6. Evaluate the improvement results	Evaluate the effectiveness of the improvement using time series data	◎					◎						
	Evaluate the scattering of the data					◎	○						
	Confirm the results	○	◎		○	○	○	○					
7. Make the improvement permanent	Manage the implementation of the improvement	○			◎		○						
	Detect abnormalities	○			◎		◎						
	Report on the improvement activity	◎	◎	◎	○	◎	○	○			○	○	○

Note: ◎ = particularly effective   ○ = general use

Table 8-1: **QC Tools for the Seven Improvement Steps**

the actual situation — not convenient but unreliable data that conceals it.

3. Understand the advantages of a method. You should meet the preconditions for using statistical methods and use the methods in the most effective manner. You will be better able to apply QC methods if you know their range of applicability, proper procedures for using the methods, and how to explain the results you obtain.

4. Make the appropriate explanation for the results you obtain. If statistical methods show a deviation, a correlation, or an abnormality, determine the technical significance of these statements, the premises upon which these evaluations are based, and the technical and economic effects of a decision and action based on the conclusion. You must find a way to combine the new method with existing technology if you are to use it effectively.

9

How to Collect Data

The Goal of Data Collection

Quality control stresses "fact control." You must have the facts if you are to rely on abstract concepts, experience, or intuition to save you from making mistaken judgments and taking mistaken actions. Thus you need data that reveals the condition of products and processes.

Many different types of data are collected in the workplace every day. Data on factors such as quality, quantity, cost, and safety are recorded for the quality of materials and products, operating conditions, the quantity produced, and the number of processes involved. Data on problems and accidents that occur is also collected. The purpose of this data is to:

- grasp the current situation
- adjust the process
- control the process
- inspect and evaluate
- analyze and improve the process

Often it is unclear why a great deal of the data is collected and what purpose it serves. Conversely, much useful data does not get collected. Good data is data that has a clearly defined purpose and can fulfill the purpose for which it is intended. The conditions that data should meet are:

1. The purpose of the data and the object to be acted upon should be clear.
2. The history of the data should be clearly defined, including 5W1H:
   - What was collected
   - Why it was collected
   - When it was collected
   - Who collected it
   - Where it was collected from
   - How/by what method was it collected

3. Collect data on the relationship between quality (results) and the various factors that influence it.
4. Collect data impartially. Do not collect only data that is easy or convenient to collect.

Populations and Samples

Data is collected to understand the actual situation and to determine the proper action to take with respect to a process or product. Products are taken randomly from a process or a lot not to obtain information about these products themselves but about the population to which they belong. The condition of a process or a lot is inferred from measurements made on these products, which are then generalized to the entire process or lot.

The products from which observations are generalized are called a *population*. Products taken from a population are called *samples*. The relationship between a population and a sample is shown in Figure 9-1.

The number of units or unit quantities in a population is called the "population size" and is represented by N.

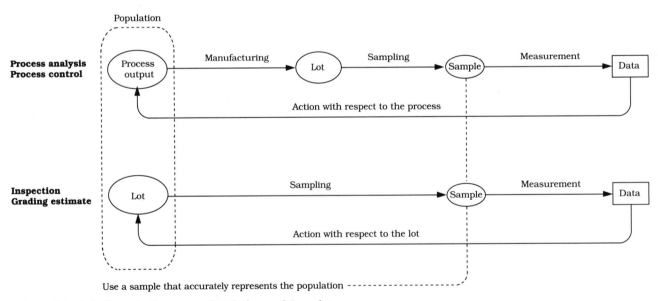

Figure 9-1: **Relationship Between a Population and Samples**

The number of units or unit quantities in the sample extracted from the population is called the "sample size" and is represented by n.

Sampling and Sampling Error

The act of taking samples from a population is called *sampling*. If your sampling method is unsuitable, you will make incorrect judgments about and take improper actions with respect to the population.

Sampling must be appropriate to its purpose, reliable, unbiased, accurate, speedy, and economical. Random sampling ensures that the ideas of the person doing the sampling do not affect it. However, since measurement data for every product is not obtained, there is some deviation from the true condition of the process and lot in the sample data. This error created by sampling is called *sampling error*.

Measurements and Measurement Error

You get data by measuring samples taken from a population. Therefore *measurement error* is always involved in these measurements. If the measurement error is not extremely small, it will lead to incorrect judgments about processes and lots and incorrect actions with respect to them. Check your measuring instruments and measurement methods daily to keep your measurement error very small.

Bias and precision are two elements of measurement error. *Bias* is the difference between the average result of many repeated measurements and the true value of the measured quantity. The degree to which repeated measurements give the same result is called *precision*.

Once you know the bias you can compensate for it. Precision, however, is affected by variables such as the person doing the measurement, the weather conditions, or the maintenance of the measuring instrument. Improve precision by standardizing a method for determining the causes of various deviations and confining them to a specified narrow range.

Types of Data

Data can be classified by statistical characteristics such as measured values and counted (numerical) values. *Measured values* are data on continuous quantities such as weight, length, time, or temperature, which have units and are obtained by measurements made by measuring instruments. *Counted values* are non-continuous data such as numbers of defective products, absent workers, or accidents, which are collected as numbers. (See Table 9-1.) Data may also be expressed as points on a graded scale (e.g., 1 to 10 from worst to best) to rate the quality characteristics of a sampled object.

Recording Data

Record measured data immediately on a data sheet. Make an effort to develop data sheets and check sheets on which you can record data simply. Clearly define your purpose before recording data. Design a data sheet suited to this purpose.

You should always clearly record the history of the data. This includes:

- product name and quality characteristics of the measured object
- sampling period and method
- measuring instrument, units of measurement, method of measurement, day and time of measurement, and person taking the measurement

It is important to collect data in a form that is appropriate for the type of analysis you want to do. Often this means developing data sheets and check sheets that organize the data in a particular way to help you isolate specific causes of defects or deviations.

1. *Investigating deviations from the process mean values:* If you are investigating deviations from such mean measured values as length, weight, time, and temperature, record the measured values on the chart in

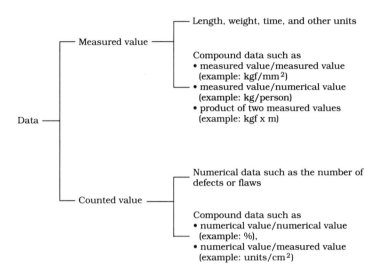

Data
- Measured value
  - Length, weight, time, and other units
  - Compound data such as
    - measured value/measured value (example: kgf/mm²)
    - measured value/numerical value (example: kg/person)
    - product of two measured values (example: kgf x m)
- Counted value
  - Numerical data such as the number of defects or flaws
  - Compound data such as
    - numerical value/numerical value (example: %),
    - numerical value/measured value (example: units/cm²)

Table 9-1: **Types of Data**

a way that facilitates the calculation of the deviation from the mean value.

    If you want to make a hypothesis about the range of the deviation, make a check sheet in frequency table format beforehand, and from time to time record the data you obtain (see Chapter 13, Figure 13-4).

2. *Investigating changes in a data series:* Pay close attention to the time and the order in which you take measurements when investigating changes and variations in values over time. This is important whether the data is measured (such as dimensions or strength) or counted (such as the number of defects or points where cracks occur). Design your check sheet so you can easily record measurements in that order. You can use columns to stratify data according to changing conditions, such as the day of the week, temperature, or a tool change or adjustment.

3. *Investigating the kind and frequency of defects and flaws:* If several different kinds of defects and flaws occur, investigate their trends and frequency separately — different defects and flaws usually have different causes. Design a check sheet with the various kinds of defects and flaws arranged in parallel columns. You can then enter the data directly on the check sheets as you get it.

4. *Investigating the cause of defects and flaws based on the situation in which they occur:* Defects and flaws always have a cause. To determine their cause, you should investigate not only the circumstances under which they arose but also a stratification of causes of defects and flaws such as materials, machines and equipment, personnel, and methods. For this analysis, make a column for each of these causal elements to stratify the data.

5. *Investigating the position at which the flaw occurs:* Check the position at which a flaw occurs as well as its frequency when trying to find its cause. Examine the distribution of the flaw. If you consider why the distribution bunches up at a certain point and observe the process closely and thoughtfully, you will usually find the cause.

In this case, use a diagram format check sheet to mark the location of the detected flaw on a pre-printed drawing of the object (see Chapter 13, Figure 13-3).

10

Graphs

Graph Classification

Graphs represent data pictorially so the overall situation can be understood easily. "Graph it as you collect it" is a good rule to remember. Properly used graphs are indispensable tools for the management and improvement of the workplace.

- A graph attracts the attention of people viewing it and makes them feel familiar with the subject of the graph.
- A graph is visual, which makes the information easier to remember.
- A graph helps the user pick out trends, patterns, and other characteristics.
- A graph can reveal hidden facts and relationships not previously recognized.

Table 10-1 shows the types of graphs most commonly used in QC and their applications.

Bar Graphs

Bar graphs are suitable for comparing the size of several quantities. They are often used to analyze quantitative relationships in the workplace such as the number of proposals, number of failures by machine, the number of defects that occur by process.

HOW TO MAKE A BAR GRAPH

STEP 1: Deciding which items to include

Determine the items to be included in the bar graph, such as the number of proposals, the number of failures by machine, and the number of defects, as well as the size of the workplace and the period concerned.

Example: An office product manufacturing company that has had an improvement proposal system for more than three years wants to sur-

Application	Graph Type		Characteristics
Compare the size of two quantities.	Bar graph		Bar graphs use parallel bars of identical width but differing lengths to compare the size of different quantities.
Look at changes over a time series.	Line graph		Line graphs manifest the overall trend in time series data by the direction of their lines.
Look at a breakdown of the components of a quantity.	Pie chart		Pie charts make it easy to grasp the breakdown of the components of a quantity over a certain period.
	Band graph		Band graphs make it easy to grasp the breakdown of the components of a quantity. Placing two or more band graphs in parallel makes it easy to compare them.
Examine the balance between items.	Radar chart		Radar charts make it easier to observe characteristics and trends as well as the balance between several items.
Examine the progress of a daily plan.	Gantt chart		Gantt charts make it easy to understand the details of a plan and progress in its implementation schedule.
Examine time series data on the achievement of a goal.	Z diagram		Use Z diagrams to track changes in the achievement of a plan or progress in meeting an objective.

Table 10-1: **Common Graph Types and Their Applications**

vey the actual results of the previous year because the number of proposals is increasing very slowly. Supervisor P surveyed her own workplace:

- *Survey item:* number of proposals
- *Object of survey:* assembly and testing workplace
- *Survey period:* January to December 1989

STEP 2: Collecting and tabulating data

Collect data in categories such as workplace, individual, machine, or process and record it on a data sheet (see sample data in Table 10-2). If the categories have no implicit numbering or order, place the data in order of descending magnitude (such as oldest to youngest worker or largest to smallest machine shop). In some cases you may need to make an "Other" column at the very end for data samples that do not fit into the categories.

(units: cases)

Employee	Age	Check	Total
A	42	〃〃 〃〃 //	12
B	38	〃〃 〃〃 〃〃 〃〃 〃〃 〃〃 ///	33
C	37	〃〃 〃〃 〃〃 〃〃 /	21
D	32	〃〃 〃〃 〃〃 〃〃 〃〃 〃〃 〃〃 ///	38
E	31	〃〃 (on leave May - November)	5
F	25	〃〃 〃〃 〃〃 /	16
G	23	〃〃 〃〃 ///	13
H	21	〃〃 ///	8
Total			145

Table 10-2: **Number of Proposals**

STEP 3: Determining the spacing of gradations along the vertical axis scale

Find the maximum and minimum values of the data and determine the spacing of gradations needed along the vertical axis scale, using a scale unit close to the minimum value.

Since the maximum number of improvement proposals in Table 10-2 is 38 and the minimum number is 5, the example uses an 8 cm vertical axis for a maximum of 40 proposals (1 cm = 5 proposals).

STEP 4: Determining the spacing of gradations along the horizontal axis scale

To balance with the vertical axis, choose horizontal axis gradations that will produce a square graph. Category labels are generally placed along the horizontal axis of a bar graph. The spacing between bars is one-half the width of a bar so that the graph will be easy to read.

Since there are eight employees tracked here, the example uses a bar width of .6 cm, with .4 cm space between bars, making the horizontal axis 7.5 cm. See Figure 10-1.

STEP 5: Drawing the horizontal and vertical axes

Use graph paper to draw the horizontal and vertical axes. Label the vertical axis and write the number values next to the gradations. Write the category items along the horizontal axis.

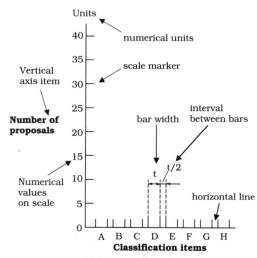

Figure 10-1: Filling in the Vertical and Horizontal Axes

STEP 6: Entering the data by drawing bars of different heights

If you have collected several types of data for each category, use shading, etc., to show stratification within the bar. See Figure 10-2.

STEP 7: Writing in related items

Enter the title, workplace name, process name, survey period, creator, and the date of creation.

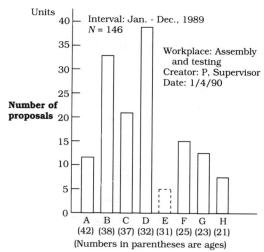

Figure 10-2: Bar Graph of Number of Proposals Made by Each Person

STEP 8: Examining the graph

Think about the information you got from the bar graph.

Every year 146 proposals are submitted, for an annual average of 18 proposals per person. This is a monthly rate of 1.5 proposals per person, just one-half the target rate of three proposals per person per month. Employee D, however, made an average of 38 proposals per year for a monthly average of over 3. Supervisor P took D's 38 proposals as the maximum, although there are large individual differences. Employee E, who left the workplace during the survey period, made the fewest number of proposals.

WAYS TO READ AND USE BAR GRAPHS

1. Use graphs to evaluate the overall situation. They are not for comparing small differences but for giving an overview of the situation.
2. Compare the height of graphs and discuss the differences between different categories.
3. Put a target line or a standard line in the bar graph and discuss differences between the bars and the line.
4. Place two bar graphs side by side horizontally for comparison. (see Figure 10-3).

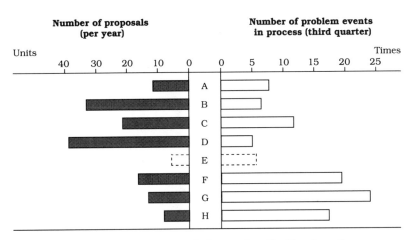

Figure 10-3: **Horizontal Bar Graph Comparing the Number of Proposals vs. Number of Process Problems**

Line Graphs

Line graphs are best suited for displaying changes in time series quantities. These graphs are used for examining changes in worker attendance, machine utilization ratio, the defect rate, and the flaw rate. Time is noted on the horizontal axis and the quantities being compared are noted on the vertical axis. You create a graph showing variations in these quantities by drawing lines to join together plotted points that represent time and quantity.

HOW TO MAKE A LINE GRAPH

STEP 1: Determining an item to track

You can choose an item such as the assembly defect rate, the number of painting defects, or the temperature within a furnace for a certain workplace or product and set the survey period.

Example: A study was made because of defects in electronic circuits used in telephone exchanges.

- *Survey subject:* defect rate (percent defective). The defect rate — (number of defects/total production) x 100 — is used rather than the number defective because the number of units produced each day varies.
- *Object of the survey:* electronic circuit packages.
- *Survey period:* two weeks (9/2 to 9/13).

STEP 2: Collecting and tabulating data

Data for the horizontal axis of the graph can be collected in units of years, quarters, months, weeks, mornings or afternoons, hours, etc. Table 10-3 shows a sample set of data.

Date/Day	9/2 (M)	3 (T)	4 (W)	5 (R)	6 (F)	9 (M)	10 (T)	11 (W)	12 (R)	13 (F)
Number of units produced	4200	4300	4400	4500	4500	4500	5400	5600	5800	5800
Number of defects	20	8	22	23	37	19	41	49	36	68
Defect rate (%)	0.48	0.19	0.50	0.51	0.82	0.42	0.76	0.88	0.62	1.17

Table 10-3: **Data on Improper Component Mounting**

STEP 3: Determining the spacing of gradations along the vertical axis scale

Find the maximum and minimum values of the data and set an appropriate interval for gradations on the vertical axis scale using a scale unit close to the minimum value.

In Table 10-3, since the maximum value is 1.17% and the minimum value is 0.19%, the maximum value on the vertical scale is set at 1.2%, with 0.2% as the unit for the scale marks. A 12 cm line will be drawn for this axis.

STEP 4: Determining the spacing of gradations along the horizontal axis scale

Choose an interval between gradations of the horizontal axis that will produce a square graph.

Since a 10 cm vertical axis was used, a 10 cm horizontal axis will be drawn, with gradations of 1 cm for each day on which data was recorded.

STEP 5: Drawing the vertical and horizontal axes

Use graph paper to draw the vertical and horizontal axes and their scales. The scales for the vertical and horizontal axes are as a rule drawn on the inside of the axes. Then enter the units for the quantities along the vertical axis and the units for time along the horizontal axis. See Figure 10-4.

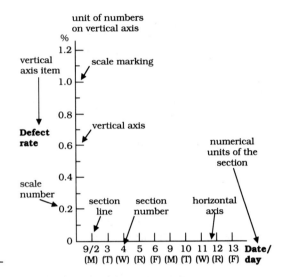

Figure 10-4: **Filling in the Vertical and Horizontal Axes**

STEP 6: Plotting data points and connecting with lines

Figure 10-5 shows a line graph made from the sample data. If you are entering two or more types of data, show the stratification with different types or colors of lines, and create a key such as the one shown in Figure 10-6.

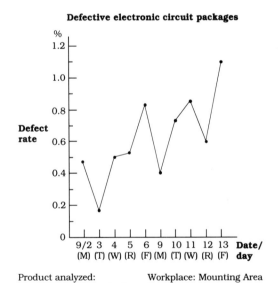

Product analyzed:
electronic circuit package
Investigation period:
9/2 - 13 (two weeks)

Workplace: Mounting Area
Creator: G, Supervisor
Date made: 9/18

Figure 10-5: **Line Graph of the Defect Rate**

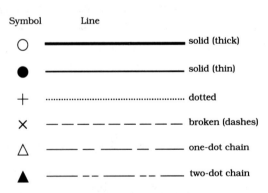

Figure 10-6: **Lines and Symbols for Stratifying Data**

STEP 7: Writing in related items

Enter the title, workplace name, product name, process name, survey period, and operator as well as the date of manufacture.

STEP 8: Examining the graph

Think about the information you got from the graph.

We see from Figure 10-5 that the defect rate is rising. We want to find out if this tendency is related to the increase in production. Last week the defect rate was about 0.5%; this week it was 0.8%. Moreover, although there is a wide day-to-day variation in the defect rate, the rate climbs steeply at the end of the week.

WAYS TO READ AND USE LINE GRAPHS

1. Consider the overall situation. Don't look at individual points but at the whole and changing picture. Keep in mind the following points as you inspect the graph:
   - Is there a tendency to increase or decrease?
   - Is there a pattern over time?
   - Does one point deviate radically from the pattern of the other points?
2. Draw a target, specification, or standard line and compare it with the movement of the points around it (see Figure 10-7).
3. Record countermeasures or changed conditions on the graph and compare the movement of the points before and after the change.
4. If you are recording two or more different kinds of data, compare them.

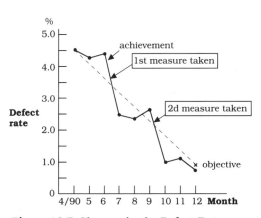

Figure 10-7: **Changes in the Defect Rate**

Pie Charts

Pie charts compare sectors of a data set represented as a circle. They can be used for breaking down product sales figures, analyzing the defect rate by the type of defect, comparing the relative number of certain categories of QC circle themes, etc.

HOW TO MAKE A PIE CHART

STEP 1: Deciding which items to include

Decide what items to include, such as a proportional breakdown of product sales, a proportional breakdown of product prices, a proportional breakdown of product defects, etc., as well as the workplace, product, and the survey period.

Example: QC circle activities are in a rut and the promotion committee makes a survey of problems of QC circle leaders.

- *Survey item:* Problems of QC circle leaders (three or fewer responses from each person surveyed)
- *Survey object:* QC circle leaders of the entire factory (120 people)
- *Survey period:* one month (9/1 to 9/30)

STEP 2: Collecting and tabulating data

Decide how you will break down the data, collect the data, and list the items in descending order from the most frequent response down. Place "other" last even if many responses fall into that category. Table 10-4 shows a sample data collection.

Item	Cases
Team members' capabilities inadequate	66
Absences from meetings	26
Supervisors don't understand problem	43
Too busy; no time to get work done	109
Own capabilities inadequate	14
Other	30
Total	**288**

Table 10-4: **Results of Investigation**

STEP 3: Determining the relative proportion of the various items and the corresponding angle of their sectors of the circle

Express the breakdown of the data into individual items as a proportion of the whole (%), the cumulative total, and the cumulative angle.

- Proportion = $\dfrac{\text{quantity of item within data}}{\text{total quantity}} \times 100$ (%)

- Cumulative number = previous cumulative numbers + quantity of this item

- Cumulative angle = $\dfrac{\text{cumulative number}}{\text{total quantity}} \times 360$ (degrees)

Table 10-5 shows these calculations for the sample data.

Item	Cases	Proportion	Cumulative cases	Cumulative angle
Too busy	109	38%	109	136°
Members' capabilities inadequate	66	23	175	219
Supervisors don't understand problem	43	15	218	272
Absences from meetings	26	9	244	305
Own capabilities inadequate	14	5	258	322
Other	30	10	288	360
Total	**288**	**100**	**288**	

Table 10-5: **Calculation of Cumulative Angle**

STEP 4: Drawing the pie chart

Draw a circle of the proper size. Starting from a baseline at the twelve o'clock position and moving clockwise, divide the circle into sectors at the cumulative angles. See Figure 10-8.

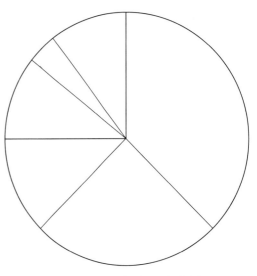

Figure 10-8: **Draw a Circle and Divide It into Sectors**

STEP 5: Labeling the sectors

Within each sector, write the name and proportions (percentage) of the item. If the sector is too small, write this information outside the circle and draw an arrow connecting it to the appropriate sector. If necessary, use cross-hatching, shading, or color to distinguish the different sectors. Figure 10-9 shows the labeled pie chart.

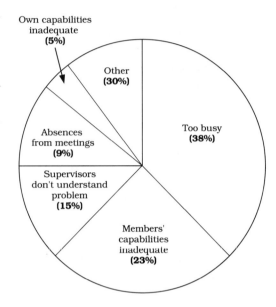

Survey period: 9/1 - 9/30
Leaders surveyed: 120
Items: 288
Creation date: 10/3
Creator: Y, Supervisor

Figure 10-9: **Survey Results on a Pie Chart**

STEP 6: Writing in related items

Add the title, survey period, totals, the date the chart was made, the maker, etc. Titles, totals, and the data collection period can be put in a circle in the middle of the chart for easy reference (see Figure 10-10).

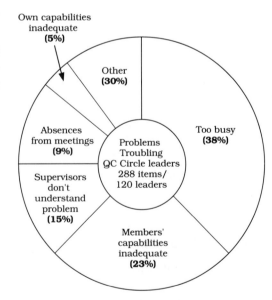

Figure 10-10: **Showing Results on a "Doughnut" Pie Chart**

STEP 7: Examining the chart

Think about the information you got from the pie chart.

The matter that most troubles QC circle leaders is "I don't have enough time to do my work," accounting for 38% of all responses. Next comes "the capabilities of the members of the group are not equal to the task" at 23%, and "supervisors don't understand my problems adequately" at 15%. Since these three items constitute 76% of all responses, they should be studied carefully to find a solution.

WAYS TO READ AND USE PIE CHARTS

1. Consider what items the pie chart is composed of.
2. Recognize which items make up a large proportion of the total.
3. Consider the relative proportions of various items in the total.
4. Compare two pie charts (see Figure 10-11). If you compare two pie charts that have different totals, make the relative areas of the circles proportional to the totals, as Figure 10-11 shows.

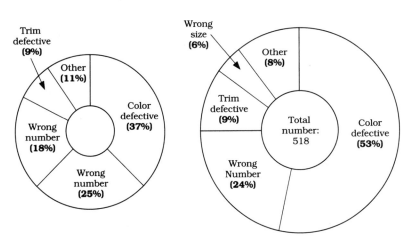

Factory A   Factory B

Figure 10-11: **Pie Chart Comparing Breakdown of Types of Errors at Two Factories**

Band Graph

Band graphs express their internal composition and proportions by the length of a band. One band graph serves the same function as a pie chart. Drawing several parallel band graphs makes it easy to compare quantities and proportions.

HOW TO MAKE A BAND GRAPH

STEP 1: Deciding which items to include

Decide what items to include, such as an internal breakdown of product sales, an internal breakdown of product prices, an internal breakdown of product defects, etc., as well as the workplace, product, and the survey period.

Example: To make up the budget for the next accounting period, a study is made of the components of product costs over the last six months.

- *Survey subject:* Breakdown of manufacturing costs (material costs, labor costs, tool and equipment costs, and indirect costs)
- *Survey object:* Components and products made by a machine processing plant
- *Survey period:* The six months prior to this month

STEP 2: Collecting and tabulating data

Decide on a method for classifying the components of the data, collect the data, and list them in descending order. List "other" last even if there are many items in this category. You may list the results in other than descending order if another order would be more useful. Table 10-6 shows a sample collection of data.

Expense Item	Cost
Materials costs	$159,600
Labor costs	102,600
Tool and equipment costs	38,000
Indirect costs	79,800
Total	**380,000**

Table 10-6: **Survey Results**

STEP 3: Finding the proportion of each item and the cumulative percentage

Find the proportion (%) of each of the components of the data you obtain, the cumulative number, and the cumulative percentage.

- Proportion = $\dfrac{\text{quantity of item within data}}{\text{total quantity}} \times 100 \ (\%)$

- Cumulative number = previous cumulative number + quantity of this item

- Cumulative percentage = $\dfrac{\text{cumulative number}}{\text{total quantity}} \times 100 \ (\%)$

Table 10-7 shows these for the sample data.

Cost Item	Cost	Proportion	Cumulative Cost	Cumulative Percentage Rate
Materials costs	$159,600	42%	$159,600	42%
Labor costs	102,600	27	262,200	69
Tool and equipment costs	38,000	10	300,200	79
Indirect costs	79,800	21	380,000	100
Total	**380,000**	**100**	**380,000**	

Table 10-7: **Calculation of Cumulative Percentage Rate**

STEP 4: Drawing a horizontal axis and scale

Using graph paper, draw a horizontal axis. Divide the axis in gradations from 0 to 100%, left to right. Write percent

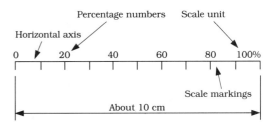

Figure 10-12: **Horizontal Axis and Scale**

STEP 5: Drawing a band and displaying the data on its length

Draw a rectangular band of constant width from left to right. Divide the band at the marks for the cumulative percentages of each category of your data. Figure 10-13 shows the divided band.

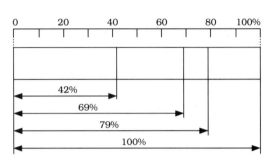

Figure 10-13: **Draw a Band and Divide It into Sections**

STEP 6: Labeling the sections of the band

Write the names of the component items and their proportion to the whole in the divided rectangular band. If the rectangle is too narrow, write the information outside the band and connect it to the appropriate section with an arrow. Use cross-hatching, shading, or colors to make the various parts of the rectangular bands easy to distinguish. Figure 10-14 shows the labeled band.

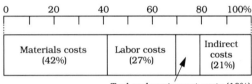

Tool and equipment costs (10%)

Plant: Machine processing plant
Period: February - July 1989
Creation Date: 8/16
Total expenses: $380,000
Creator: T, Supervisor

Figure 10-14: **Survey Results on a Bar Graph**

STEP 7: Writing in related items

Write in the title, period, total, date the graph was created, the creator, etc.

STEP 8: Examining the graph

Think about the information you get from the graph.

The largest component in the manufacturing costs of the machine processing plant is materials cost at 42%. Labor costs come next at 27%, followed by indirect costs at 21% and machinery and equipment costs at

10%. Thus the proportion of materials cost : labor cost : machinery and equipment cost : indirect costs is 4 : 3 : 1 : 2.

WAYS TO READ AND USE BAND GRAPHS

1. Consider what items make up the band graph.
2. Recognize which items make up a large proportion of the total.
3. Consider the relative proportion of various items in the total.
4. Compare two band graphs by placing one below another, connecting cumulative percentages with dotted lines (see Figure 10-15).

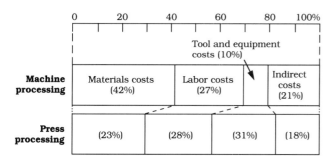

Figure 10-15: **Parallel Comparison of Two Band Graphs**

References

Chiba, Rikio, Atsushi Otaki, and Susumu Yazu. *QC Introductory Series 5: Arranging and Using Data I.* Japanese Standards Association, 1983.

Ishihara, Katsukichi, Kazuo Hirose, Katsuya Hosotani, and Hidenori Yoshida. *An Easy Approach to the Seven Tools of QC.* Japanese Standards Association, 1980.

11

Pareto Diagrams

Pareto diagrams are specialized bar graphs that can be used to show the relative frequency of events such as bad products, repairs, defects, claims, failures, or accidents. A Pareto diagram presents information in descending order, from the largest category to the smallest. Points are plotted for the cumulative total in each bar and connected with a line to create a graph that shows the relative incremental addition of each category to the total.

How to Make a Pareto Diagram

STEP 1: Deciding which items to study and collecting data

Decide the categories of the data items and the period over which you will collect data, then collect the data. The item categories will usually be content or causal factors.

- *Content categories:* type of defect, place, position, process, time, etc.
- *Cause categories:* materials, machinery and equipment, operating method, operator, etc.

Choose a data collection period similar to the period in which the problem appears, such as a week or a month. Table 11-1 shows a sample set of data.

Example: A metal fixture stamped in a particular shape is covered with an adhesive and placed in a mold into which rubber is injected to make the product. A recent study was made to investigate a rise in the number of defects.

- *Survey item:* number of defects
- *Process:* molding process
- *Item category:* by defect
- *Period:* 6/1 to 6/30
- *Data:* survey record

Defective Items	Number of Defects
Bad rubber	91
Poor adhesion	128
Cracks	9
Voids	36
Impurities	15
Cuts	23
Other	12

Table 11-1: **Survey Data**

STEP 2: Tabulating data and calculating the cumulative number

Arrange the item categories in order of the number of items and enter the data in a table. Categories that contain few items are combined in the "other" category and listed at the very end. (The "other" category may be larger than the smallest separate category.)

Starting with the category containing the most items and working in descending order, calculate the cumulative numbers and write them in the table. Table 11-2 shows the cumulative table from the sample data.

No.	Defective Items	Number of Defects	Cumulative Number
1	Poor adhesion	128	128
2	Bad rubber	91	128 + 91 = 219
3	Voids	36	219 + 36 = 255
4	Cuts	23	255 + 23 = 278
5	Impurities	15	278 + 15 = 293
6	Cracks	9	293 + 9 = 302
7	Other	12	302 + 12 = 314
	Total	**314**	**314**

Table 11-2: **Arrangement of Data and Calculation of Cumulation**

STEP 3: Drawing the vertical and horizontal axes

Determine a gradation interval on the vertical axis suitable for the data total. Choose a horizontal axis gradation interval so that the Pareto diagram will have a square shape. Draw the vertical and horizontal axes on graph paper, marking the gradations for the vertical axis scale (generally marked on the inside of the axes).

Write the item name, gradation numbers, and the units used. Label the horizontal axis with the data categories, in descending order from left to right. In a Pareto diagram, the bars are drawn next to each other, with no space between, so do not leave spaces when you draw the horizontal scale.

Since the cumulative number in Table 11-2 is 314 units, we will make a vertical scale for 300 units, using a 10 cm line (part of the line extends beyond the last scale mark). To make the horizontal scale roughly the same length, we use 1 cm for each of the seven categories, making a 7 cm line. See Figure 11-1.

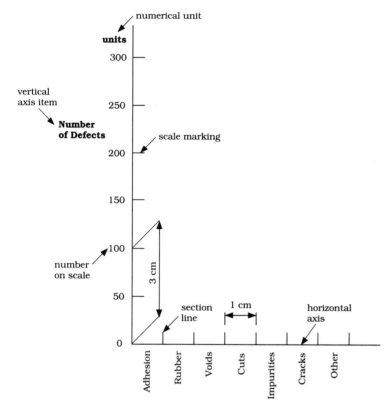

Figure 11-1: **Fill in the Vertical and Horizontal Axes**

STEP 4: Displaying the data as a bar graph

Draw the bar graph along the horizontal axis, in descending order as you have labeled it. Figure 11-2 shows the bar graph for the sample data set.

STEP 5: Drawing a cumulative curve

Plot the point representing the cumulative total in the upper right corner of each bar and connect the points to make a broken line graph (see Figure 11-2). This broken line is called a cumulative curve.

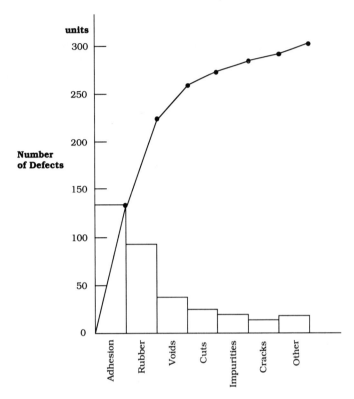

Figure 11-2: **Fill in the Bar Graph**

STEP 6: Creating a percentage scale on a vertical axis on the right side

Taking the starting point of the broken line graph as 0 and the ending point as 100%, divide the range into equal gradations (such as 10% or 20%) and label them. Figure 11-3 shows the percentage scale drawn in.

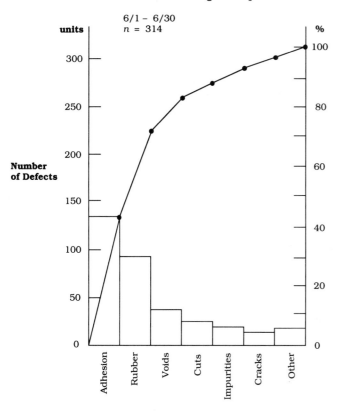

Figure 11-3: **Pareto Diagram: Defective Molded Components**

STEP 7: Labeling the diagram

Write in necessary items such as the title, the data collection period, the total number of data, the process name, the collector's name, etc.

STEP 8: Examining the diagram

Think about the information you got from the Pareto diagram.

Items associated with defective molding include bad adhesion, defective rubber, voids, cuts, impurities, and cracks. Poor adhesion, at 41% of the total, is the most common defect. Next comes defective rubber at 29%. These two defective items together constitute 70% of the total. Future improvement efforts will focus on these two defects to identify the causes and find countermeasures.

Ways to Use Pareto Diagrams

1. *Use a Pareto diagram to focus on the principal aspect of a problem.* By making a chart, you can determine which is the key problem and concentrate your efforts on making improvements in that area.
2. *Decide the objective of your improvements and your improvement items.* A Pareto diagram helps you select specific items or causes to make the most effective improvements toward your objective.
3. *Predict the effectiveness of the improvement.* By showing the relative importance of various causes of problems, a Pareto diagram helps you predict the effectiveness of various proposed improvements.
4. *Make a Pareto diagram arranged by cause.* Pareto diagram categories are not limited to types of defects. You can also create Pareto diagrams using causal factors as categories — materials, methods, machines and equipment, or operator problems, for example.
5. *Understand the effectiveness of the improvement.* Align the vertical axis scales of pre-improvement and post-improvement Pareto diagrams in order to check the effectiveness of the improvement. See Figure 11-4 for an example. Note how the shading is used to keep track of categories, which are in a different order in the "after" diagram.

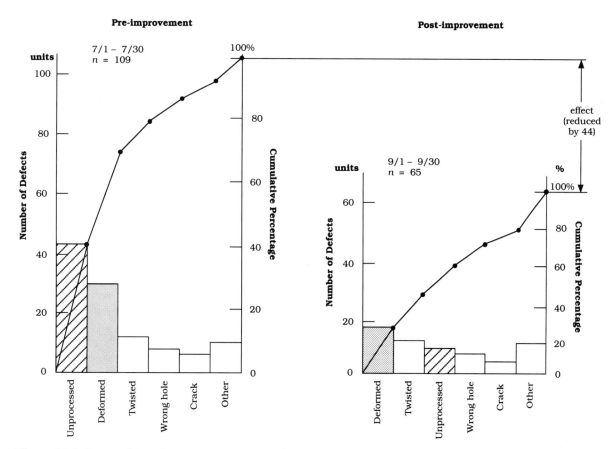

Figure 11-4: **Pre- and Post-improvement Pareto Diagrams**

6. *Make easy improvements right away, even if they have lower priority.* You should immediately make improvements that are easy to implement, even if the items have lower priority. This way benefits can be realized immediately from the improvements.

7. *Make a Pareto diagram using monetary losses as the measure rather than units or cases.* Financial loss can be a better measure of the severity of a problem than units or cases. Although Figures 11-5 and 11-6 show the same categories, they are in a different order of significance. "Breaks" is the most significant as far as monetary loss, even though it is not the category with the largest number of occurrences.

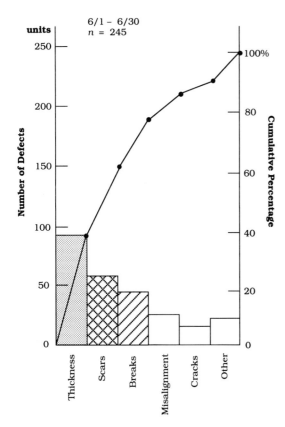

Figure 11-5: **Pareto Diagram: Number of Defects**

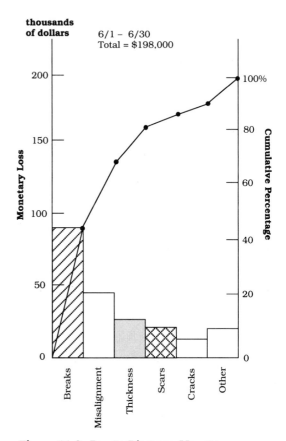

Figure 11-6: **Pareto Diagram: Monetary Losses**

8. *Use Pareto diagrams in your explanations and records.*
Pareto diagrams are more useful for delineating problems and their severity than simply comparing data. Pareto diagrams enable the reader to understand the problems and their relative severity at a glance.

References

Ishihara, Katsukichi, Kazuo Hirose, Katsuya Hosotani, and Hidenori Yoshida. *An Easy Approach to the Seven Tools of QC*. Japanese Standards Association, 1980.

Otaki, Atsushi and Susumu Yazu. *QC Introductory Series 6: Arranging and Using Data II*. Japanese Standards Association, 1983.

12

Cause-and-effect Diagrams

A *cause-and-effect diagram* is a useful method for clarifying the causes of a problem. It classifies the various causes thought to affect the results of work, indicating with arrows the cause-and-effect relationship among them. Figure 12-1 shows the basic structure of a cause-and-effect diagram.

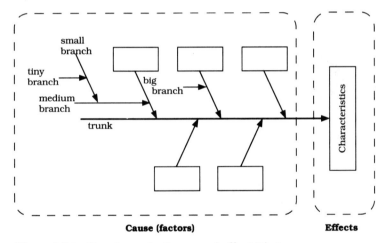

Cause (factors)   **Effects**

Figure 12-1: **Structure of a Cause-and effect Diagram**

The cause-and-effect diagram is sometimes called a "fishbone diagram," an "Ishikawa diagram" (after the late Kaoru Ishikawa, the quality expert who championed its use), or a "characteristics diagram" (referring to its use in identifying the cause of various quality characteristics, including problems).

Notice that the diagram has a "cause" side and an "effect" side. *Effects* are stated as particular quality characteristics or problems resulting from work. Examples include problems involving product quality, cost, quantity of production, delivery, workplace safety, and QC circle activities.

On the "cause" side are the *factors* that influence the stated effects or characteristics. Difficulties involving materials, machinery and equipment, operating methods, operators, or the environment are examples of some main categories, although you can use any breakdown that is relevant to your analysis. The branches of the diagram are arrows indicating the relationship between the effect and the causal factors. The thick arrows branch off the center line like limbs branching from a tree trunk.

Cause-and-effect diagrams are valuable to any process to which they can be applied. Everyone involved with the problem should participate, offering his or her opinions to uncover the factors involved in a problem.

How to Make a Cause-and-effect Diagram

STEP 1: Clarifying the characteristics of the problem and writing a title

Make sure everyone concerned understands the problem well, decide which characteristics to examine, and write a title for your investigation on a blackboard or large sheet of paper. Process data showing bad characteristics helps uncover the factors involved in a problem. You can also do this after an improvement to determine how much the process has actually improved.

Example: Cracks on the front surface of contact lenses have increased recently to become the most common defect. Until now, this problem has been solved immediately with a manual adjustment, but the problem recurs—the basic problem has not been solved. Accordingly, a survey of the causes of cracks during grinding was carried out.

STEP 2: Writing in the effect characteristics and drawing the spine

Write the characteristics to be examined in a box on the right side (see Figure 12-2). Be specific in describing the effect characteristics. Don't just say, "Component X is defective"; instead say, "Component X is thin" or "Component X is weak." Next, draw a thick arrow running from left to right (to the characteristics box). This arrow is the trunk.

STEP 3: Clarify the factors affecting the characteristic

The usefulness of your cause-and-effect diagram depends on how well you do this step. Methods for defining the factors include:

1. The big branch expansion method
2. The small branch expansion method (brainstorming)
3. The small branch expansion method (affinity diagram)

The Big Branch Expansion Method:

1. Divide the factors you believe affect the characteristic into categories that contain four to six items. Draw a big branch for each category, placing the category name in a box at the end (see Figure 12-3).
2. For each big branch, draw medium, small, and tiny branches based on the suggestions of participants to get to the cause of that characteristic. See Figure 12-4. In discussions, it is essential to repeatedly ask "why" until you get to the root cause.

"Contact Lens Grinding Cracks"

Figure 12-2: **Fill In Title, Effect Characteristics, And Trunk**

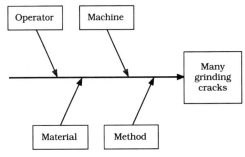

Figure 12-3: **Factor Classification (Big Branch Expansion Method)**

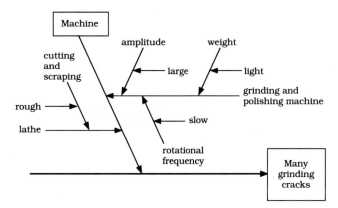

Figure 12-4: **Identifying the Cause
(Big Branch Expansion Method)**

The Small Branch Expansion Method (Brainstorming):

1. Everyone considers the factors thought to influence the characteristic. The group brainstorms to synthesize ideas. These items are then written on the blackboard or large paper prepared earlier. See Table 12-1.

2. As the participants discuss the relationships, group the factors into small categories on the basis of their suggestions. You can further group these small categories into medium and large categories. See Table 12-2.

3. Arrange the categories in the format of a cause-and-effect diagram. The large categories become the big branches, the medium categories become medium branches, and the small categories become small branches.

Factors responsible for "many grinding cracks"
lathe cutting roughly
leftover shavings from cutting
grinding time too long
cracks caused by crack removal fluid
crack removal fluid not applied long enough
untrained operator
careless operator
grinding machine not heavy enough
machine's rotational frequency too low
machine amplitude is too high
filter water depleted
grinding agent particles too large
P block is soft
pitch dish is hard
tired operator
nervous operator
pitch dish does not join when pressed together
pitch is filled up
contaminants enter pitch dish when it is pressed
contaminants enter during grinding
mixing ratio of grinding agent

Table 12-1: **Factor List
(Brainstorming Method)**

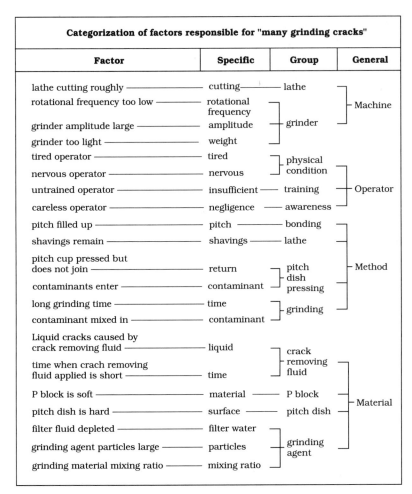

Table 12-2: **Factor Classification (Brainstorming Method)**

The Small Branch Expansion Method (Affinity Diagram):

1. Distribute about 50 index cards equally among all members of the group.
2. Ask members of the group to write down factors they believe influence the characteristic.
3. Place the cards on a table and based on the opinions of the group, group related cards together. These become small branches. Next, relationships are found

among the small branch headings, which are then joined together to make a medium branch. Similarly, relationships are found among the medium branch headings, which are then joined together to make a big branch. See Table 12-3.

4. Arrange the grouped cards in cause-and-effect diagram format and place them on a large sheet of paper.

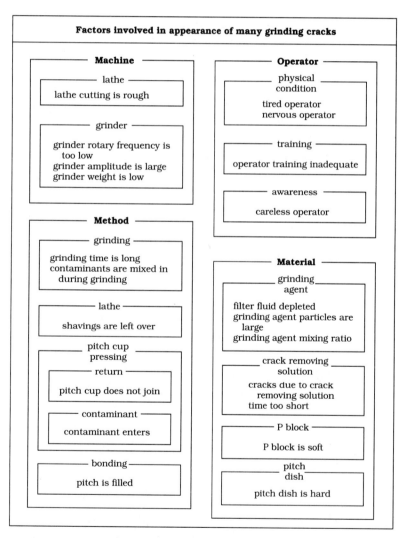

Table 12-3: **Factor Classification**
           (Affinity Diagram Method)

STEP 4: Checking for omitted factors

Once the format of the cause-and-effect diagram has been set, all the participants should make sure that no factor has been left out. If a factor has been omitted, insert it in the diagram. Figure 12-5 shows the factors written in the diagram.

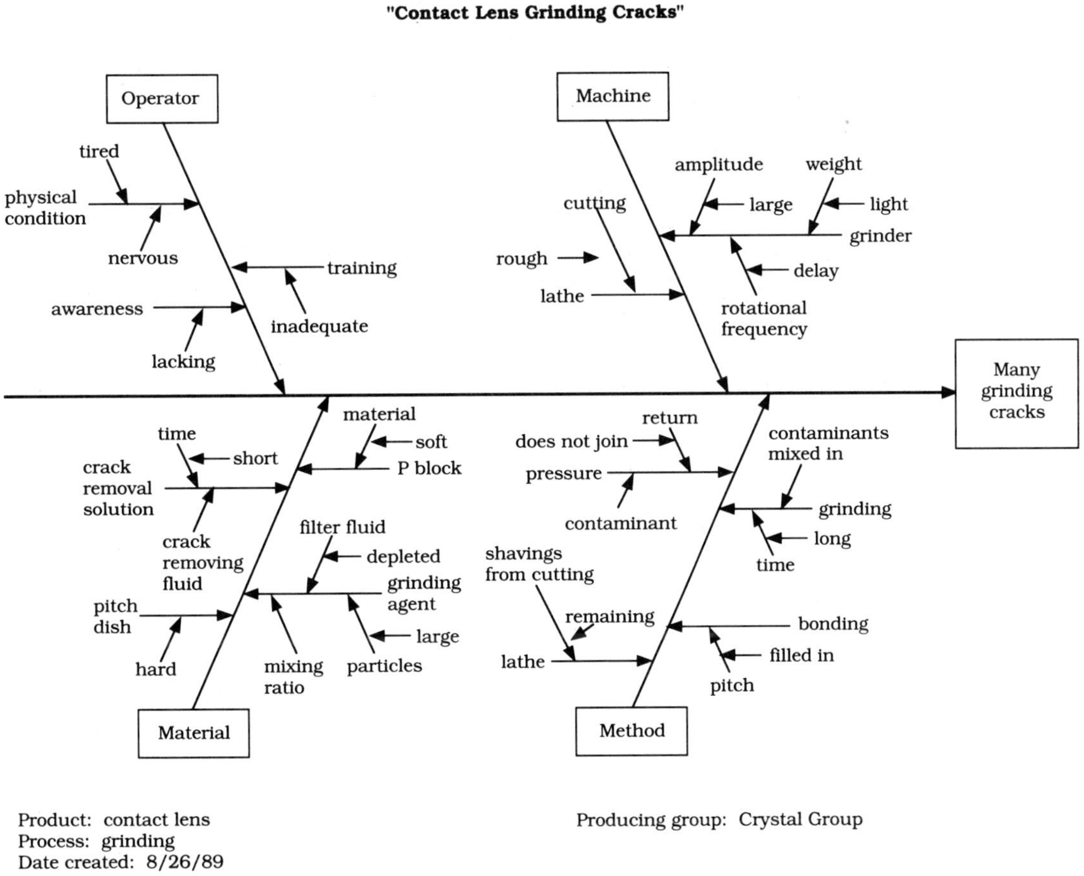

"Contact Lens Grinding Cracks"

Product: contact lens
Process: grinding
Date created: 8/26/89

Producing group: Crystal Group

Figure 12-5: **Cause-and-effect Diagram: Contact Lens Grinding Cracks**

STEP 5: Identifying factors that strongly affect the characteristic

Check the workplace and the data once more and discuss them with all participants. Circle factors that strongly affect the characteristic (circle between five and eight items). See Figure 12-6.

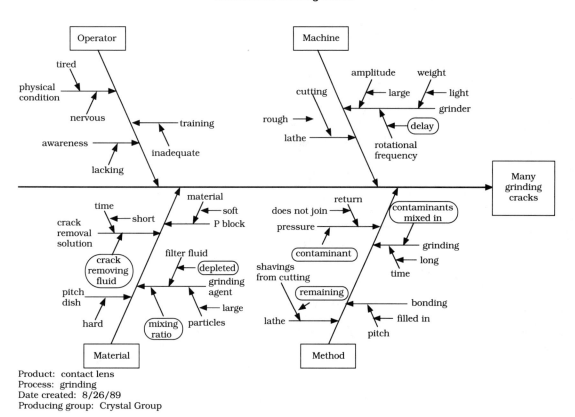

Product: contact lens
Process: grinding
Date created: 8/26/89
Producing group: Crystal Group

Figure 12-6: **Cause-and-effect Diagram: Contact Lens Grinding Cracks (Major Factors Circled)**

STEP 6: Writing in related information

Write in the product name, process name, the work station where it was made, the group name, the names of participants, the date of creation, etc.

Ways to Use Cause-and-effect Diagrams

1. *Use a cause-and-effect diagram to help guide discussion.* Sometimes group discussion doesn't stay on the topic. A discussion centered on a cause-and-effect diagram can keep the discussion on the topic and focus everyone's intelligence on the problem.

2. *Use a diagram as a study aid.* By participating in the construction of a cause-and-effect diagram and discussing it with other members of the group, people notice new things and learn from one another.

3. *Use a diagram to understand the actual situation.* Using a cause-and-effect diagram will make you look carefully around the workplace and think about the cause.

4. *Use a diagram for factors management.* Once you have made a cause-and-effect diagram, use it for daily factors management. If a quality characteristic is bad or an accident occurs, search for the cause. Each time you find a cause factor that applies, make a check mark next to it on the diagram (see Figure 12-7). In this manner, you will manage factors daily according to their priority.

5. *Use a diagram as technical material when creating and revising manufacturing standards.* Someone who writes a good cause-and-effect diagram understands the work well. Detailed diagrams are technical material useful for making and revising technical standards, QC process tables, operating standards, inspection standards, equipment inspection standards, and other standard references.

"Defects Due to Filling by Neutral Dust"

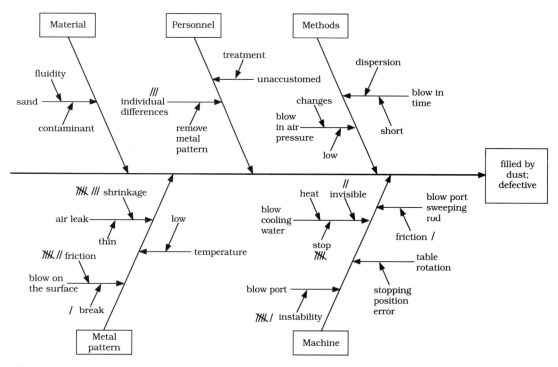

Figure 12-7: **Cause-and-effect Diagram Used for Factor Checking**

References

Chiba, Rikio, Atsushi Otaki, and Susumu Yazu. *QC Introductory Series 5: Arranging and Using Data I.* Japanese Standards Association, 1983.

Ishihara, Katsukichi, Kazuo Hirose, Katsuya Hosotani, and Hidenori Yoshida. *An Easy Approach to the Seven Tools of QC.* Japanese Standards Association, 1980.

13

Check Sheets

In constantly busy workplaces, if data is not gathered simply, the data will be delayed in processing and your action will not be effective. You must consider how data is gathered and processed in your operations. Gathering and processing data suited to your objectives is essential even in simple operations.

A *check sheet* is a form, in diagram or table format, prepared in advance for recording data. You can thus take down necessary information by just making a check mark on the page. Check sheets are used in the following forms:

1. Check sheets for recording data and making surveys
   - Defective item check sheet (Figure 13-1)
   - Defect factor check sheet (Figure 13-2)
   - Defect position check sheet (Figure 13-3)
   - Process distribution check sheet (Figure 13-4)
2. Inspection and validation check sheet (Figure 13-5)

Purpose of Checking	Type of Check Sheet
1. Determine defect details	Defective item check sheet
2. Determine occurrence of defects by day of the week, operator, machine, etc.	Defect factor check sheet
3. Determine where defects occur	Defect position check sheet
4. Determine dispersion of dimensions, hardness, weight, etc.	Process distribution check sheet
5. Inspect machines or equipment or check the operating procedure	Inspection and validation check sheet

Table 13-1: **Types of Check Sheets for Various Purposes**

How to Make a Check Sheet

STEP 1: Clarifying your objective

Think about and clarify objectives such as "we want to investigate the defect in detail," "we want to determine the position of the flaw," and "we want to determine the distribution of the measurements."

Example: Three-color lenses are glued to the dial of a meter of a children's bicycle in a process. Once a fastening jig presses the color lenses onto the aluminum dial and they are covered with an adhesive bond, they are placed next to a special box for natural drying. After drying, they are sent on to the next process. The number of lenses that were defective because of poor adhesion in the following process has increased lately. Therefore this defect was investigated.

- *Objective:* Determine the cause of defective lenses

STEP 2: Determining the type of check sheet to use

As Figures 13-1 through 13-5 show, there are several different kinds of check sheets. Decide which type of check sheet best suits your purpose (see Table 13.-1)

- *Check sheet type:* Defective item check sheet

STEP 3: Deciding which items to check

Discuss a method for classifying data suited to your objective in making the checks and decide which items to check. If you are investigating defects or the location of flaws, make a category for each item and each flaw location. The check item, however, should not be too narrowly defined.

- *Items checked:* lens peeling defect (peeling), lens aberration (aberration), lens cracks (cracks), contaminant on lens (contaminant), lens in wrong position (position), incorrect number of tapes (tapes), other

STEP 4: Creating the check sheet

Design your check sheet format on a piece of paper. Make sure it is easy to record data on your check sheet, that the entire situation can be taken in by glancing at the check sheet, and that the data on the check sheet is easy to process. See Table 13-2 for items that should be included in a check sheet.

1. Title:	To express clearly the purpose of the inspection
2. Object, item:	What to check and where to check it
3. Checking method:	What you should use and what procedure to follow when making checks
4. Date and time of check:	At what interval checks should be made and when they should begin and end
5. The checker:	Who performed the checks
6. The location:	Where checks are made
7. Summary of conclusions:	Total, mean, calculation of proportions within the total, and observations

Table 13-2: **Items Recorded on a Check Sheet**

STEP 5: Recording the data

Make observations and record them on the check sheet. Make simple notes using symbols rather than letters or numbers. Besides the symbols ✔ and /, use additional symbols (such as ○,●, △, ▲, ✕, ❑, and ■) to record several different types of data in one check sheet column.

Defect Item	9/2 (M)	3 (T)	4 (W)	5 (R)	6 (F)	9 (M)	10 (T)	11 (W)	12 (R)	13 (F)	16 (M)	17 (T)	18 (W)	19 (R)	20 (F)	Total
Peeling																
Aberration																
Crack																
Contaminant																
Position																
Tape																
Other																
Total																
Weekly total																

Table 13-3: **Lens Glass Defect Item Inspection Check Sheet**

STEP 6: Tallying the check results

Assemble the check results and then perform calculations on them to find totals, averages, proportions, etc. While you are making checks, record in the blank space any idea that occurs to you so that you can use it when you are searching for the cause.

Defect Item	9/2 (M)	3 (T)	4 (W)	5 (R)	6 (F)	9 (M)	10 (T)	11 (W)	12 (R)	13 (F)	16 (M)	17 (T)	18 (W)	19 (R)	20 (F)	Total
Peeling		/				/							/		/	4
Aberration						///	//	7HL	////	7HL /	7HL //	7HL /	7HL ////	7HL //	7HL 7HL	59
Crack				//	////					7HL				/	///	15
Contaminant		/	/	//		//	7HL	///		//	///		///	////	///	29
Position	//		/						//			/	//			8
Tape	//		/						///			/	//			9
Other			//	///		/	/		////		/	///		//		17
Total	4	2	5	7	4	6	9	8	13	13	11	11	17	14	17	141
Weekly total				22						49					70	

*Hitomi Ishikura, "Reducing Defects in Dials of Children's Bicycles," *FQC*, 189 (JUSE Press Ltd., 1978).

Table 13-4: **Lens Glass Defect Item Inspection Check Sheet, Filled In***

STEP 7: Examining the check sheet

Think about the information you got from the check sheet.

Lens aberration is the most common defect (59 cases); contaminants stuck to the lens comes in second (29 cases). These two items account for 88 cases or 62% of the total. Lens aberration increased rapidly from 0 cases the first week to 20 cases the second week and 39 cases the third week.

Contaminants on the lenses also increased from the second week on. There were 4 cases of lens contamination during the first week, 12 cases during the second week, and 13 cases during the third week.

Overall, there were 22 cases of defects during the first week, increasing to 49 cases the second week and 70 cases during the third week. Lens aberration and contaminants had a strong influence on defects.

There were 15 cases of cracks, which occurred at the same rate every week. Moreover, lens position errors and the wrong number of tapes occurred on the same day.

Ways to Use Check Sheets

1. *Discuss check sheet results.* Total the results and discuss overall trends, the data distribution, the relative proportion of each item, etc. Analyze for each check item the manifestation of the defect or flaw (several simultaneously, scattered, sudden, gradual increase, gradual decrease, etc.), spread of the distribution, bias, and form.
2. *Search for the cause.* From your analysis of the check sheet results, discuss separately how people, machines, materials, methods, etc., cause defects, flaws and deviations in measurements.
3. *Check up on the results of an improvement.* You should always check up on the results of an improvement. Use the check sheet to determine if the results of the action improved results. If results do not improve, the action was not effective.
4. *Make certain that the defect does not recur.* It is essential, once you have achieved good results with an improvement, to make certain that the bad result never recurs. From then on, check the item on your check sheet to make sure that the problem will not recur.

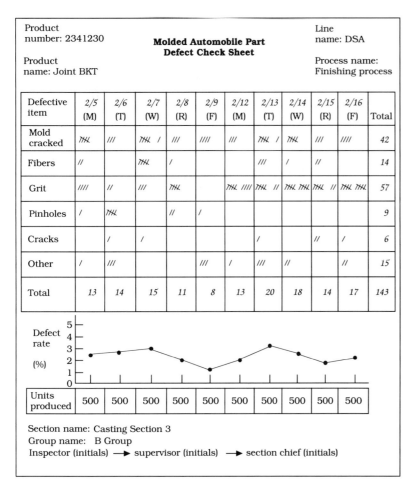

| Product number: 2341230 | | **Molded Automobile Part Defect Check Sheet** | | | | Line name: DSA | | | | |
| Product name: Joint BKT | | | | | | Process name: Finishing process | | | | |

Defective item	2/5 (M)	2/6 (T)	2/7 (W)	2/8 (R)	2/9 (F)	2/12 (M)	2/13 (T)	2/14 (W)	2/15 (R)	2/16 (F)	Total
Mold cracked	7HL	///	7HL /	///	////	///	7HL /	7HL	///	////	42
Fibers	//		7HL	/			///	/	//		14
Grit	////	//	///	7HL		7HL ////	7HL //	7HL 7HL	7HL //	7HL 7HL	57
Pinholes	/	7HL		//	/						9
Cracks		/	/				/		//	/	6
Other	/	///			///	/	///	//		//	15
Total	13	14	15	11	8	13	20	18	14	17	143

Defect rate (%)
5 4 3 2 1 0

| Units produced | 500 | 500 | 500 | 500 | 500 | 500 | 500 | 500 | 500 | 500 |

Section name: Casting Section 3
Group name: B Group
Inspector (initials) ➞ supervisor (initials) ➞ section chief (initials)

Figure 13-1: **Defective Item Check Sheet**

Product number: G100B9991		Gas Meter Body Defect Occurrence Status Survey Check Sheet			Process name: FL-SK						
Product name: F-type gas meter body					Inspector: (initials)						

Operator	Jig	1/22 (M)		1/23 (T)		1/24 (W)		1/25 (R)		1/26 (F)		Total	
		a.m.	p.m.	a.m.	p.m.	a.m.	p.m.	a.m.	p.m.	a.m.	p.m.		
A	JF-3	ooooo o △ ×	oooo ● □	ooooo o	oo ● △	ooooo oo ×	oooo ● ×	ooooo ooo ●	ooo □	ooooo oo ●●	ooooo △	66	106
	KF-3	o △△△ □	oo ● △△△	×	ooo ● △△	oo ×	●	o △	oo ●●	oo △△△△ ×	o ● △△△	40	
B	JF-3	ooo △ ×	●● ×	●● ×	ooo ●	o	o ●●● △		oo ●●	●●● △△	oo ●● △ ×	37	87
	KF-3	o ● △△△△△	oo ● △△	oo □	●● × □	o ● △	oo ●● □	o ● ×	●●● △△ ×	o ●● △△△ □	oo ●●● △△	50	
Total		25	20	13	17	16	17	15	18	28	24	193	
		45		30		33		33		52			

(Symbol)
{ o = deviation in thickness
  ● = scratch
  △ = crack
  × = porosity
  □ = other

Figure 13-2: **Defect Factor Check Sheet**

Automobile Painting Defect Location Check Sheet				Approvals ___(section chief) ___(supervisor) ___(group leader)
Vehicle Type: GM-2300	Place of inspection: Station M	Inspection period: 3/3 - 3/5	Number of units inspected: 1200	
Process: B520	Inspection method: visual	Sampling method: all	Inspector N	Symbol ● = surface paint defect x = string-like defect Δ = other

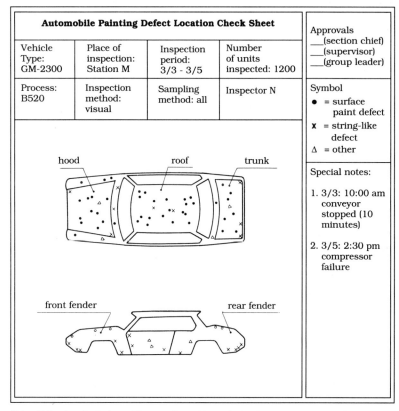

Special notes:

1. 3/3: 10:00 am conveyor stopped (10 minutes)

2. 3/5: 2:30 pm compressor failure

*Rikio Chiba, Atsushi Otaki, and Susumu Yazu, *QC Introductory Series 5: Arranging and Using Data I* (Japanese Standards Association, 1983), 41.

Figure 13-3: **Defect Position Check Sheet***

Wire Thickness Inspection Check Sheet			
Product number: 100543201	Characteristics: Thickness (μm)		Measured machine: TW05
Product name: Wire	Standard value 410 $^{+69}_{0}$		Date: 2/20/90
Process: Edging	Sample: 120° (all)		Person taking measurements: T

Specification	Thickness (μm)	Check 10	20	30	40						Total
	520~529										
	510~519										
	500~509	//									2
	490~499	7HŁ	/								6
	480~489	7HŁ	7HŁ	////							14
▶	470~479	7HŁ	///								8
	460~469	7HŁ	7HŁ								10
	450~459	7HŁ	7HŁ	7HŁ	///						18
	440~449	7HŁ	7HŁ	7HŁ	7HŁ	7HŁ	7HŁ	//			32
	430~439	7HŁ	7HŁ	7HŁ	7HŁ	/					21
	420~429	7HŁ	///								8
	410~419	/									1
▶	400~409										
	390~399										
	380~389										
	370~379										

Notes

Figure 13-4: **Process Distribution Check Sheet**

Check Sheet for Preventing the Admixture of Impurities

| Process: | | Date: | | Inspector: | | | | Work record: |

Inspection point	No.	Inspection Contents	Pre-treatment	Post-treatment	Check	Action	Pre-cleaning treated rubber
Workplace	1	Are other types of rubber removed from the workplace before treating B rubber? Is B rubber removed from the workplace before treating N rubber?	✓		○		
Finished rubber	2	Are the various types of specialized rubbers placed where B rubber, C rubber, and N rubber were before treatment?	✓		○		
Finished rubber sack	3	Is finished rubber stuck to the front or back of the sack? Front → ⊟ ← Back	✓	✓	○		
Between metal surfaces	4	Use the light bulb test to check whether residual rubber has come between the metal casings.		✓	○		
Roller saucer	5	Has rubber or oil on the front, back, and sides of the roller saucer been cleaned off? saucer	✓		○		
Work surface	6	Is there waste rubber or contaminants on the front or rear surfaces of the rolling machine?	✓	✓	✗	○	
Truck	7	Is the loading platform contaminated with waste rubber?	✓	✓	○		

Figure 13-5: **Inspection and Validation Check Sheet**

References

Chiba, Rikio, Atsushi Otaki, and Susumu Yazu. *QC Introductory Series 5: Arranging and Using Data I* . 41. Japanese Standards Association, 1983.

Ishihara, Katsukichi, Kazuo Hirose, Katsuya Hosotani, and Hidenori Yoshida. *An Easy Approach to the Seven Tools of QC*. 78. Japanese Standards Association, 1980.

Ishikura, Hitomi. "Reducing Defects in Dials of Children's Bicycles." *FQC*, 189 (1978, JUSE Press Ltd.).

14

Histograms

A *histogram*, or frequency distribution diagram, is a graph that displays the distribution of data. It is constructed from data collected in a frequency table, which is a chart that divides the range of data into several equal sections to compare the frequency of occurrence in each section. The histogram drawn from the frequency table resembles a bar graph, composed of columns representing the frequency at which data appears in various sections of the range.

How to Make a Histogram

STEP 1: Gathering data

Gather at least 50 and if possible over 100 data items. Express the overall number of data items as N.

Example: The length (in mm) of 80 samples of a component were measured, producing the results shown in Table 14-1. The specified value is 30.2 ± 0.9 mm, but there is a lot of variation. A histogram will show the range of variation in this data set.

units = mm

29.9	30.1	○ 30.3	30.2	30.1	30.0	29.9	29.7
○ 30.6	30.4	29.9	× 29.5	30.4	29.7	30.0	○ 30.5
29.9	29.7	⊗ 29.1	30.2	30.3	29.4	30.2	29.8
× 29.6	30.6	29.8	29.9	29.8	30.0	30.3	30.0
30.1	29.9	29.3	29.8	30.4	× 29.2	29.8	30.0
29.9	30.0	29.6	○ 30.5	× 29.8	29.8	30.4	29.9
30.4	× 29.4	30.3	30.0	29.9	○ 30.3	30.0	× 29.5
30.0	30.4	29.4	30.0	30.0	29.6	× 29.7	29.9
30.5	29.7	29.9	30.1	○ 30.6	29.5	○ 30.4	29.7
30.2	◎ 30.8	29.5	29.9	30.2	29.8	30.1	29.9

Table 14-1: **Measurement Data**

STEP 2: Finding the maximum and minimum values

Find the maximum value L and the minimum value S in the data. Mark the maximum value (○) and the minimum value (×) in each column (or row) of the data table. Find

Find the maximum value (○) and the minimum value (×) in each column.

the maximum value among the maximum values ($\bigcirc = L$) and the minimum value among the minimum values ($\otimes = S$). This method is both fast and accurate.

The following values were obtained:
- Maximum value: $L = 30.8$
- Minimum value: $S = 29.1$

STEP 3: Determining the width of the section

Divide the distance between the maximum value and the minimum value into a suitable number of equal intervals. First, divide the difference (range) between L and S into a number k of sections and find the width of each section h. Ten is the usual value selected for k to produce an integral multiple h of the unit of measure.

Note: You do not have to precisely calculate the number of sections k. You can use the formula $k = \sqrt{N}$ and round off to the nearest integer the value of h you obtain. After determining a value for k that is an integral multiple of the unit of measure, you will obtain the results shown in Table 14-2.

Divide the range ($L - S$) into 10 sections and round off the result to an integral multiple of the unit of measure (here, 0.1 mm):

$$\frac{L-S}{10} = \frac{30.8 - 29.1}{10} = 0.17 \rightarrow 0.2 = h$$

- Section width: $h = 0.2$

Number of data points N	Number of data sections k
50 — 100	6 — 10
100 — 250	7 — 12
> 250	10 — 20

Table 14-2

STEP 4: Determining the section boundary values

The boundary value of a section is specified to an accuracy of one-half the smallest unit of measure. The first section has the minimum value as the low boundary. Calculate the high boundaries by adding the width of a section to the lower boundary.* Make the specified values as close to the boundary values as possible to make it easy to compare the actual values with specified values.**

Since the unit of measurement is 0.1 mm, one-half that value (0.05 mm) is subtracted from the lowest value (29.1) to create the lower boundary

$$29.1 - \frac{0.1}{2} = 29.05$$

*In general, the starting point of the section boundary value = minimum value - $\frac{unit}{2}$.

**Use an integral multiple of the unit of measurement as your boundary value to make clear its relationship with the specified value.

No.	Section Boundary Values	Median Value	Check	Frequency
1	29.05 ~ 29.25	29.15	//	2
2	29.25 ~ 29.45	29.35	////	4
3	29.45 ~ 29.65	29.55	ＨＩＬ ///	8
4	29.65 ~ 29.85	29.75	ＨＩＬ ＨＩＬ ////	14
5	29.85 ~ 30.05	29.95	ＨＩＬ ＨＩＬ ＨＩＬ ＨＩＬ ///	23
6	30.05 ~ 30.25	30.15	ＨＩＬ ＨＩＬ	10
7	30.25 ~ 30.45	30.35	ＨＩＬ ＨＩＬ //	12
8	30.45 ~ 30.65	30.55	ＨＩＬ /	6
9	30.65 ~ 30.85	30.75	/	1
Total				80

Table 14-3: **Frequency Chart**

STEP 5: Determining the median value of the sections

Determine the median value lying halfway between the section boundaries. Use this value when calculating the average value and the standard deviation from the frequency table.

for the first section.
See the values in the frequency table shown in Table 14-3.

Adding the section width $h = 0.2$ to this result makes the upper boundary value of the first section 29.25. The range of the first section is thus 29.05 to 29.25. Find the boundary values of the remaining sections by successively adding $h = 0.2$.

Note: Here, 29.3 or above is a good product. Thus, the first section shown in the diagram is just below the lower limit of the specification.

Use Table 14-3 to find the median value of each section. For example, the median value of the first section is

$$\frac{29.05 + 29.25}{2} = 29.15$$

Use the same method to calculate the median value of subsequent sections.

STEP 6: Making a frequency table

List the boundary values and median value of sections in columns running from small to large values. Assign data items one by one to the appropriate sections by placing a mark in the check column. Total the data in the frequency column to make certain that the number of data items equals N.

Make a mark in the check column, determine the frequency, and complete the frequency table (Table 14-3).

STEP 7: Making a histogram

Write the ranges of values for the sections along the horizontal axis and the frequency scale along the vertical axis. Your horizontal scale will be easier to understand if you use values such as 1.0, 1.5, and 2.0, rather than values based on the boundaries or median values of the sections.

Construct a diagram that has a square proportion (axes of approximately equal length).

Draw vertical lines corresponding to the specification boundaries. Use the space below the diagram to record essential items such as the data history (product name, when the data was taken, etc.), the number of data items, the average value, the standard deviation, and so on.

Note: See Chapter 16 for methods of using the frequency table to determine the average value and the standard deviation.

Write the dimensions along the horizontal axis and the frequency scale along the vertical axis to create the histogram (see Figure 14-1). Record information on items outside the upper and lower specifications limits.

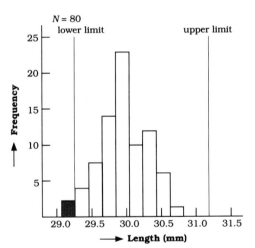

Product name: Component X
Period: 6/3 ~ 6/28
$N = 80$ $\bar{x} = 29.965$ $s = 0.350$
Specified value: 30.2 ± 0.9

Figure 14-1: **Histogram**

Ways to Use Histograms

Determining the Distribution Pattern from the Shape of the Histogram

You may not notice the many small variations in your data. Viewing a histogram draws your attention to the distribution of the data as a whole.

1. *Normal histograms.* Data obtained from a stable process usually produces a histogram that is highest in the center and tapers off symmetrically to the left and right.

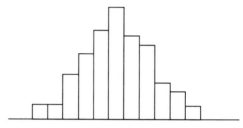

Figure 14-2: **Normal Histogram**

2. *Double peak histograms.* Double peaks appear if you mix data from different materials that have different averages. Correct this problem by stratifying the data and making two new histograms. The right-hand and the left-hand peaks will then resemble the normal histogram and the differences between the different data strata will become clear.

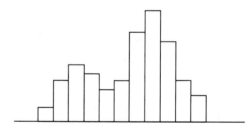

Figure 14-3: **Double Peak Histogram**

3. *Isolated island histograms.* A small isolated island appears beside a normal histogram. Accidental mixing of data from another distribution produces this type of histogram.

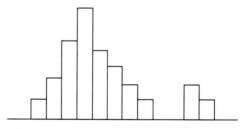

Figure 14-4: **Isolated Island Histogram**

4. *Cliff histograms.* The slope of the histogram ends abruptly in a steep cliff. Eliminating all items that do not meet specifications is one way to produce this type of histogram.

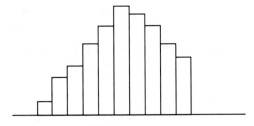

Figure 14-5: **Cliff Histogram**

5. *Cogwheel histograms.* Alternating peaks and depressions in adjacent sections produce a pattern resembling a cogwheel. Section widths that are integral multiples of the unit of measurement of the scale produce this shape as an artifact of the way the scale is read during measurement.

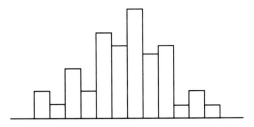

Figure 14-6: **Cogwheel Histogram**

Using Histograms to Determine Whether Specifications Are Satisfied

Keep the following points in mind as you determine if the histogram falls well within the upper and lower limits of the specifications:

1. Is the center of the distribution exactly halfway between the upper and lower limits of the specification (or target value)?
2. Is the spread of the distribution too large or too small?
3. Does any data appear beyond the upper limit or the lower limit of the distribution?
4. Is there ample space for the distribution within the specified limits?

See Figure 14-7.

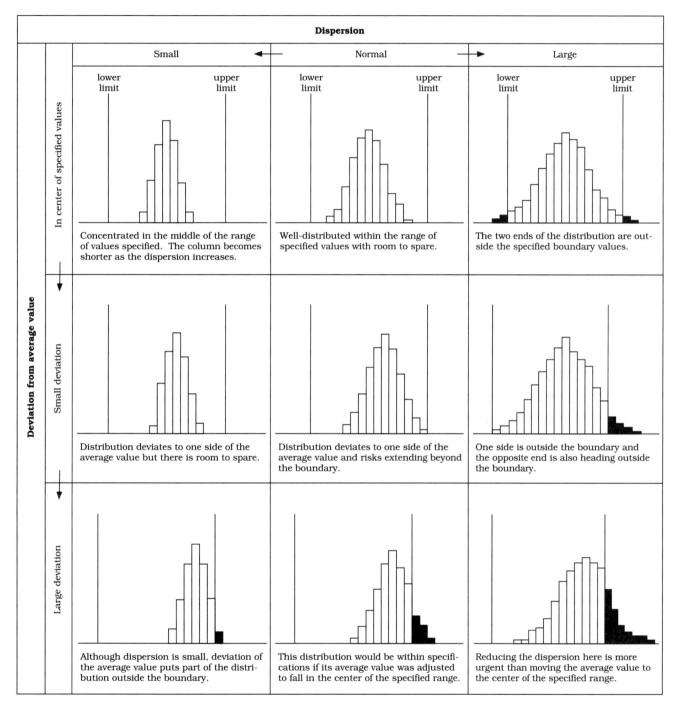

Figure 14-7: **Correspondence with Specified Values**

Comparing Data by Stratifying and Investigating Differences between Strata

Stratify data by machine, material, work shift, and so on, make histograms for each data set, and compare. Use the same horizontal characteristic scale on the histograms and place them next to each other for easy comparison. See Chapter 15, Figure 15-4. You can also use histograms to evaluate the effectiveness of improvement measures by comparing histograms that show the situation both before and after the improvement measure was implemented.

15

Stratification

When investigating the cause of a defect or the scatter of distribution of a component's measurements, the need often arises to examine data grouped by the type of machine, type of material, method of operation, or operator. The method of grouping data by common points or characteristics to better understand similarities and characteristics of data is called *stratification*.

Stratification and comparison of data is an effective method for isolating the cause of a problem. You can stratify the data you collect for the QC tools such as graphs, Pareto diagrams, check sheets, histograms, scatter diagrams, and control charts. Table 15-1 shows examples of the types of stratification commonly used in the workplace.

1. By material	Manufacturer, buyer, brand, place of production, purchase date, lot received, production lot, components, purity, size, parts, time stored, storage place, etc.
2. By machine, equipment, or tool	Machine type, number, model, performance, and age; by factory, line, tool, size, mold, and die.
3. By operator	Individual, team, group, age, experience, gender, etc.
4. By operating procedures and by operating conditions	Temperature, pressure, speed, rotational frequency, line speed, location of operation, illumination, air temperature, humidity, weather, operating procedure, etc.
5. By measurement and inspection	Instrument, measurement procedure, place of measurement, person making the measurement, inspection tools, inspection procedure, place of inspection, inspector, etc.
6. By time	Time, morning, afternoon, evening, night, day, week, month, period, season, etc.; just before starting and just after finishing the operation.
7. By environment and weather	Air temperature, humidity, clear, cloudy, rainy, windy, snowy, rainy season, dry season, sound, illumination, etc.
8. Other	New vs. previous product, unit product vs. continuously produced product, good product vs. defective product, packing method and transportation method, etc.

Table 15-1: **Stratification of data**

Using Stratification with the QC Tools

Stratified Graph

In an iron forging plant, molds A and B are used alternately in lot production. Three samples were pulled from each lot to measure the thickness of the product's central section, which is one of the most important quality characteristics relating to the dimensions of the product. A broken line graph was made of the results.

A large scatter appears above the specified value of $30 \, ^{+2.5}_{0} \,$ mm. These are thickness defects. Products made with mold A are marked with a Δ and products made with mold B are marked with a $\times$. As shown in Figure 15-1, products made with mold A were within specifications but some products made with mold B were outside the specifications.

Graphs stratified by mold were produced to make this fact more evident. The mean value of products made with mold B ($\bar{x}_B = 32.63$) is 1.4 mm more than the mean value of mold A products ($\bar{x}_A = 31.23$), as Figure 15-2 shows. Since this value is outside the specified limits, mold B must be repaired to reduce the scatter of the data. (See Chapter 16 for more about the mean and other average values.)

Stratified Histogram

Optical equipment is spot welded in this process. The welding strength rating of the product is shown in a histogram. The shaded area of Figure 15-3 shows that some welds are not strong enough to meet the lower

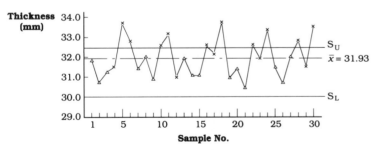

Figure 15-1: Line Graph Before Stratification

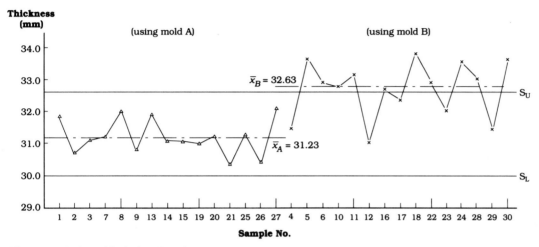

Figure 15-2: **Stratified Line Graph**

boundary of the 65 kgf/cm² specification. Since operators A and B alternate on a single spot welding machine, histograms stratified by operator were made.

The stratified histogram in Figure 15-3 shows that some of operators A's welds are too weak, while operator B's welds are sufficiently strong. The search for the cause of the weak welds can then focus on operator A's methods. Further investigation showed that the method for adjusting the applied pressure had not been standardized (see Figure 15-4).

Stratified Scatter Diagrams

A heat treatment plant purchases materials from companies A and B. Although heat treatment conditions were held constant according to the standard, there was a large dispersion in the hardness. Since the hardness increased when material from company B was used, the heat treatment plant made a scatter diagram of the hardness of the material, stratified by material manufacturer.

Figure 15-5 is a scatter diagram stratified by materials manufacturer. This diagram shows that the materials from both companies become harder as the heat treating temperature increases. Although both materials were heat treated at the same temperature, however, the material from company B has a hardness about 5 degrees more than that of company A's materials.

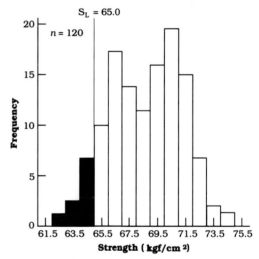

Figure 15-3: **Combined Histogram**

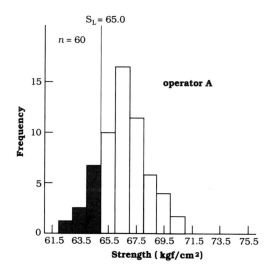

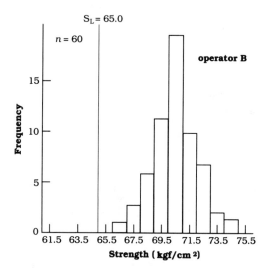

Figure 15-4: **Stratified Histogram**

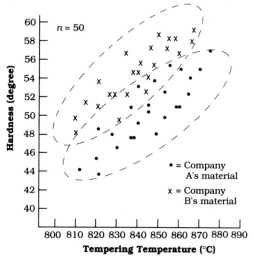

Figure 15-5: **Stratified Scatter Diagram**

References

Chiba, Rikio, Atsushi Otaki, and Susumu Yazu. *QC Introductory Series 5: Arranging and Using Data I.* Japanese Standards Association, 1983.

Ishihara, Katsukichi, Kazuo Hirose, Katsuo Hosotani, and Hidenori Yoshida. *An Easy Approach to the Seven Tools of QC.* Japanese Standards Association, 1980.

16

Quantitative Expressions of the Data Distribution

Data distributions are usually evaluated quantitatively by looking at an average value or at the spread of the distribution of the values. This chapter introduces the expressions commonly used to describe these aspects of the distribution.

Expressing the Average Value of a Distribution

MEAN VALUE: $\bar{x}$

The *mean value* or *mean* is the simple arithmetic average of the total of the sample values.

Direct Calculation Method

STEP 1:

Arrange the measured values (x) as shown in Table 16-1.

Example: Five samples are taken from a lot of pins. The length of each sample is measured (units = mm), with the results shown in Table 16-1a.

No.	Measured value x
1	x_1
2	x_2
$\vdots$	$\vdots$
n	x_n
Total	Σ_x
Average	$\bar{x}$

Table 16-1

No.	x
1	52.14
2	52.03
3	52.10
4	52.25
5	52.16
Total	260.68
Average	52.136

Table 16-1a

STEP 2:

Find the total (summation or Σx) of x.

$$\Sigma x = x_1 + x_2 + \cdots + x_n$$

$$\Sigma x = 260.68$$

STEP 3:

$$\bar{x} = \frac{\Sigma x}{n}$$

$$\bar{x} = \frac{260.68}{5} = 52.136 \text{ (mm)}$$

Calculation Using Data Transformation

Data transformation refers to methods of manipulating measured values to make them easier to use in calculations. In this case, an amount a (52) is subtracted from each measured value to make a smaller number, which is multiplied by b (100) to eliminate decimal places. The formulas are modified accordingly.

STEP 1:

Transform each of the measured values and arrange them as shown in Table 16-2.

Example:

No.	x	$u = (x - a) \times b$
1	x_1	u_1
2	x_2	u_2
⋮	⋮	⋮
n	x_n	u_n
Total	—	Σx
Average	—	$\bar{u}$

Table 16-2

No.	x	$u = (x - 52) \times 100$
1	52.14	14
2	52.03	3
3	52.10	10
4	52.25	25
5	52.16	16
Total	—	68
Average	—	13.6

Table 16-2a

STEP 2:

$$\bar{u} = \frac{\Sigma u}{n}$$

$$\bar{u} = \frac{68}{5} = 13.6$$

STEP 3:

$$\bar{x} = \bar{u} \times \frac{1}{b} + a$$

$a = 52$
$b = 100$
$\bar{x} = 13.6 \times \dfrac{1}{100} + 52$
$= 52.136 \text{ (mm)}$

MEDIAN VALUE: $\tilde{x}$

The *median value* is found by arranging the data values in order and determining the middle value. It is sometimes used in place of the mean.

For an Odd Number of Values

STEP 1:

List the measured values in order of their size.

Example: Determine the value of x from the data given in Table 16-1a.

52.03
52.10
<u>52.14</u>
52.16
52.25

STEP 2:

The value at the center is taken as the median value.

$\tilde{x} = 52.14$

For an Even Number of Values

STEP 1:

List the measured values in order of their size.

Example: Determine the value of $\tilde{x}$ when $x_6 = 52.24$ is added to the data given in Table 16-1a.

52.03
52.10
<u>52.14</u>
<u>52.16</u>
52.24
52.25

STEP 2:

The two central values are determined, and their average is taken as the median.

$$\tilde{x} = \frac{52.14 + 52.16}{2}$$

$$= 52.15 \text{ (mm)}$$

Expressing the Spread of the Distribution

RANGE: R

The *range* is the difference between the smallest and largest values in the sample. It is calculated simply by subtraction.

STEP 1:

Determine the maximum value x_{max} and the minimum value x_{min} among the measured values.

Example: In the case of Table 16-1a,

$$x_{max} = 52.25$$
$$x_{min} = 52.03$$

STEP 2:

$$R = x_{max} - x_{min}$$

$$R = 52.25 - 52.03 = 0.22 \text{ (mm)}$$

VARIANCE: V
Direct Calculation Method

STEP 1:

The measured value x and the square of the measured value x^2 are shown in Table 16-3.

No.	x	x^2
1	x_1	x_1^2
2	x_2	x_2^2
⋮	⋮	⋮
n	x_n	x_n^2
Total	Σx	Σx^2

Table 16-3

Example:

No.	x	x^2
1	52.14	2,718.5796
2	52.03	2,707.1209
3	52.10	2,714.4100
4	52.25	2,730.0625
5	52.16	2,720.6656
Total	260.68	13,590.8386

Table 16-3a

STEP 2:

Calculate the summation (total) of the squares.

$$S = \Sigma x^2 - \frac{(\Sigma x)^2}{n}$$

$$S = 13{,}590.8386 - \frac{(260.68)^2}{5}$$
$$= 0.02612$$

STEP 3:

Calculate the variance (V).

$$V = \frac{S}{(n - 1)}$$

$$V = \frac{(0.02612)}{(5 - 1)}$$
$$= 0.00653 \text{ (mm)}$$

Calculation Using Data Transformation

To simplify the calculations, a (52) is subtracted and the result multiplied by b (100) to eliminate decimal places. The formulas are modified accordingly.

STEP 1:

Transform each of the measured values and arrange them as shown in Table 16-4.

No.	x	$u = (x - a) \times b$	x^2
1	x_1	u_1	u_1^2
2	x_2	u_2	u_2^2
:	:	:	:
n	x_n	u_n	u_n^2
Total	—	Σu	Σu^2

Table 16-4

Example:

No.	x	$u = (x - 52) \times 100$	u^2
1	52.14	14	196
2	52.03	3	9
3	52.10	10	100
4	52.25	25	625
5	52.16	16	256
Total	—	68	1,186

Table 16-4a

STEP 2:

Calculate the sum of the squares.

$$S = \frac{1}{b^2} \left\{ \Sigma u^2 - \frac{(\Sigma u)^2}{n} \right\}$$

$$S = \frac{1}{(100)^2} \left\{ 1,186 - \frac{(68)^2}{5} \right\}$$
$$= 0.02612$$

STEP 3:

Calculate the variance V.

$$V = \frac{S}{(n-1)}$$

$$V = \frac{(0.02612)}{(5-1)}$$
$$= 0.00653 \text{ (mm)}$$

STANDARD DEVIATION: *s*

STEP 1:

Determine the variance *V*.

Example: According to the previous calculation,

$$V = 0.00653$$

STEP 2:

Calculate the standard deviation (*s*).

$$s = \sqrt{V}$$

$$s = \sqrt{0.00653}$$
$$= 0.0808 \text{ (mm)}$$

Determining Mean Value and Standard Deviation Using a Frequency Table

You can use the method just described to calculate the mean value and the standard deviation even if you have made many individual measurements. However, if you can section the data and make a frequency table (as in the case of constructing a histogram), you can use a simpler method for calculating these values.

STEP 1: Making a frequency table

Make a frequency table with *f*, *u*, *uf*, and u^2f columns on its right side.

Example: The lengths of eighty component samples were measured (unit: mm) and the frequency of the various measurements was recorded on the frequency table (Table 16-5). (This table uses the same data as the table for preparing the histogram in Chapter 14, Table 14-3.)

No.	Section Boundary Values	Median Value	Check	*f*	*u*	*uf*	u^2f
1	29.05 ~ 29.25	29.15	//	2	-4	- 8	32
2	29.25 ~ 29.45	29.35	////	4	-3	-12	36
3	29.45 ~ 29.65	29.55	〜〜 ///	8	-2	-16	32
4	29.65 ~ 29.85	29.75	〜〜 〜〜 ////	14	-1	-14	14
5	29.85 ~ 30.05	29.95	〜〜 〜〜 〜〜 〜〜 ///	23	0		
6	30.05 ~ 30.25	30.15	〜〜 〜〜	10	1	10	10
7	30.25 ~ 30.45	30.35	〜〜 〜〜 //	12	2	24	48
8	30.45 ~ 30.65	30.55	〜〜 /	6	3	18	54
9	30.65 ~ 30.85	30.75	/	1	4	4	16
Total				80	—	6	242

Table 16-5: Frequency Table for Calculation of $\bar{x}$ and *s*

(a) If the numerical value of the $(n + 1)$th and subsequent places is less than one-half the value of the nth unit, then drop it.

Example 1: 1.23 rounded off to two significant digits becomes 1.2.

Example 2: 1.2343 rounded off to three decimal places becomes 1.234.

(b) If the numerical value of the $(n + 1)$th and subsequent places is greater than one-half the value of one nth place unit, then increase the value of the nth place by 1.

Example 1: 1.26 rounded off to two significant digits becomes 1.3.

Example 2: 1.2967 rounded off to three decimal places becomes 1.297.

(c) If the numerical value of the $(n + 1)$th and subsequent places equals one-half the value of one nth place unit or if you don't know whether to drop it or not, then take one of the following steps:

• If the value of the nth place is 0, 2, 4, 6, or 8, drop it.

Example 1: 1.25 rounded off to two significant places, becomes 1.2.

Example 2: 0.625 rounded off to two decimal places becomes 0.62.

• If the value of the unit in the nth place is 1, 3, 5, 7, or 9, then increase the value of the nth place by one unit.

Example 1: 1.350 rounded off to two significant digits becomes 1.4.

Example 2: 0.095 rounded off to two decimal places becomes 0.10.

(d) If you know that the numerical value of the $(n + 1)$th and subsequent places is to be carried or discarded, you must use either method (a) or (b).

Example 1: 2.347 --> 2.35 --> 2.3.
Example 2: 2.452 -->2.45 --> 2.5.

17

Process Capability

Process capability, for a stable manufacturing process, is the capacity of the process to reach a certain level of quality. For a stabilized process in which factors affecting the standard deviation are properly controlled, process capability, as measured by the quality characteristics of the products of the process, is usually expressed as the mean value plus or minus three times the standard deviation ($x \pm 3s$). If you can freely set a mean value (such as a standard temperature setting), then you can express process capability as six times the standard deviation from that mean value.

Process capability can be shown graphically using histograms and process capability charts. Process capability indices numerically express the relation between the distribution and the specification limits.

Process Capability Charts

A *process capability chart* is a graphic plot of the stability or variation in dispersion of quality over time, relative to a specified or target value.

How to Draw a Process Capability Chart

1. Collect about 100 data points from the process according to the production sequence or over a certain period of time.
2. Using graph paper, draw a scale of measured values (usually time) along the horizontal axis and a scale of characteristic (quality) values along the vertical axis.
3. Plot the data sequentially. Create a plot by joining together the data points.
4. Draw lines representing the specified or target values.
5. Create a horizontal histogram on the right side of the chart to highlight the distribution pattern. See Figure 17-1.

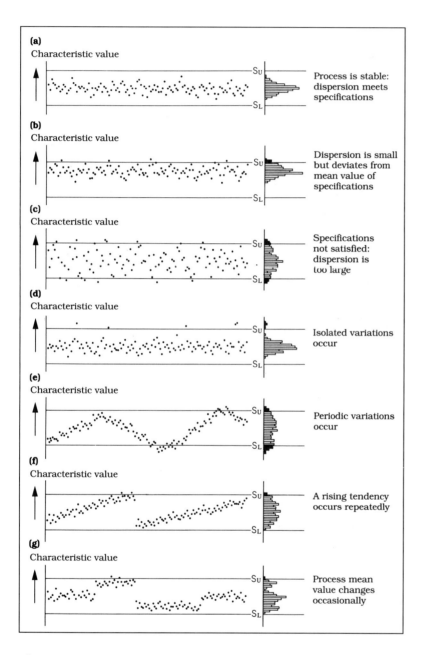

Figure 17-1: **Process Capability Chart (Examples)**

How to Read Process Capability Charts

1. Check to see if the points you have plotted fall between the upper and lower limits specified (see Figure 17-1). Is there enough room for the dispersion of the points within the upper and lower limits?
2. Does the arrangement of the plotted points change over time? For example, do the plotted points tend to rise or fall over time? Is there a pattern in the changes in the placement of the points? Are there abrupt changes in the position of the points?

Process Capability Index

The *process capability index* (C_p) is expressed as a ratio to the specified value. It is used to quantitatively evaluate the adequacy of the process capability — whether the variation in the process is within the limits of the specifications. The following sections give formulas for determining the process capability index and related indices. See Table 17-1 for a guide to interpreting indices in various ranges of value.

C_p	Evaluation	Assessment
$C_p > 1.33$	Good	• Process capability completely meets specifications.
$1.33 \geqq C_p > 1.0$	Acceptable	• Process capability does not completely meet specifications; process control should be continued.
$1.0 \geqq C_p$	Inadequate	• Process capability inadequate; improvements should be made.

Table 17-1

USING TWO SPECIFICATIONS

Evaluating the dispersion

If upper and lower specification limits are given, to set and adjust the average value you need only evaluate the width of the dispersion within the limits:

$$C_p = \frac{T}{6s}$$

where T is the width of the specification limits and s is the standard deviation (the spread of the characteristic measured in the process — see Chapter 16 for directions on calculating).

$$T = S_U - S_L$$

where S_U is the upper limit of the specification and S_L is the lower limit.

Note: When determining standard deviation s, sample the material over a certain period. Using this quality characteristics data, draw a histogram to evaluate the process capability. Calculate the standard deviation from this data. For proper evaluation of the process capability and standard deviation, make sure the sampling period is not biased.

Example 1: The external diameter specification of a component in an external grinding process is 78.000 ±0.012 mm. This process is controlled using an $\bar{x} - R$ (mean and range) control chart to standardize the process. From data collected during the previous month,

$$\bar{x} = 78.002, \, s = 0.0032$$

we determine

$$T = 0.012 \times 2 = 0.024$$

$$\therefore C_p = \frac{0.024}{(6 \times 0.0032)}$$

$$= 1.25$$

See Figure 17-2.

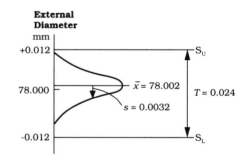

Figure 17-2: **Two Limits Specified (Grinding)**

Accordingly, although the process capability is not perfect, management of the dispersion always keeps the mean value at the center of the dispersion so that it meets the specifications.

Using C_{pk}

The expression C_{pk} is often used instead of C_p to evaluate the centering of the process within the specification at the same time as the variation.

$$C_{pk} = (1 - K)\frac{T}{6s}$$

where

$$K = \frac{|\text{ the mean value of the specification} - \bar{x} \, |}{\dfrac{T}{2}}$$

If $K \geq 1$, $C_{pk} = 0$. If $C \leq 1$, compare it with C_p. If C_p is acceptable, then the problem can be improved by changing the center. If it too is unacceptable, the amount of variation must be corrected.

Example 2: For a carburizing heat treatment process, the effective depth of carburization specified is 1.1 mm to 1.3 mm. The quality distribution determined for this process is

$$\bar{x} = 1.224 \text{ mm}$$
$$s = 0.031 \text{ mm}$$

See Figure 17-3.

$$T = 1.3 - 1.1 = 0.2$$

$$K = \frac{|\, 1.2 - 1.224 \,|}{\dfrac{0.2}{2}} = 0.24$$

$$\therefore C_{pk} = (1 - 0.24)\frac{0.2}{6 \times 0.031} = 0.82$$

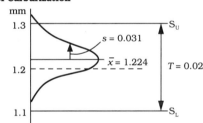

Effective Depth of Carburization

Figure 17-3: **Two Limits Specified (Carburization)**

The C_{pk} index indicates a problem here with process capability. However, the C_p is greater than 1:

$$C_p = \frac{0.2}{6 \times 0.031} = 1.08$$

This indicates not only that the process variation is only slightly smaller than the specifications, but also that the distribution itself is poorly centered. An improved procedure that revises heat treatment conditions must be developed to improve the process capability.

USING A SINGLE SPECIFICATION

Upper limit specified

If only the upper limit is specified, use the following formula:

$$C_{pU} = \frac{S_U - \bar{x}}{3s}$$

Example 3: For a planar grinding process, the ends of a component must be parallel to within 8 μm or less. The quality distribution here has the value

$$\bar{x} = 2.91 \ \mu m \ and \ s = 1.26 \ \mu m$$

$$C_{pU} = \frac{8 - 2.91}{3 \times 1.26} = 1.35$$

This value indicates that the process capability is completely adequate (well within the specifications limits). (Use Table 17-1 to interpret the index for single-limit specifications as well.)

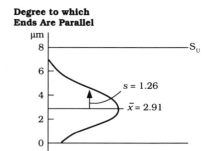

Figure 17-4: **Upper Limit Specified**

Lower limit specified

If only the lower limit is specified, use the following formula:

$$C_{pL} = \frac{\overline{x} - S_L}{3s}$$

Example 4: The specified tensile strength after heat treatment is 63 kgf/mm². The result of the process capability study is $\overline{x}$ = 68.12 kgf/mm², s = 2.41 kgf/mm².

$$C_{pL} = \frac{68.12 - 63}{3 \times 2.41} = 0.71$$

Here the process capability is inadequate (see Figure 17-5). Changes must be made in heat treatment conditions to reduce the dispersal and change the average value target to slightly increase the tensile strength.

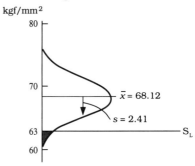

Tensile Strength
kgf/mm²

Figure 17-5: **Lower Limit Specified**

Estimating Percentage Defective

When the process capability is too low, a number of the products made will be outside the specification limits. The normal distribution table (see Table 17-2) is used to estimate the probability that for a specification limit that is u times the standard deviation s from the process average, a value will fall outside the specified limits. This probability is the percentage defective. You can estimate the percentage defective using the following procedure:

STEP 1:

Use the following formula to determine the value of u (using the specified boundary values S_U and S_L):

$$u = \frac{S_U - \bar{x}}{s} \quad \text{or} \quad u = \frac{\bar{x} - S_L}{s}$$

STEP 2:

Using the value of u (read down the left column, then in to the numerical value of the second decimal place), determine P from the normal distribution table (see Table 17-2). P is the probability that the value of u is exceeded in the standard normal distribution (a normal distribution in which the average value = 0 and the standard deviation = 1). Therefore,

$$P = \text{the estimated percentage defective}$$

Examples:

1. We can estimate the percentage defective of the effective carburization depth of Example 2 above:

    $$u = \frac{(1.3 - 1.224)}{0.031} = 2.45$$

    From the normal distribution table, we determine that $P = 0.0071$. Thus we get an estimated percentage defective of about 0.7%.

2. We can estimate the percentage defective of the tensile strength of Example 4 above:

    $$u = \frac{(68.12 - 63)}{2.41} = 2.12$$

    From the normal distribution table, we determine that $P = 0.0170$. Thus we get an estimated percentage defective of about 1.7%.

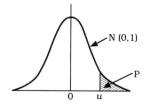

(A table for determining the value of *P* from *u*)

u	＊ = 0	1	2	3	4	5	6	7	8	9
0.0 *	.5000	.4960	.4920	.4880	.4840	.4801	.4761	.4721	.4681	.4641
0.1 *	.4602	.4562	.4522	.4483	.4443	.4404	.4364	.4325	.4286	.4247
0.2 *	.4207	.4168	.4129	.4090	.4052	.4013	.3974	.3936	.3897	.3859
0.3 *	.3821	.3783	.3745	.3707	.3669	.3632	.3594	.3557	.3520	.3483
0.4 *	.3446	.3409	.3372	.3336	.3300	.3264	.3228	.3192	.3156	.3121
0.5 *	.3085	.3050	.3015	.2981	.2946	.2912	.2877	.2843	.2810	.2776
0.6 *	.2743	.2709	.2676	.2643	.2611	.2578	.2546	.2514	.2483	.2451
0.7 *	.2420	.2389	.2358	.2327	.2296	.2266	.2236	.2206	.2177	.2148
0.8 *	.2119	.2090	.2061	.2033	.2005	.1977	.1949	.1922	.1894	.1867
0.9 *	.1841	.1814	.1788	.1762	.1736	.1711	.1685	.1660	.1635	.1611
1.0 *	.1587	.1562	.1539	.1515	.1492	.1469	.1446	.1423	.1401	.1379
1.1 *	.1357	.1335	.1314	.1292	.1271	.1251	.1230	.1210	.1190	.1170
1.2 *	.1151	.1131	.1112	.1093	.1075	.1056	.1038	.1020	.1003	.0985
1.3 *	.0968	.0951	.0934	.0918	.0901	.0885	.0869	.0853	.0838	.0823
1.4 *	.0808	.0793	.0778	.0764	.0749	.0735	.0721	.0708	.0694	.0681
1.5 *	.0668	.0655	.0643	.0630	.0618	.0606	.0594	.0582	.0571	.0559
1.6 *	.0548	.0537	.0526	.0516	.0505	.0495	.0485	.0475	.0465	.0455
1.7 *	.0446	.0436	.0427	.0418	.0409	.0401	.0392	.0384	.0375	.0367
1.8 *	.0359	.0351	.0344	.0336	.0329	.0322	.0314	.0307	.0301	.0294
1.9 *	.0287	.0281	.0274	.0268	.0262	.0256	.0250	.0244	.0239	.0233
2.0 *	.0228	.0222	.0217	.0212	.0207	.0202	.0197	.0192	.0188	.0183
2.1 *	.0179	.0174	.0170	.0166	.0162	.0158	.0154	.0150	.0146	.0143
2.2 *	.0139	.0136	.0132	.0129	.0125	.0122	.0119	.0116	.0113	.0110
2.3 *	.0107	.0104	.0102	.0099	.0096	.0094	.0091	.0089	.0087	.0084
2.4 *	.0082	.0080	.0078	.0075	.0073	.0071	.0069	.0068	.0066	.0064
2.5 *	.0062	.0060	.0059	.0057	.0055	.0054	.0052	.0051	.0049	.0048
2.6 *	.0047	.0045	.0044	.0043	.0041	.0040	.0039	.0038	.0037	.0036
2.7 *	.0035	.0034	.0033	.0032	.0031	.0030	.0029	.0028	.0027	.0026
2.8 *	.0026	.0025	.0024	.0023	.0023	.0022	.0021	.0021	.0020	.0019
2.9 *	.0019	.0018	.0018	.0017	.0016	.0016	.0015	.0015	.0014	.0014
3.0 *	.0013	.0013	.0013	.0012	.0012	.0011	.0011	.0011	.0010	.0010

Table 17-2: **Normal Distribution Table**

18

Control Charts

A *control chart* is a type of line graph used to assess and maintain the stability of a process. A center line and upper and lower control limits (collectively called control lines) are drawn on a graph. Data is collected over time and the values are plotted on the graph.

The control limits serve as guides to the control state of the process, distinguishing random causes of variation from specific causes that should be investigated. If the points plotted to express the condition of a process fall within the control limits and the distribution of the points is not abnormal, then variation is considered to be from random causes and the process is considered stable. Plotted points that fall outside the control limits or in an abnormal distribution pattern signify an unstable, out-of-control process. You can make the process more stable by identifying and eliminating the cause of the abnormality and taking action to prevent its recurrence.

Control charts are also used to analyze processes to understand the state of a process, the factors involved in the dispersion of data points, and so on. Table 18-1 describes the most commonly used charts and when to use them.

Making Control Charts with Measured Values

$\bar{x}$ – R CONTROL CHARTS

STEP 1: How to collect data

Collect about 100 data points. Organize this data into four or five groups of 20 to 25 data points. Enter the data on a data sheet. Some notes on the sampling process:

Example 1: In a guide roller grinding process, the external diameter of the guide roller is the characteristic

1. Choose the samples to minimize variation within each group and highlight variations between groups. This usually means taking sequential samples so that values in each group should be similar.
2. Although it is helpful to use more than 100 data points, it is important that the data represent the latest state of the process.
3. The number of groups is usually between two and six; four or five groups is the most common case.
4. Enter important process control information, such as the product name, the quality characteristics, the sampling method, and the method of measurement, on the data sheet.

value. Five samples ($n = 5$) are measured every hour to determine the external diameter of the roller. The five samples from products produced during the same hour constitute a group. Thirty data groups ($k = 30$) are gathered during the time period and entered in the data sheet (see Table 18-2). The 150 data points shown on the data sheet will be used to make the $\bar{x} - R$ control chart to determine the state of the process.

Category	Chart Type	Statistical Quantity	Application
Measured values	$\bar{x} - R$ chart	mean value and range	• Charts dimensions and their precision, weight, time, strength, and other measurable quantities.
	$\tilde{x} - R$ chart	median and range	• Charts measurable quantities; similar to $\bar{x} - R$ but requires fewer calculations to plot.
	x chart	individual measured values	• Used when obtaining measured values is expensive and quick action is desired (data measured individually rather than in sample sets).
Counted (numerical) values	pn chart	number of defective units	• Charts the number of defective units in samples of fixed size.
	p chart	percent defective	• Charts the number of defective units in samples of varying size (fraction defective).
	c chart	number of defects	• Charts the number of flaws appearing in a product of fixed size or previously defined unit over a certain period of time (e.g., the number of cracks in a metal plate or glass product).
	u chart	number of defects per unit area	• Charts the number of flaws that appear on a product of varying size over a period of time (e.g., bruises in wire material and irregularities in fabrics).

Table 18-1: **Types of Control Charts and Their Uses**

$\bar{x} - R$ **Control Chart Data Sheet** No. _____

Product name	guide roller		Manufacturing order number	54-A-105	Time period		7-16
Characteristics	outer diameter (designation 18.5 mm)		Workplace	Grinding No. 1			7-20
Unit of measurement	0.001 mm		Specified daily production	7,500	Machine number		GD - 5
Specified limits	max.	+ 30	Sample	Size	n = 5	Operator	$\mathcal{AK}$
	min.	+ 20		Interval	1 hr	Signature of inspector	$\mathcal{KY}$
Spec. no.	G - 5210		Measuring instrument number	D = 2010			

Date	Group No.	Measured Values					Sum Σx	Mean Value $\bar{x}$	Range R	Comments
		x_1	x_2	x_3	x_4	x_5				
7/16	1	27	24	28	27	26	132	26.4	4	
	2	25	26	29	28	23	131	26.2	6	
	3	23	27	25	24	27	126	25.2	4	
	4	26	25	28	25	27	131	26.2	3	
	5	25	29	25	26	24	129	25.8	5	
	6	22	23	29	24	23	121	24.2	7	
7/17	7	28	27	25	26	26	132	26.4	3	
	8	24	27	27	26	24	128	25.6	3	
	9	24	27	26	24	23	124	24.8	4	
	10	26	26	25	27	25	129	25.8	2	
	11	25	30	23	28	27	133	26.6	7	
	12	23	28	25	24	22	122	24.4	6	
7/18	13	25	26	23	26	24	124	24.8	3	
	14	25	27	23	26	27	128	25.6	4	
	15	24	24	25	25	23	121	24.2	2	
	16	24	27	23	28	27	129	25.8	5	
	17	28	29	25	26	24	132	26.4	5	
	18	26	28	27	25	28	134	26.8	3	
7/19	19	30	26	30	28	32	146	29.2	6	
	20	26	29	27	27	28	137	27.4	3	
	21	28	26	24	25	25	128	25.6	4	
	22	25	27	24	26	27	129	25.8	3	
	23	27	29	26	25	23	130	26.0	6	
	24	25	24	28	26	21	124	24.8	7	
7/20	25	26	25	26	27	25	129	25.8	2	
	26	23	24	27	24	28	126	25.2	5	
	27	25	26	30	20	27	128	25.6	10	
	28	23	27	24	28	22	124	24.8	6	
	29	27	23	24	25	24	123	24.6	4	
	30	25	25	26	24	28	128	25.6	4	

			Total	771.6	136
			$\bar{\bar{x}} = 25.72$		$\bar{R} = 4.53$

$\bar{x}$ control chart $A_2\bar{R} = 2.61$

UCL = $\bar{\bar{x}} + A_2\bar{R} = 28.33$

LCL = $\bar{\bar{x}} + A_2\bar{R} = 23.11$

R control chart

UCL = $D_4\bar{R} = 9.56$

LCL = $D_3\bar{R} = $ —

n	A_2	D_4	D_3
4	0.729	2.28	—
5	0.577	2.11	—

Table 18-2: $\bar{x}$–R Control Chart Data Sheet

STEP 2: Calculating $\bar{x}$

Determine the mean value $\bar{x}$ for each data group.

$$\bar{x} = \frac{x_1 + x_2 + \dots + x_n}{n}$$

Here,

x_1 = first measured value
x_2 = second measured value
x_n = nth measured value
n = number of groups

Usually the measured value is determined to the nearest whole unit.

For example, for group no. 1,

$$\bar{x} = \frac{27 + 24 + 28 + 27 + 26}{5}$$
$$= 26.4$$

Use the same method to calculate $\bar{x}$ for the other groups.

STEP 3: Calculating R

Determine the range R for each group.

$$R = (\text{maximum value of } x) - (\text{minimum value of } x)$$

For group no. 1, we obtain

$$R = 28 - 24 = 4$$

and likewise for the other groups.

STEP 4: Calculating the control lines

Median line:

$\bar{x}$ control chart:

$$\bar{\bar{x}} = \frac{\Sigma \bar{x}}{k}$$

R control chart:

$$\bar{R} = \frac{\Sigma R}{k}$$

where k is the number of groups.

(Here the values of the control lines are determined to two decimal places more than the measured values.)

Control limits:

Find the values for the factors A_2, D_3, and D_4 that correspond to the size n of the group in Table 18-3. These are factors used in calculating the control limits for R charts.

$$\bar{\bar{x}} = \frac{771.6}{30} = 25.72$$

$$\bar{R} = \frac{136}{30} = 4.53$$

Table 18-3 states values for the A_2, D_4, and D_3, used in the next calculation. If $n = 5$, then

$\bar{x}$ control chart:

Upper control limit (UCL) = $\bar{\bar{x}} + A_2\bar{R}$

Lower control limit (LCL) = $\bar{\bar{x}} - A_2\bar{R}$

R control chart:

Upper control limit (UCL) = $D_4\bar{R}$
Lower control limit (LCL) = $D_3\bar{R}$

(The range R is usually determined to one digit more than the measured value.)

$A_2 = 0.577$
$D_4 = 2.11$
$D_3 = —$

Accordingly, for an $\bar{x}$ control chart:

UCL = 25.72 + (0.577 x 4.53)
= 28.33
LCL = 25.72 – (0.577 x 4.53)
= 23.11

For an R control chart:

UCL = 2.11 x 4.53 = 9.56 ◊ 9.6
LCL = — (ignore)

Sample Size n	$\bar{x}$ Control Chart	R Control Chart	
	A_2	D_3	D_4
2	1.880	—	3.27
3	1.023	—	2.57
4	0.729	—	2.28
5	0.577	—	2.11
6	0.483	—	2.00
7	0.419	0.076	1.92
8	0.373	0.136	1.86
9	0.337	0.184	1.82
10	0.308	0.223	1.78

Table 18-3: $\bar{x}$– R Control Limits Factor Table

STEP 5: Drawing the control chart

Using graph paper or a special chart form, draw an $\bar{x}$ scale on the left of the upper portion of the vertical axis and an R scale on the left of the lower portion of the vertical axis. Draw a group number scale along the horizontal axis. Next plot the values of $\bar{x}$ and R found in steps 2 and 3 and connect the points. Draw in the median lines, UCL, and LCL determined in step 4 and write in the numerical values of these lines.

Create the chart on $\bar{x}$ – R control chart paper. Write in essential information such as the median line and control limit lines. See Figure 18-1.

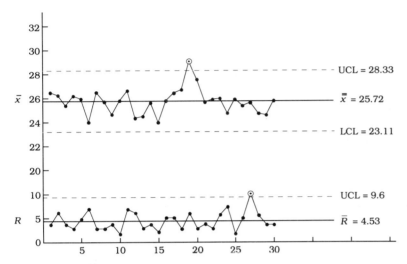

Figure 18-1: $\overline{x}$ – **R Control Chart**

STEP 6: Assessment and examination

Determine whether the process is stable.

Item 19 exceeds the UCL in the $\overline{x}$ control chart, while Item 27 exceeds the UCL line in the R control chart. This indicates that this process is not stable.

$\tilde{x}$ – *R* CONTROL CHARTS

STEP 1: How to collect data

This is the same as for $\overline{x}$ – R control charts. For a group of size n, it is more convenient for n to be an odd number when determining the median value $\tilde{x}$. Frequently used values for n are $n = 3$ and $n = 5$.

Example 2: Using values of $n = 5$, and $k = 30$ and a total of 150 data points for analyzing the guide roller grinding process of the previous item (see Table 18-4), draw $\tilde{x}$– R control charts and examine them.

STEP 2: How to determine the value of $\tilde{x}$

List each measured value of a group from smallest to largest. When n is odd, take the middle value as $\tilde{x}$. When

Here, $n = 5$. In group no. 1, for example, the measured values arranged in ascending order are:

n is even, add the two middle values and take their average as $\tilde{x}$.

24 26 27 27 28

The median $\tilde{x}$ is the middle value in the sequence, which is 27.

Group Number	Measured Value					Median	Range	Notes
	x_1	x_2	x_3	x_4	x_5	$\tilde{x}$	R	
1	27	26	28	27	26	27	4	
2	25	26	29	28	23	26	6	
3	23	27	25	24	27	25	4	
4	26	25	28	25	27	26	3	
5	25	29	25	26	24	25	5	
6	22	23	29	24	23	23	7	
7	28	27	25	26	26	26	3	
8	24	27	27	26	24	26	3	
9	24	27	26	24	23	24	4	
10	26	26	25	27	25	26	2	
11	25	30	23	28	27	27	7	
12	23	28	25	24	22	24	6	
13	25	26	23	26	24	25	3	
14	25	27	23	26	27	26	4	
15	24	24	25	25	23	24	2	
16	24	27	23	28	27	27	5	
17	28	29	25	26	24	26	5	
18	26	28	27	25	28	27	3	
19	30	26	30	28	32	30	6	
20	26	29	27	27	28	27	3	
21	28	26	24	25	25	25	4	
22	25	27	24	26	27	26	3	
23	27	29	26	25	23	26	6	
24	25	24	28	26	21	25	7	
25	26	25	26	27	25	26	2	
26	23	24	27	24	28	24	5	
27	25	26	30	20	27	26	10	
28	23	27	24	28	22	24	6	
29	27	23	24	25	24	24	4	
30	25	25	26	24	28	25	4	
					Sum	768	136	

Table 18-4: $\tilde{x} - R$ Control Chart Data Sheet

STEP 3: Calculating R

Range R is the maximum value of x minus the minimum value of x.

This is determined the same way as for the $\bar{x} - R$ control chart.

STEP 4: Calculating the control lines

Median line for $\tilde{x}$ control chart:

$$\bar{\tilde{x}} = \frac{\Sigma \tilde{x}}{k}$$

$$\bar{\tilde{x}} = \frac{768}{30} = 25.60$$

Median line for R control chart:

$$\bar{R} = \frac{\Sigma R}{k}$$

$$\bar{R} = \frac{136}{30} = 4.53$$

Here k is the number of groups. Values are usually determined to two places more than the measured values.

Control limits for $\tilde{x}$ control chart:

According to Table 18-5, if $n = 5$:

$$m_3 A_2 = 0.691$$

Determine the values of m_3 and $m_3 A_2$ according to the group size n as shown in Table 18-5.

Thus, in the $\tilde{x}$ control chart:

$$\text{UCL} = \tilde{x} + m_3 A_2 R$$

$$\text{LCL} = \tilde{x} - m_3 A_2 R$$

$$\begin{aligned} \text{UCL} &= 25.60 + 0.691 \times 4.53 \\ &= 28.73 \\ \text{LCL} &= 25.60 - 0.691 \times 4.53 \\ &= 22.47 \end{aligned}$$

Values are usually determined to two places more than the measured values.

Sample Size n	$\tilde{x}$ Control Chart	
	$m_3 A_2$	m_3
2	1.880	1.000
3	1.187	1.160
4	0.796	1.092
5	0.691	1.198
6	0.549	1.135
7	0.509	1.214
8	0.432	1.160
9	0.412	1.223
10	0.363	1.176

Table 18-5: $\tilde{x}$ Control Chart Factors (a)

Control limits for R control chart:

$$UCL = D_4\bar{R}$$
$$LCL = D_3\bar{R}$$

Control limits for R control charts are calculated just as for $\bar{x} - R$ control charts:

$$UCL = 9.6$$
$$LCL = — \text{ (ignore)}$$

STEP 5: Drawing the control chart

Using graph paper, draw an $\tilde{x}$ scale to the left of the upper portion of the vertical axis and an R scale to the left of the lower portion of the vertical axis. Draw a group number scale along the horizontal axis.

Next, plot the values of $\tilde{x}$ and R found in Steps 2 and 3. Plot all the measured values x on the control chart. In each group, if n is an odd number take the middle value; if n is an even number take the average of the two middle values as the median. Connect the median and R points for quick visual reference. Write in the median line, UCL, and LCL determined in Step 4, along with their numerical values.

Plot the measured values on graph paper. Then determine and connect the values of $\tilde{x}$ and R on the graph to make an $\tilde{x} - R$ control chart (see Figure 18-2).

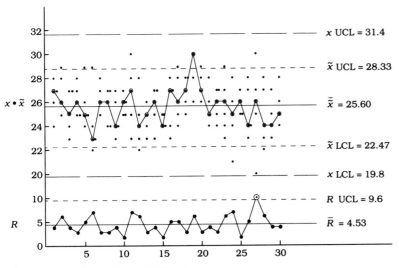

Figure 18-2: $\tilde{x} - R$ Control Chart

STEP 6: Assessment and evaluation

Determine whether the process is stable.

The $\tilde{x}$ control chart UCL line is exceeded in group no. 19, and the R control chart UCL line is exceeded in group no. 27. This example, like the $\bar{x}$-R control chart, shows a deviation from the control limits, indicating that the process is not stable.

x CONTROL CHARTS

For Groups of Samples

You can use an x-R control chart with averages of multiple groups of samples. This is a way of managing individual measured values so that abnormalities are detected early and action can be taken quickly. This kind of control chart is not useful alone, but is used together with an $\bar{x}$-R control chart or an $\tilde{x}$-R control chart.

STEP 1: How to collect data

Using a sample group size of 4 or 5, measure at least 20 to 25 groups.

Example 3: Analyze data from the guide roller grinding process of the previous item, $n = 5$ and $k = 30$, using an x control chart together with an $\tilde{x}$-R control chart.

STEP 2: Calculating $\bar{x}$

$$\bar{x} = \frac{(x_1 + x_2 + \ldots + x_n)}{n}$$

Determine $\tilde{x}$ using Step 2 of the previous instructions.

STEP 3: Calculating R

$$R = (\text{maximum value of } x) - (\text{minimum value of } x)$$

STEP 4: Calculating the control lines

Center line:

$$\overline{\overline{x}} = \frac{\Sigma \overline{x}}{k}$$

Center line for $\tilde{x}$ chart:

$$\overline{\overline{x}} = \frac{\Sigma \tilde{x}}{k}$$

Control limits:

$$UCL = \overline{\overline{x}} + E_2 \overline{R}$$

$$LCL = \overline{\overline{x}} - E_2 \overline{R}$$

If used with an $\tilde{x}$ control chart, $\overline{\overline{x}}$ is used instead of $\overline{\overline{x}}$. The values are generally determined to one place beyond the measured value.

Find E_2 from Table 18-6, using the value corresponding to the size of the group. *Note:* Since $E_2 = nA_2$, you can determine the value of E_2 if you know the value of A_2.

Since in this case we are using an $\tilde{x}$ – R control chart with the x control chart, the center line:

$$\overline{\overline{x}} = 25.60$$

$$E_2 = 1.29$$
$$UCL = 25.60 + 1.29 \times 4.53$$
$$= 31.44 \lozenge 31.4$$
$$LCL = 25.60 - 1.29 \times 4.53$$
$$= 19.76 \lozenge 19.8$$

Sample Size n	$\tilde{x}$ Control Chart E_2
2	2.66
3	1.77
4	1.46
5	1.29
6	1.18
7	1.11
8	1.05
9	1.01
10	0.98

Table 18-6: $\tilde{x}$ **Control Chart Factors (b)**

STEP 5: Drawing the control chart

Figure 18-2 shows an x control chart, together with the $\tilde{x}$– R control chart. When plotting each measured value on the $\tilde{x}$ control chart, the values of x and $\tilde{x}$ are superimposed. When using an $\overline{x}$ – R control chart together with an x control chart, set the corresponding upper and lower limits and plot the values in the order x, $\overline{x}$, and R.

STEP 6: Drawing the control chart

Draw an $x - Rs$ control chart like the chart shown in Table 18-3.

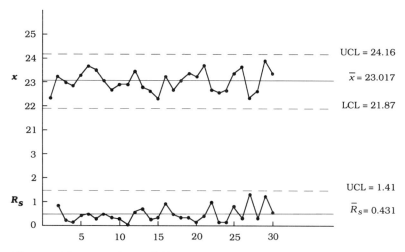

Figure 18-3: x - Rs Control Chart

STEP 7: Assessment and evaluation

Check whether the process is stable.

Since there are no points outside the control limits, the process is essentially stable. However, points 27 and 29 of Rs are near the limit. You should notice this wide variation.

Making Control Charts with Counted (Numerical) Values

pn CONTROL CHARTS

STEP 1: How to collect data

Take a sample of a fixed size from at least 20 to 25 groups. Determine the number of defects *pn* in each group. The size of the sample is based on the expected defect rate. Set your sample size so that it will contain between one and five defects.

Example 5: In a component shot peening process, surface treatment was performed on each of 150 components. External visual inspections were made of each of the 150 components to determine the number of defects produced. Table 18-8 shows the *pn* defect data where $n = 150$ and $k = 30$. (*Note:* In control charts for numerical values, n represents the size of the sample, not the number of samples taken.)

No.	pn	No.	pn	No.	pn	No.	pn	No.	pn	No.	pn
1	1	6	2	11	1	16	6	21	3	26	3
2	3	7	4	12	1	17	4	22	1	27	3
3	1	8	3	13	2	18	1	23	1	28	2
4	0	9	1	14	5	19	3	24	2	29	3
5	2	10	2	15	3	20	2	25	4	30	1
										Sum	70
										Mean	2.33

Table 18-8

STEP 2: Calculating the control lines

Center line:

$$\bar{p}n = \frac{\Sigma pn}{k}$$

This computation is carried out to two decimal places.

Control limits:

$$UCL = \bar{p}n + \sqrt{\bar{p}n\,(1-\bar{p})}$$

$$LCL = \bar{p}n - \sqrt{\bar{p}n\,(1-\bar{p})}$$

$$\bar{p} = \frac{\Sigma pn}{(n \times k)}$$

Here, n = sample size and k = number of groups. Compute the values of the UCL and the LCL to one decimal place. If LCL is negative, do not consider it.

$$\bar{p}n = \frac{70}{30} = 2.33$$

$$\bar{p} = \frac{70}{(150 \times 30)}$$

$$= 0.0156$$

$$3\sqrt{\bar{p}n\,(1-\bar{p})} = 3\sqrt{2.33\,(1-0.0156)}$$

$$= 4.54$$

Control limits are:

UCL = 2.33 + 4.54 = 6.87 ◊ 6.9
LCL = 2.33 − 4.54 = − 2.21 ◊ (ignore)

STEP 3: Drawing the control chart

Using graph paper, write the number of defects on the vertical scale and the group numbers on the horizontal scale. Plot the number of defects in each group. Then draw the control chart and write in the numerical values.

Create a *pn* control chart as shown in Figure 18-4.

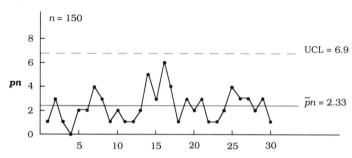

Figure 18-4: pn Control Chart

STEP 4: Assessment and evaluation

Determine whether the process is stable.

In this example, all the points are within the control limits. There is no abnormality in the distribution of the points; thus this process is judged to be stable.

p CONTROL CHARTS

STEP 1: How to collect data

Predict the process defect rate and choose a sample size that will produce between one and five defects in each sample. Take samples from at least 20 to 25 groups and check the number of defects *pn* in each group.

Naturally, it is preferable to have a sample size that is fixed or varies very little. However, this procedure can be used even when the sample size varies.

Example 6: In a press process, products in lever A molding are inspected for abrasion. All of the material charges are inspected and the number of defects is calculated. The defect rate *p* is used to make a control chart.

Table 18-9 shows n and pn data for $k = 25$. (*Note:* In control charts for numerical values, n represents the size of the sample, not the number of samples taken.)

STEP 2: Calculating p

Calculate the defect rate p for each group.

$$p = \frac{pn}{n}$$

Calculate the percentage (%) p to two significant places.

First, calculate p for each group as shown on the data sheet for Table 18-9. For example, in no. 1,

$$p = \frac{3}{526} = 0.6\%$$

Follow the same procedure to calculate p for the remaining values.

STEP 3: Calculating the control lines

Center line:

$$\bar{p} = \frac{\Sigma pn}{\Sigma n}$$

Center line:

$$\bar{p} = \frac{130}{12{,}711} = 0.0102$$

$$= 1.02 \ (\%)$$

Control limits: Since group size n is different for each group, each group will have its own individual control limit values. To determine them, first transform each individual value of n into a factor A for each group, using the formula:

$$A = \frac{3}{\sqrt{n}}$$

See Table 18-9. The values for A are then used in the following equation and the resulting limits drawn above each group:

$$\text{UCL} = \bar{p} + A \sqrt{\bar{p} \ (1 - \bar{p})}$$

$$\text{LCL} = \bar{p} - A \sqrt{\bar{p} \ (1 - \bar{p})}$$

Control limits: First, determine whether you can use the simplified calculation method described on page 223. Since the values of n in this case (206 to 906) vary more than $+ 50\% \ n$ (508.4 ± 50% = 254 to 763), the simplified method of calculating the control limits cannot be used here. See Table 18-9 for the individual control limit values that were calculated for these data.

p Control Chart Data Sheet   No. _____

Product name		Lever A	Manufacturing order number		P7-18	Time period	7/2
Quality characteristic		Rubbing	Workplace		Press Group 3		7/14
Method of measurement		Visual	Specified daily production		1,100	Machine number	CP-302
Specification limits	Maximum	Limit sample	Material sampling interval		Each charge of material	Operator	𝒥𝒦
	Minimum	—	Measuring instrument number		—	Signature of inspector	ℋ𝒮
Specification number		P-552A					

Date	Lot number	Group number	Sample size n	Number of defects pn	Defect rate p	$A = \dfrac{3}{\sqrt{n}}$	$A \times \sqrt{\bar{p}(1-\bar{p})}$	UCL $\bar{p} + A\sqrt{\bar{p}(1-\bar{p})}$	LCL $\bar{p} - A\sqrt{\bar{p}(1-\bar{p})}$
7/2	#5	1	526	3	0.6	0.131	1.32	2.34	—
	6	2	483	6	1.2	0.137	1.38	2.40	—
3	7	3	602	5	0.8	0.122	1.23	2.25	—
	8	4	479	2	0.4	0.137	1.38	2.40	—
4	9	5	531	9	1.7	0.130	1.31	2.33	—
	10	6	527	4	0.8	0.131	1.32	2.34	—
5	11	7	206	8	③.9	0.209	2.10	3.12	—
	12	8	395	6	1.5	0.151	1.52	2.54	—
	13	9	610	4	0.7	0.121	1.22	2.24	—
6	14	10	608	2	0.3	0.122	1.23	2.25	—
	15	11	586	10	1.7	0.124	1.25	2.27	—
9	16	12	212	3	1.4	0.206	2.07	3.09	—
	17	13	231	6	2.6	0.197	1.98	3.00	—
	18	14	571	2	0.4	0.126	1.27	2.29	—
10	19	15	550	4	0.7	0.128	1.29	2.31	—
	20	16	382	2	0.5	0.153	1.54	2.56	—
	21	17	415	6	1.4	0.147	1.48	2.50	—
11	22	18	906	11	1.2	0.100	1.01	2.03	0.01
	23	19	249	7	2.8	0.190	1.91	2.93	—
12	24	20	611	4	0.7	0.121	1.22	2.24	—
	25	21	524	5	1.0	0.131	1.32	2.34	—
13	26	22	887	7	0.8	0.101	1.02	2.04	0
	27	23	479	6	1.3	0.137	1.38	2.40	—
14	28	24	538	3	0.6	0.129	1.30	2.32	—
	29	25	603	5	0.8	0.122	1.23	2.25	—
Total			12711 (Σn)	130 (Σpn)					

$\bar{p} = \Sigma pn / \Sigma n = 0.0102 = 1.02\%$ $\sqrt{\bar{p}(1-\bar{p})} = 0.1005 = 10.05\%$

Table 18-9: p Control Chart Data Sheet

(The values for the other elements of this equation, which remain the same for the entire data set, are show at the bottom of Table 18-9.)

Note: If the size of each group varies only ± 50% from $\bar{n}$ (the average value of the size of the group n), you can use a simplified method to calculate the control limits, using the value of n:

$$\left.\begin{array}{c} \text{UCL} \\ \text{LCL} \end{array}\right\} = \bar{p} \pm 3 \ \sqrt{\frac{\bar{p}(1-\bar{p})}{n}}$$

Using

$$\bar{n} = \frac{\Sigma n}{k}$$

when plotting points near the boundary, you can make a precise calculation whether a particular point falls within the limits.

STEP 4: Drawing the control chart

Using graph paper, put the defect rate p on the vertical axis and the group numbers on the horizontal axis. Draw lines representing the individual control limits. Then plot the defect rate points for each group.

Note: Since the control limits vary for each group, do not write numerical values next to the control limits.

Create a p control chart as shown in Figure 18-5.

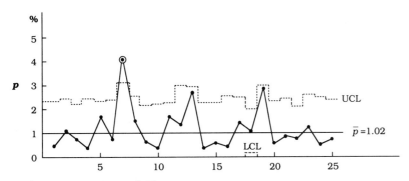

Figure 18-5: p Control Chart

STEP 5: Assessment and evaluation

Check whether the process is stable.

Since a point exceeds the control limits of group no. 7, the process is not stable.

c CONTROL CHARTS

STEP 1: How to collect data

Take a sample of a fixed size from at least 20 to 25 groups and determine the number of defects in each group. The size of the sample should be chosen so that one to five defects occur in the average sample.

Example 7: A *c* control chart was made of the cracks in the surface of stainless steel plates of a certain size. Data on the number of defects for $k = 30$ is shown in Table 18-10. *c* represents the number of cracks in each sample.

No.	c	No.	c	No.	c	No.	c	No.	c	No.	c
1	3	6	1	11	2	16	2	21	1	26	2
2	1	7	0	12	0	17	1	22	0	27	4
3	0	8	1	13	0	18	3	23	2	28	1
4	2	9	0	14	1	19	0	24	1	29	0
5	1	10	2	15	1	20	1	25	6	30	2
										Total	41
										Mean	1.37

Table 18-10

STEP 2: Calculating the control lines

Center line:

$$\bar{c} = \frac{\Sigma c}{k}$$

Control limits:

$$UCL = \bar{c} + 3\sqrt{\bar{c}}$$

$$LCL = \bar{c} - 3\sqrt{\bar{c}}$$

Control line:

$$\bar{c} = \frac{41}{30} = 1.37$$

Since $3\sqrt{\bar{c}} = 3.51$, the control limits are

$$UCL = 1.37 + 3.51 = 4.88 \rightarrow 4.9$$
$$LCL = 1.37 - 3.51 = -2.14 \rightarrow \text{(ignore)}$$

Calculate the median line to two significant places and the control limits to one significant place. If LCL has a negative value, do not consider it.

STEP 3: Drawing the control chart

Draw a c control chart as shown in Figure 18-6.

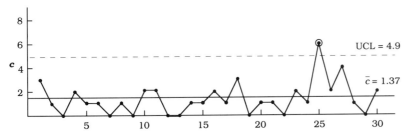

Figure 18-6: c Control Chart

STEP 4: Assessment and evaluation

Check whether the process is stable.

Since a point in group no. 25 is outside the control limits, the process is not stable.

u CONTROL CHARTS

STEP 1: How to collect data

Take samples of size n (here, representing length, area, time, etc.) from at least 20 to 25 groups and determine the number of defects in each sample. The size of the sample should be chosen so that one to five defects occur in the average sample.

Example 8: During the production process of a nonwoven fabric used in carpets, the surface of the material is visually inspected for defects. Because there are many different carpet sizes, the number of defects per unit area is used to create a u control chart. The n and c data for $k = 27$ are shown in Table 18-11.

Material number	Material size n	Number of defects c	Number of defects per unit u	$\frac{1}{\sqrt{n}}$	UCL $\bar{u}+3\sqrt{\bar{u}}\times\frac{1}{\sqrt{n}}$	LCL $\bar{u}-3\sqrt{\bar{u}}\times\frac{1}{\sqrt{n}}$
1	180	1	0.006	0.0745	0.0383	—
2	180	0	0		↑	
3	180	2	0.011		↑	
4	180	1	0.006		↑	
5	180	3	0.017		↑	
6	180	3	0.017		↑	
7	150	2	0.013	0.0816	0.0407	—
8	150	0	0		↑	
9	150	4	0.027		↑	
10	150	2	0.013		↑	
11	150	0	0		↑	
12	150	3	0.020		↑	
13	150	1	0.007		↑	
14	150	0	0		↑	
15	200	3	0.015	0.0707	0.0370	—
16	200	5	0.025		↑	
17	200	1	0.005		↑	
18	200	4	0.020		↑	
19	200	3	0.015		↑	
20	120	2	0.017	0.0913	0.0440	—
21	120	0	0		↑	
22	120	5	0.042		↑	
23	120	1	0.008		↑	
24	120	1	0.008		↑	
25	200	6	0.030	0.0707	0.0370	—
26	200	3	0.015		↑	
27	200	2	0.010		↑	
Total	**4,480**	**58**				

Table 18-11: **Control Chart Data Sheet**

Note: In control charts for numerical values, n represents the size of the sample, not the number of samples taken.

STEP 2: Calculating u

Determine the number of defects u per unit area for each group.

$$u = \frac{c}{n}$$

Determine the value of u to two significant figures.

Calculate the value of u for each group, as shown in Table 18-11. For example, in the first group,

$$u = \frac{1}{180} = 0.006$$

Follow the same formula to calculate all the values of u.

STEP 3: Calculating the control lines

Center line:

$$\bar{u} = \frac{\Sigma c}{\Sigma n}$$

Control limits:

$$UCL = \bar{u} + 3\sqrt{\bar{u}} \times \frac{1}{\sqrt{n}}$$

$$LCL = \bar{u} - 3\sqrt{\bar{u}} \times \frac{1}{\sqrt{n}}$$

Determine the control limits to three significant figures. If LCL is negative, do not consider it.

Although the sample size n varies for each sample, as long as these variation fall within ±50% of $\bar{n}$ (the average value of n), you can use $\bar{n}$ and the simple method to calculate the control limits just as you do for p control charts.

$$\left. \begin{array}{c} UCL \\ LCL \end{array} \right\} = u \pm 3\sqrt{\frac{\bar{u}}{\bar{n}}}$$

Here, you can use the expression

$$\bar{n} = \frac{\Sigma n}{k}$$

to determine the control limits. You will thus be able to determine precisely whether a point is inside the control limits when you are plotting points near the limits.

Center line:

$$\bar{u} = \frac{58}{4,480} = 0.0129$$

Control limits: Determine whether you can use the simple method to calculate the control limits. In this case, n varies between a minimum of 120 and a maximum of 200. Since

$$\bar{n} = \frac{4480}{27} = 165.9$$

the variation falls within the ± 50% (83 to 249) range, and you can use the simple method.

$$3\sqrt{\frac{\bar{u}}{\bar{n}}} = 3\sqrt{\frac{0.0129}{165.9}} = 0.0264$$

Accordingly,

UCL = 0.0129 + 0.0264 = 0.0393
LCL = 0.0129 − 0.0264 = − 0.0135 ◊ (ignore)

The precisely calculated values of the control limits for each group are calculated for $n = 120, 150, 180$, and 200 for four different control limits as shown in Table 18-11.

STEP 4: Drawing the control chart

Create a *u* control chart as shown in Figure 18-7.

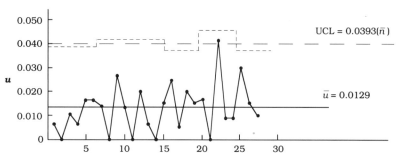

Figure 18-7: u Control Chart

STEP 5: Assessment and evaluation

Determine whether the process is stable.

Using *n* and the simple method, it was determined that point no. 22 is slightly outside the control limit. However, when the control limits are calculated precisely, point no. 22 is found to be within the control limits. Accordingly, you can consider the process to be stable.

How to Read Control Charts

Criteria for Determining Process Stability

A process is stable when it meets the following criteria:

1. No points are outside the control limits. (If a point is on the control limit, consider it to be outside the limit.)
2. There is no abnormality in the distribution of the points.

A *controlled state* is "a stable state at a desirable level in view of technical and economical considerations."* Figure 18-8 shows examples of stable and unstable process states.

---

* Japanese Industrial Standard JIS Z 8101-1981, "Glossary of Terms Used in Quality Control."

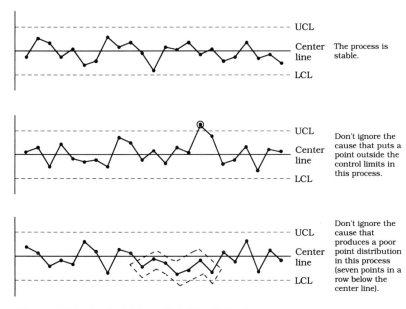

Figure 18-8: **Control Chart Stability Criteria**

Two basic types of errors can be made when evaluating control charts. The first kind is judging a stable process to be unstable because a point lies outside the control limits. The second kind is mistakenly judging a process to be stable because all of the points fall within the control limits, although an abnormality in fact exists.

Using control charts makes the first type of error rare, but the second type appears in cases where the variation in the process is small. In such cases, you can determine whether there is in fact a problem by evaluating the distribution of points within the control limits. A distribution can be abnormal even if no points are outside the control limits.

Evaluating Abnormal Distribution Patterns

1. *Sequence:* If a continuous sequence of points exists on one side of the center line then the average value of the distribution may have shifted. If there are seven or more consecutive points, then you may judge that the average value of the distribution has shifted towards

the side of the center line on which the consecutive points are found. See Figure 18-9(a).

2. *Bias:* If there are fewer than seven consecutive points on one side of the center line, but most of the points are on that side, assume there is an abnormality if you find on that side:

    • 10 of 11 consecutive points
    • 12 or more of 14 consecutive points
    • 14 or more of 17 consecutive points or
    • 16 or more of 20 consecutive points

    See Figure 18-9(b).

3. *Trend:* A steady gradual rise or fall in the position of the points is called a trend. A trend consisting of seven or more consecutive rising or falling points is a sign of an abnormality. Trends sometimes show that changes are occurring in the average value. Often the points pre-ceding the trend are outside the limit and the trend shows a movement towards the limit. See Figure 18-9(c).

4. *Approaching the limit:* If two out of three consecutive points or three or more out of seven points are either approaching a control limit or are more than two-thirds of the distance between the center line and the control limit, you can consider that an abnormality exists. See Figure 18-9(d). (*Note:* Since the control limit lines are the average value ± 3 standard variations (3s), the two-thirds line is the value of ± 2s.) This line is called the *warning limit*.

5. *Periodicity:* The position of data points may rise and fall in a periodic waveform. Sometimes a large-wave periodicity contains smaller-wave periodicity. Determining the period, amplitude, and causes of these periodic phenomena is often useful in process analysis. See Figure 18-9(e).

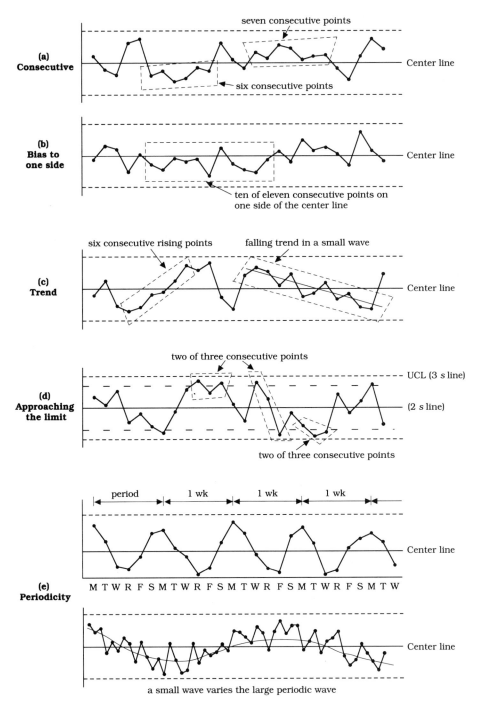

Figure 18-9: **Poor Distribution of Points**

Ways to Use Control Charts

FOR ANALYZING THE PROCESS

Step 1: Identifying the Characteristics for Control

Use the following guidelines to select the characteristics for your measurement:

1. Identify the important technical characteristics suitable to the intended use of the product and its quality functions.
2. Use the quality characteristics of the product sent to the next process as well as of the finished product.
3. Use multiple characteristics for analysis.
4. Use closely related substitute characteristics for characteristics that are difficult to measure for technical or economic reasons.
5. Use characteristics that facilitate measurements you will need for process control or improvement action.
6. Use easily quantifiable characteristics. Where possible, use measured values rather than numerical (counted) values.

Step 2: Choose the Control Chart

Choose the appropriate type of control chart for the characteristics you want to control (see Table 18-1).

Step 3: Determine the Methods for Sampling and Making Groups

A few guidelines follow for dividing the groups to be sampled:

1. Try to eliminate variations within groups so that the process state within the group will be as homogeneous as possible. Only random factors should be involved in dispersion within the group. Picking sequential samples is a common way to ensure that variability within a group is based on chance only.
2. Make a clear technical distinction between causes that create dispersion within a group and causes that create dispersion between groups.

3. Divide the groups so that the dispersion in the process you want to control is manifested in the dispersion between groups.

These factors will determine the size of the sample taken, the sampling time interval, the data collection method, and so on.

Step 4: Use the Data Collected in the Survey Analysis Stage to Make a Control Chart

Record the source of the data, how and when it was collected, and other historical information. Construct a stratified control chart if necessary to clarify distinct elements of the data.

Step 5: Use the Control Chart to Analyze the Process and Make Improvements

Follow these guidelines when interpreting and applying the results of the chart:

1. Determine the cause of each abnormality and take measures to prevent it from recurring.
2. Examine the difference between stratified data and take action to eliminate that difference. When two processes are manufacturing the same product, control each of the processes individually using stratification to prevent differences from arising.
3. Analyze variations within and between groups. Adopt measures for reducing the dispersion in cases of large variations.
4. Clearly understand the relationships between an effect and its causes and between quality character-istics and substitute characteristics.

Step 6: Compare Measured Values with Specified Values and Determine the Process Capacity

1. Make histograms and compare measured values with the specified values. Determine the process capacity index and check whether the measured value meets the specified value by a satisfactory margin.
2. If the measured values are unsatisfactory relative to specified values, the situation must be managed with

process improvements, adjustments, and 100% inspection of products from the entire production run. In some cases, you may have to reconsider the specification.

3. Evaluate the process to determine whether it is stable and whether it meets the specifications. Although these two objectives are interdependent, your first priority should be to make the process stable within the control limits (note the arrows in the matrix in Table 18-12).

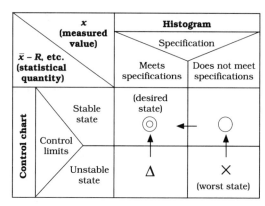

→ indicates direction of improvement

Table 18-12: **Evaluation Using Histogram and Control Chart Specifications/ Control Matrix**

FOR MANAGING THE PROCESS

Step 1: Set Control Limits as a Process Control Step

During the process analysis stage, measures are adopted to prevent abnormalities from recurring and to improve the process in various ways. Control limits are set to control the process and maintain the improved condition.

1. In this case, once actions have been taken to prevent the problem from recurring and to improve the process, abnormality data from the previous analytical stage is discarded and new control limits are calculated

2. If you can set and adjust the average value, use the median value of a technical standard as the $\bar{x}$ or $\tilde{x}$ center line and set control limits from that.

3. If stratification, group division, sampling, and other methods are carried out differently during the process control stage than they were during the analysis stage, reset the control limits using preparatory data taken during appropriate periods.

4. If there are no significant abnormalities in the control chart created during the analysis stage, you can use the control limits of that control chart during the process management stage.

Note: If only one out of 35 consecutive points or two out of 100 consecutive points are outside the control limits, you can consider the process stable and may continue to use those control limits. However, you should obtain additional data and recalculate the control limits as soon as possible.

Step 2: Collect Data and Plot It on the Control Chart

Using a control chart with preliminary process management control lines, plot the position of samples as they are measured. Use this plot to determine whether the process is stable.

Step 3: Determine the Cause of an Abnormality and Take Action

Take immediate action when an abnormality is detected. In addition to restoring the process to its normal state, adopt measures that will prevent the problem from recurring. New abnormalities should have different causes from abnormalities previously dealt with. As you carry out more measures to prevent abnormalities, the dispersion of the process will become smaller and the process will become more stable.

Step 4: Recalculate to Revise the Control Lines

Revise the control lines under the following circumstances:

1. When you make modifications to make the process clearer from a technical and equipment standpoint.
2. When an abnormality appears on the control chart, to clarify how the process has changed.
3. After a certain period of time, although there have been no changes in the process.

Scatter Diagrams and Correlation

What Is Correlation?

If two types of data, x and y, are related in that x increases or decreases with y, a correlation exists between them. A scatter diagram is a chart that expresses the relationship between two such data types. As Figure 19-1 shows, a scatter diagram depicts the relationship as a pattern that can be directly read.

If y increases with x, then x and y are *positively correlated*. If y decreases as x increases, then the two types of data are *negatively correlated*. If no significant relationship is apparent between x and y, then the two data types are *not correlated*.

Determining correlations can be useful in the following ways:

1. For choosing factors strongly correlated with quality characteristics among several factors that affect quality characteristics.
2. For determining the optimal range for variables to set the conditions for controlling characteristics.
3. For comparing the results of precise measurements and simple measurements, destructive testing and nondestructive testing, and for choosing substitute characteristics and methods for carrying out measurements and experiments.

How to Make a Scatter Diagram

STEP 1:

Collect 30 to 50 pairs of quantitative data (x and y).

Example: A certain material has an A content (percent $\times 10^{-2}$) of x and

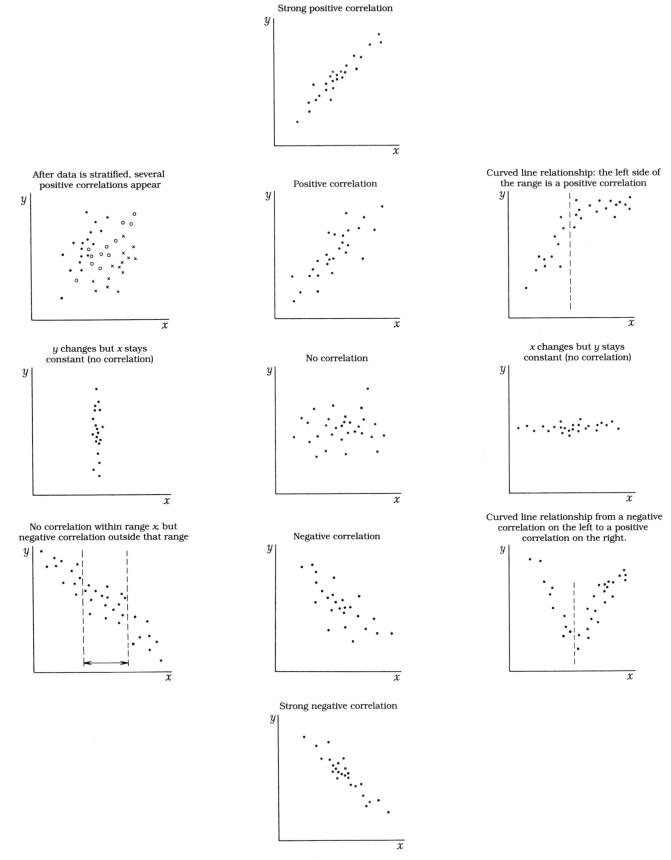

Figure 19-1: **Dispersion Diagrams and Correlations for Various Cases**

No.	x	y	No.	x	y	No.	x	y	No.	x	y
1	21.8	15.7	11	21.3	14.5	21	21.6	15.1	31	20.7	12.8
2	22.3	15.1	12	22.2	14.7	22	22.3	15.5	32	22.4	12.7
3	20.7	13.5	13	24.8	17.8	23	19.1	10.8	33	19.7	13.8
4	21.9	14.6	14	22.0	15.4	24	23.9	18.5	34	23.1	15.4
5	21.1	14.9	15	20.4	13.4	25	20.9	13.4	35	21.9	13.8
6	23.6	15.7	16	21.3	11.9	26	20.2	11.8	36	21.2	16.4
7	20.3	13.9	17	23.3	15.0	27	22.2	14.1			
8	20.9	13.2	18	20.6	13.8	28	21.5	14.9			
9	22.7	16.2	19	23.2	15.3	29	22.1	14.7			
10	23.9	15.4	20	22.6	12.2	30	23.3	16.6			

Table 19-1

a Charpy shock value (kg • m/cm²) of y. The data pairs x and y (n = 36) shown in Table 19-1 are obtained.

STEP 2:

Choosing units that express the range of the x and y values, draw an x scale along the horizontal axis and a y scale along the vertical axis. Try to draw the scales so that the axes are approximately equal length.

STEP 3:

Plot the data pairs (x, y) as points on a scatter diagram. If two points have the same coordinates, make two marks very close together.

The scatter diagram for this data set is shown in Figure 19-2. It shows a positive correlation between x and y.

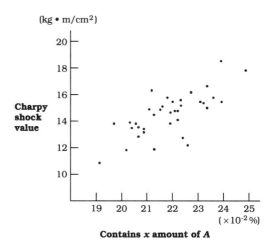

Figure 19-2: **Dispersion Diagram**

How to make a correlation table

When you have a large number of data items, a correlation table may be easier to make than a scatter diagram. A correlation table is a two-dimensional frequency table. The procedure is similar to making a one-dimensional frequency table (see Chapter 14 on histograms).

First, divide the dispersion of x into equal intervals. Do the same for the dispersion of y. Then create a matrix table with columns and rows for each data interval. Enter marks representing the coincidence of data pairs in the boxes of this table.

See Table 19-2 for an expression of this data in a correlation table.

y \ x	19.05 ~ 19.55	19.55 ~ 20.05	20.05 ~ 20.55	20.55 ~ 21.05	21.05 ~ 21.55	21.55 ~ 22.05	22.05 ~ 22.55	22.55 ~ 23.05	23.05 ~ 23.55	23.55 ~ 24.05	24.05 ~ 24.55	24.55 ~ 25.05	Total
18.05 ~ 19.05										/			1
17.05 ~ 18.05												/	1
16.05 ~ 17.05				/				/	/				3
15.05 ~ 16.05					///	//			//	//			9
14.05 ~ 15.05					///	/	///		/				8
13.05 ~ 14.05		/	//	////		/							8
12.05 ~ 13.05				/			/	/					3
11.05 ~ 12.05			/	/									2
10.05 ~ 11.05	/												1
Total	1	1	3	5	5	5	6	2	4	3	0	1	**36**

Table 19-2: Correlation Table

The Correlation Sign Test

A method exists for mathematically calculating and checking the "correlation factor" to specifically analyze the relationship between a pair of variables x and y. However, you can determine whether the data shown on the scatter diagram is correlated without performing calculations, using a simple "correlation sign test method."

STEP 1:

Draw lines to divide all the plotted data points into equal groups (the y median line $\tilde{y}$ and the x median line $\tilde{x}$.

Example: Check the correlation between x and y in the previous example. Draw the median lines $\tilde{x}$ and $\tilde{y}$ (see Figure 19-3).

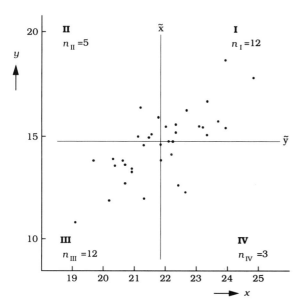

Figure 19-3: **Determining the Sign of the Dispersion Diagram**

STEP 2:

The median lines divide the scatter diagram into four areas. These areas are designated I, II, III, and IV, beginning at the top right. Count the number of points in each area (n_I, n_{II}, n_{III}, and n_{IV}). Do not count points on the median lines themselves.

$$n_I = 12$$
$$n_{II} = 5$$
$$n_{III} = 12$$
$$n_{IV} = 3$$

STEP 3:

The number of points in areas I and III (n_I and n_{III}) are added to create the sum n_+. The number of points in areas II and IV (n_{II} and n_{IV}) are added to create the sum n_-. Combine n_+ and n_- to arrive at the total N. (If there are data points on the median lines, N will be smaller than the total number of points.)

$$n_+ = n_I + n_{III} = 12 + 12 = 24$$
$$n_- = n_{II} + n_{IV} = 5 + 3 = 8$$
$$N = n_+ + n_- = 24 + 8 = 32$$

STEP 4:

Referring to the sign test table (see Table 19-3), find the row corresponding to N and read the numbers (criteria) in the columns $n_{0.01}$ and $n_{0.05}$. Compare these criteria with n_+ and n_- as shown below.

$n_{0.05}$ $n_- > n_{0.01}$ = positive correlation
$n_{0.01}$ n_- = strong positive correlation

$n_{0.05}$ $n_+ > n_{0.01}$ = negative correlation
$n_{0.01}$ n_+ = strong negative correlation

Note: Using these numerical criteria to evaluate data is called *statistical testing.* $n_{0.05}$ and $n_{0.01}$ are numerical values that have significance levels of 5% and 1%. Significance levels are measures of probability, or the risk of making an erroneous assessment. When you make judgments according to this system of criteria, the probabilities of making an error are 5% and 1%.

Generally a positive (or a negative) *correlation* is one with a level of significance of 5%. Similarly, a *strong correlation* is one with a significance level of 1%.

If $N = 32$, then $n_{0.01} = 8$ and $n_{0.05} = 9$.

$n_- = 8 = n_{0.01}$

This is a strong positive correlation, demonstrating a relationship between the A content of a material and the Charpy shock value. As the A content in the compound increases, the Charpy shock value increases.

N	$n_{0.01}$	$n_{0.05}$	N	$n_{0.01}$	$n_{0.05}$	N	$n_{0.01}$	$n_{0.05}$	N	$n_{0.01}$	$n_{0.05}$	N	$n_{0.01}$	$n_{0.05}$
			29	7	8	52	16	18	75	25	28			
			30	7	9	53	16	18	76	26	28			
8	0	0	31	7	9	54	17	19	77	26	29			
9	0	1	32	8	9	55	17	19	78	27	29			
10	0	1	33	8	10	56	17	20	79	27	30			
11	0	1	34	9	10	57	18	20	80	28	30			
12	1	2	35	9	11	58	18	20	81	28	31			
13	1	2	36	9	11	59	19	21	82	28	31			
14	1	2	37	10	12	60	19	21	83	29	32			
15	2	3	38	10	12	61	20	22	84	29	32			
16	2	3	39	11	12	62	20	22	85	30	32			
17	2	4	40	11	13	63	20	23	86	30	33			
18	3	4	41	11	13	64	21	23	87	31	33			
19	3	4	42	12	14	65	21	24	88	31	34			
20	3	5	43	12	14	66	22	24	89	31	34			
21	4	5	44	13	15	67	22	25	90	32	35			
22	4	5	45	13	15	68	22	25						
23	4	6	46	13	15	69	23	25						
24	5	6	47	14	16	70	23	26						
25	5	7	48	14	16	71	24	26						
26	6	7	49	15	17	72	24	27						
27	6	7	50	15	17	73	25	27						
28	6	8	51	15	18	74	25	28						

Table 19-3: **Sign Test Table**

Affinity Diagrams

The affinity diagram* method uses the affinity between partial, piecemeal items of verbal data to help understand systematically the structure of the overall problem. This method is used to help better understand problems that must be solved.

This method uses words that express facts, predictions, ideas, opinions, and similar expressions about fuzzy situations or subjects not previously experienced. The affinity diagram method builds a framework for verbal data from many different sources, based on similarities, common elements, and relationships expressed in the user's statement or in the background and assumptions underlying the statement. The affinity diagram method organizes data into an easily understandable diagram that gives clues about the overall nature of the object of study. It is a creative process that can break

---

* The affinity diagram method is derived from the KJ Method® developed by Dr. Kawakita Jiro.

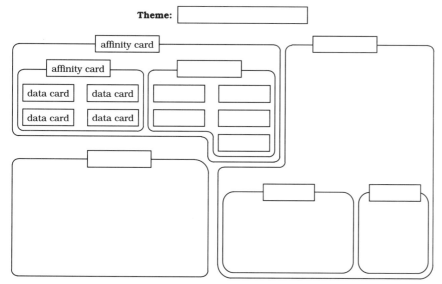

Figure 20-1: **Elements of an Affinity Diagram**

through preconceived notions about the situation. Affinity diagrams help people think more effectively about problems in three ways:

- They define the nature of the problem and bring out hidden problems.
- They help organize and order fuzzy ideas.
- They show the proper direction to take in solving problems.

Moreover, the process of creating an affinity diagram in a group helps group members better understand and teach each other. It promotes effective teamwork and enthusiasm about carrying out the group's mission.

How to Make an Affinity Diagram

STEP 1: Deciding on a theme

Select the subject or problem you want to address.

STEP 2: Collecting verbal data

Verbal data consists of categories such as facts, inferences, predictions, ideas, or opinions. Collect verbal data relevant to your theme and goals. Brainstorming is a method often used when a group meets to make an affinity diagram. Observation, research, and individual thought are other sources of data.

STEP 3: Making data cards

Write each item of verbal data you collect on a single data card. Index cards or adhesive notes make useful data cards.

STEP 4: Arranging the cards

Spread out a large sheet of paper. Place the data cards side by side so that no card is on top of another one. Read each card and try to discover which cards are alike in some way. Consider, for example, "which other cards have a similar meaning?" or "is this one connected somehow to another one?" Place cards that seem similar near one another.

STEP 5: Making affinity cards

Read and correct the verbal data in each group of cards you have arranged. If the data is not accurate enough, clarify the statements. Then, for each group, label another card with a short but complete statement of the characteristics of the group of cards. This is called an affinity card.

STEP 6: Stacking affinity cards and data cards

Stack the data cards in each related group and clip or band them with their affinity cards on top. Treat each group of stacked cards as a single card and put them back with the other cards.

STEP 7: Continuing the card arrangement

Repeat steps 4 through 6, continuing to arrange the data cards and make affinity cards. As you continue, you will find that the similarities among cards gradually become more distant. You will need to use a looser definition of what it means to "be similar," "be related," or "have common points." Continue arranging the cards until you have five or fewer stacks. Sometimes you will have "lone wolf" cards at the end that you are unable to place in relationship with other cards.

STEP 8: Distributing the cards

Distribute the stacks of cards on a large sheet of paper. Arrange the stacks according to affinities among the affinity cards. Then unclip the cards and spread out the stack on the sheet of paper, keeping the affinity groups distinct. Try to organize the different cards so that the entire arrangement will be easy to read. See Figure 20-1 for an example of how to organize the affinity and data cards.

STEP 9: Making an affinity diagram

Once you have decided on the placement of cards, attach each card in position and draw borderlines to enclose groups of stacked cards. If card stacks are enclosed by two or three borderlines, make the lines of different thicknesses or colors so that the diagram is easy to understand.

Ways to Use Affinity Diagrams

Affinity diagrams are useful when you are working on themes you don't understand, can't reach a conclusion about, or don't know what to do about. They have a wide range of applications. You can use an affinity diagram to determine how effective a problem theme you are now working on is likely to be or how effective a certain theme might be if adopted.

1. Affinity diagrams help you attack a problem in the right way.
   - Discover why careless mistakes keep happening.
   - Discover why improvement activity is not going as planned.
2. Affinity diagrams help organize ideas for decision making.
   - Understand the role personal initiative should play.
   - Understand the nature of the leadership the foreman should exercise.
3. Affinity diagrams help people reach solutions to problems.
   - Improve human relationships in the workplace.
   - Understand the issues to determine the best ways to use automation.

Figure 20-2 shows an affinity diagram constructed to help resolve problems in "autonomous management of improvement activities."

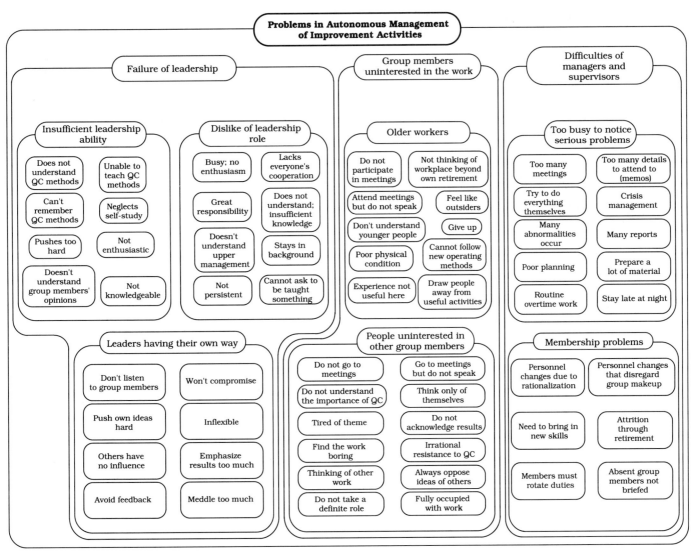

Problems in Autonomous Management
of Improvement Activities

Failure of leadership

Insufficient leadership ability

Does not understand QC methods

Unable to teach QC methods

Can't remember QC methods

Neglects self-study

Pushes too hard

Not enthusiastic

Doesn't understand group members' opinions

Not knowledgeable

Dislike of leadership role

Busy; no enthusiasm

Lacks everyone's cooperation

Great responsibility

Does not understand; insufficient knowledge

Doesn't understand upper management

Stays in background

Not persistent

Cannot ask to be taught something

Leaders having their own way

Don't listen to group members

Won't compromise

Push own ideas hard

Inflexible

Others have no influence

Emphasize results too much

Avoid feedback

Meddle too much

Group members uninterested in the work

Older workers

Do not participate in meetings

Not thinking of workplace beyond own retirement

Attend meetings but do not speak

Feel like outsiders

Don't understand younger people

Give up

Poor physical condition

Cannot follow new operating methods

Experience not useful here

Draw people away from useful activities

People uninterested in other group members

Do not go to meetings

Go to meetings but do not speak

Do not understand the importance of QC

Think only of themselves

Tired of theme

Do not acknowledge results

Find the work boring

Irrational resistance to QC

Thinking of other work

Always oppose ideas of others

Do not take a definite role

Fully occupied with work

Difficulties of managers and supervisors

Too busy to notice serious problems

Too many meetings

Too many details to attend to (memos)

Try to do everything themselves

Crisis management

Many abnormalities occur

Many reports

Poor planning

Prepare a lot of material

Routine overtime work

Stay late at night

Membership problems

Personnel changes due to rationalization

Personnel changes that disregard group makeup

Need to bring in new skills

Attrition through retirement

Members must rotate duties

Absent group members not briefed

*Seiji Hara, "Characteristics Diagrams," *FQC*, 258 (April 1979): 17 (JUSE Press Ltd.).

Figure 20-2: **Affinity Diagram for Theme "Problems in Autonomous Management of Improvement Activities"***

References

Futami, Ryoji, *Graphical Methods for TQC*. JUSE Press Ltd., 1985.

Hara, Seiji. "Characteristics Diagrams." *FQC*, 258 (April 1984): 17 (JUSE Press Ltd.).

Mizuno, Shigeru, ed. *The New Seven Tools of QC for Management and Staff*. JUSE Press Ltd., 1979. (Available in English from Productivity Press as *Management for Quality Improvement: The 7 New QC Tools* — Ed.)

Nayatani, Yoshinobu, ed. "A Lecture on the New Seven Tools of QC." Japanese Standards Association, 1987.

21

Relations Diagrams

The relations diagram method* is used to analyze problems when the causes have complex interrelationships. Making a diagram to show the cause-and-effect relationships and the relationships among different causal factors enables you to find the causes of problems and discover methods for solving them. You can also use the relations diagram method to pinpoint the elements required to achieve a certain goal. Figure 21-1 shows the basic elements of a relations diagram.

---

* The relations diagram method (also called linkage diagram method) is an application of the diagrams used in management indicator relational analysis, a methodology developed for economic engineering.

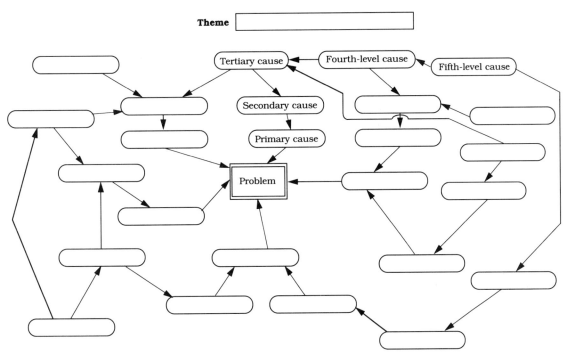

Figure 21-1: **Elements of a Relations Diagram**

The teamwork process used in making a relations diagram concerning a particular problem has the following advantages over other methods:

1. Cause-and-effect diagrams show the various factors and the causal relationships between them. Relations diagrams can express these relationships more freely since they are not limited to any particular format.
2. Affinity diagrams arrange cards representing verbal data according to the similarities perceived among different cards. A relations diagram uses arrows as well to indicate a series of cause-and-effect relationships.
3. By showing all causal relationships in a broad perspective, relations diagrams are helpful in discovering the principal causes that affect the entire situation.

How to Make a Relations Diagram

STEP 1: Describing the problem

Write on a card a specific description of the problem relating to the theme you have chosen and place the card in the center of a large sheet of paper. You might write, for example, "Why _____ doesn't work." Make your description of the problem very straightforward and easy to understand.

STEP 2: Making cause cards

Write down simply and clearly the causes you believe are affecting the problem. Write each cause on a single card. This is called a cause card. Don't make too many — no more than 50 cause cards.

STEP 3: Distributing the cards

Read all the cards you have made and group similar cards together. Place the cards side by side on a large sheet of paper so that they don't overlap.

STEP 4: Arranging the cards according to cause-and-effect relationships

Place cause cards for items that have a strong cause-and-effect relationship with the problem very close to the problem. Divide the cards into first-, second-, third-, and fourth-level causes, placing each rank a little farther from the problem card. As you come to understand the cause-and-effect relationships systematically, adjust the positions of the cards and draw arrows from causes towards effects.

STEP 5: Adding and revising cards

As you arrange the cards, sort the cause cards into related groups and add new cards to the groups as you think of things. Revise the notes on the cards and move the cards around to avoid arrows crossing when possible. Redraw the arrows as necessary.

STEP 6: Determining the relationship among all the cards

Leave the cards in position for a while. Study the card grouping as a whole to understand the relationships between groups of cards so that you can arrange the cause-and-effect relationships. Change the relationships between these groups if necessary.

STEP 7: Making the relations diagram

Once you have placed the cards in their proper positions, paste or tape them to the paper to complete the relations diagram.

STEP 8: Identifying the principal causes

Isolate the causes that have particularly important causal relationships with the problem. Highlight these cards with a colored box or thick lines; highlight the associated arrows with a thick colored line.

Ways to Use Relations Diagram

Cause-and-effect diagrams are an effective, widely used method for clarifying which causes are most responsible for the problem. However, where there is a complex relationship between many causes and effects and you can gather verbal data bearing on the problem, a relations diagram can clarify the cause-and-effect relationships and facilitate discussion about the principal causes.

Guidelines for Using Relations Diagrams

1. If you have not been able to make many cause cards, or if the notes on the cards are too abstract, take a fresh look at the problem from a different angle. For example, you could change the question written on the card from "Why doesn't the number of defects decrease?" to "Why are defects produced?"

2. If it is difficult to choose a primary cause, you might find it easier to divide the problem into two or three parts. For example, split "we can't get started on the job" into "we can't plan our work" and "although we did our planning, we can't get started on the job."

3. Use arrows to connect causes and effects. Avoid inserting unnecessary arrows to avoid confusion and unnecessary complexity. If you have a group that has arrows going around in a vicious circle, you may break the circle at any point.

4. When you are isolating the most important causes and developing solutions to the problem, go back to second, third, and fourth layers of underlying problems to discover the specific root causes that bear directly on the solution of the problem. The arrows on the diagram make it easy to trace the origins of negative influences on the process that you are studying.

5. You can also use the relations diagram method in a "positive" way to identify pathways that will produce a certain desired effect, such as "A turns B into C." Place a statement of the desired effect in the center of your chart in place of the problem statement.

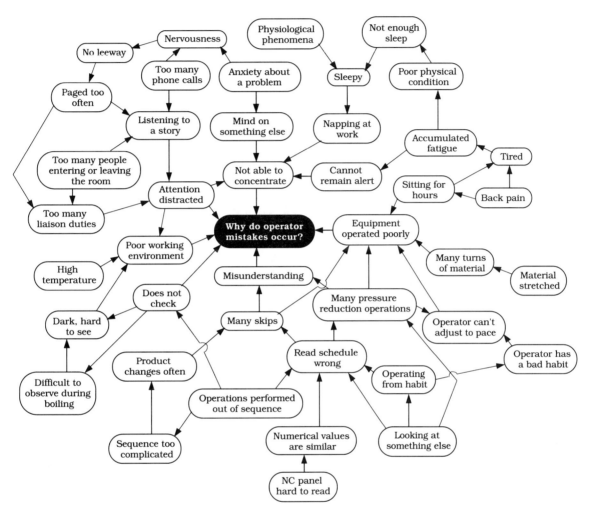

*Shigeo Kudo, "Playback 24," FQC, 270 (March 1985): 52 (JUSE Press Ltd.).

Figure 21-2: **Relations Diagram for Theme "Why Do Operator Mistakes Occur?"***

Figure 21-2 presents a relations diagram used to facilitate discussion of an improvement theme relating to a steel rolling process, "Eliminating Mistakes in the Rolling Process." Analysis of mistakes in the steel rolling process shows that mistakes occur most frequently on Mondays and during late-night work shifts, as a result of human fatigue caused by difficult physical and mental adjustments after a holiday, poor physical conditions, or poor work rhythms. Based on this relations diagram, videotaping was used to analyze the work process. A suitable operation period cycle was devised to avoid fatigue. The number of rolling errors attributable to operator errors fell to zero.

References

Futami, Ryoji. *Graphical Methods for TQC*. JUSE Press Ltd., 1985.

Kudo, Shigeo. "Playback 24." *FQC*, 270 (March 1985): 52 (JUSE Press Ltd.).

The Seven New QC Tools Research Group, ed. *The Seven New QC Tools Made Easy*. JUSE Press Ltd., 1984.

22

Systematic Diagrams

The systematic diagram method* is a technique that helps you think systematically about each aspect of solving a problem or achieving a particular goal. It resembles a tree with an increasing number of branches. By developing the root and branch relationships between the various parts of a method, this tool helps you choose the optimal method for achieving your goal.

Types of Systematic Diagrams

There are two basic types of systematic diagrams: "plan-development" and "component-development." The plan-development systematic diagram is used to develop methods and policies for systematically achieving objectives and goals (see Figure 22-1). If you find that a method you thought would directly achieve your objective does not work in practice, use this type of diagram to revise the method to better suit the objective. Think again about which method would best achieve the objective. When there are many alternative methods, work out the root and branch relationships among them to find the best one.

A component-development systematic diagram is used to develop the structural elements of the object of your improvement activity (see Figure 22-2). There are two kinds of systematic diagrams for developing these structural elements.

- If you are focusing on the required quality functions, create a quality function systematic diagram that analyzes the primary, secondary, and tertiary functions and the substitute characteristics.
- If you are working on a problem in which many factors affect the characteristics and you need to go deeper than the three levels of causal factors, a characteristics

---

*The systematic diagram method applied here to problem solving, was developed originally for functional analysis in Value Engineering.

systematic diagram will display your data in a format more easily understood than a cause-and-effect diagram.

How to Make a Systematic Diagram

To solve a problem, you need to make a plan for eliminating factors that impede the solution of the problem. The procedure for creating a plan-development systematic diagram is presented here.

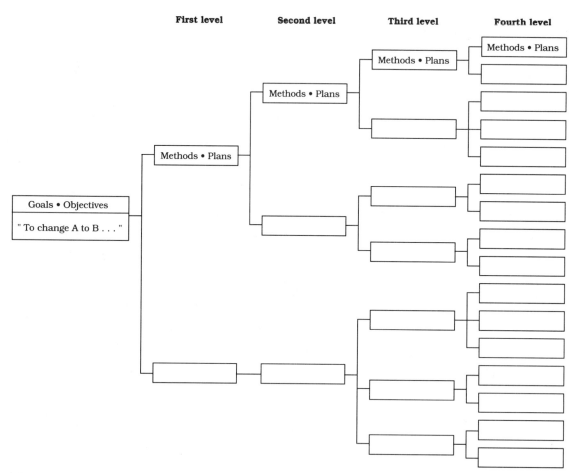

Figure 22-1: **Elements of a Plan-development Systematic Diagram**

STEP 1: Setting the objective or target

Write down on a card the theme you have adopted or the problem you want to solve. Place the card in the middle of the left-hand side of a large sheet of paper. This is the objective or the target to be reached. To make the theme or problem easier to understand, express it in the simple form "To make A do _____ . . . ."

STEP 2: Developing the primary means

Think about the primary means for achieving the objective. A primary means is one that when implemented will directly achieve the objective. Distinguishing the basic objective from subsidiary objectives, you can think of the primary means as the means to achieve the basic objective.

There may be more than one primary means that will directly achieve the objective. Write each primary means on a card. Place the cards to the right of and parallel to the card on which you wrote the objective or target, creating the first level of a root and branch configuration. Draw lines connecting the roots and branches.

STEP 3: Developing the secondary means

Turning around the primary means to view it as an objective, think of several means that would perform its function. Write them on cards in the format " *means* will lead to *objective*." Place these cards to the right of the primary means cards and draw lines connecting the roots and branches.

STEP 4: Developing higher-order means

Continue in the same manner, taking the secondary means as the objective of the third-level means, the third-level means as the objective of the fourth-level means, and so on. Ordinarily this process is carried out to the fourth order. Write down each means on a card and place the cards as shown in Figure 22-1. Carrying on group discussion during this process will produce many different ideas for your systematic diagram.

STEP 5: Check the relationship between objectives and means

Once you have developed a higher-order means that you can implement, go back to the first-, second-, and third-level means and ask, "Is this means effective in accomplishing this goal?" Make revisions as necessary. Then work backwards from the highest order and see if any conflicts develop when you ask the question, "Is that objective accomplished if I implement that means?"

STEP 6: Make a systematic diagram

Arrange the cards on the paper and paste or tape them in place. To complete the systematic diagram, draw lines to show the root and branch relationship of the means and objectives.

Ways to Use Systematic Diagrams

If you have found the causes that affect the problem but have been unable to establish a set of specific plans and methods for solving the problem, use a systematic diagram to develop an approach to identify the appropriate plans and methods. If you need to use several different methods and plans for solving a problem, you can use a systematic diagram to evaluate the methods and plans. Systematic diagrams can also be used to clarify the implementation of methods and plans.

Guidelines for Applying Systematic Diagrams

1. Many different kinds of ideas are helpful in devising methods and plans. Constructing the diagram in a large brainstorming session will take advantage of the experience and knowledge of people from other fields who are not directly involved with the problem. The group moves forward by systematically examining a problem. The members of the group teach one another.

2. Use systematic diagrams to develop plans. Make an evaluation table for the implementation plan of each

plan. Place the evaluation table on the right-hand side of the systematic diagram, to the right of the highest order plan. Use standard symbols to rate the effectiveness and practicality of each plan. Indicate the priority of each implementation plan. Making an implementation assignment table and a scheduling table are also helpful in the actual implementation of a plan.

3. If you run into constraints during plan implementation, look at things from a new angle. Consider approaches and ideas you may not have looked at before to come up with innovations.

Figure 22-2 shows how the systematic diagram method has been used in discussions and plan development. In this example, although roll crack detection equipment has been installed in a continuous hot rolling steel plant, the detection equipment is not working at its expected capacity. After determining why the detection rate is low and making a cause-and-effect diagram that shows the factors impeding detector performance, analyze the factors and use systematic diagrams to develop plans for handling the principal causes.

Evaluate the effectiveness and practicality of each measure. For example, Figure 22-2 clarifies that the reflector of the mercury vapor lamp in the detector should be made from stainless steel to prevent rust. Also, to prevent spherical cracks, the mercury vapor lamp must constantly stay in the ON position.

A systematic diagram that develops these factors is shown in Figure 22-3. It was made for an improvement activity with the objective of eliminating paint defects in an automobile anti-pitting coating process.

Although the blower air pressure was set to maintain a constant width in the sprayed paint, the pressure increased during the winter as the viscosity of the paint increased, thereby narrowing the spray width. This made the paint thicker on the surface and made paint defects occur more often.

The various factors affecting the spray width were set out in a systematic diagram. The effects of paint temperature, paint composition, and robot movements on paint defects were studied. The results led to adoption of a new

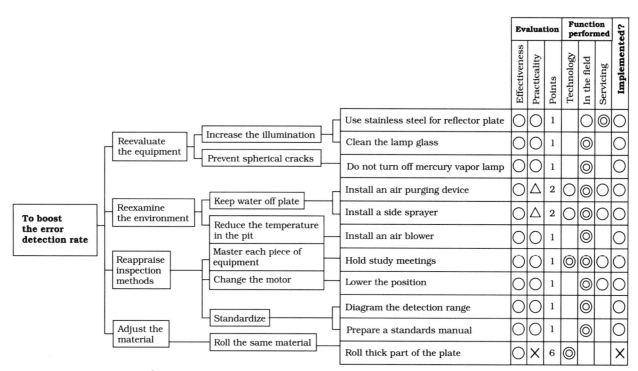

*Hiroyuki Toshimitsu, "Quality Control Methods for the Early Detection of Rolling Cracks," *FQC*, 273 (June, 1985): 53.

Figure 22-2: **Plan-development Systematic Diagram for Theme "Detection Rate Improvement"***

paint heating method, comparison of the paint with a viscosity standard, and implementation of several improvements related to the robot spray gun speed and the distance between the spray gun and the sprayed surface. With these improvements, paint defects were eliminated.

References

Futami, Ryoji. *Graphical Methods for TQC*. JUSE Press Ltd., 1985.

Mizuno, Shigeru, ed. *The New Seven Tools of QC for Management and Staff*. JUSE Press Ltd., 1979. (Available in English from Productivity Press as *Management for Quality Improvement: The 7 New QC Tools* — Ed.)

Nakajima, Yatsuhiro. "Stabilizing Anti-Pitting Paint Blowers." *FQC*, 275 (August, 1985): 47.

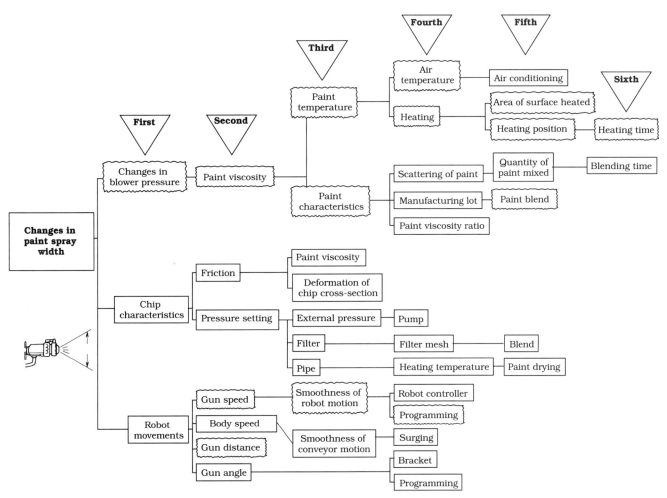

Items in wavy boxes should be investigated by the entire group.

*Yatsuhiro Nakajima, "Stabilizing Anti-Pitting Paint Blowers," *FQC*, 275 (August, 1985): 47.

Figure 22-3: **Component-development Systematic Diagram for Theme "Changes in the Spray Width of Pitting Resistant Paint"***

The Seven New QC Tools Research Group, ed. *The Seven New QC Tools Made Easy.* JUSE Press Ltd., 1984.

Toshimitsu, Hiroyuki. "Quality Control Methods for the Early Detection of Rolling Cracks." *FQC*, 273 (June, 1985): 53.

23

Matrix Diagrams

The matrix diagram method is used to show the relationship between results and causes, or between objectives and methods, when each of these consists of two or more elements or factors. The results and causes or objectives and methods are arrayed in a grid of rows and columns. Identifying the relationships between two elements or factors, where the rows and columns intersect, clarifies the problem and helps find measures for solving it.

Figure 23-1 shows the essential elements of a matrix diagram. Various symbols are used to indicate the presence and degree of strength of a relationship between two sets of essential items. A matrix can help you see a problem as a whole. It becomes visually clear whether a problem is localized (symbols appear isolated) or more broad-ranging (symbols appear in a row or column).

Matrix diagrams can be made in several basic configurations, named for the letters they resemble. The L-type matrix is a two-dimensional table that arranges a pair of essential elements in rows and columns. A T-type matrix is a three-dimensional table composed of two L-type matrices, with one set of factors in common between them. There are also Y-type matrices and X-type matrices, combinations of three and four L-type matrices.

Using these multidimensional composite matrices to guide your thinking has the following advantages:

1. The matrices allow you to take in all the relationships between the various factors at once. You can see the problem areas and where they are concentrated.
2. Testing and evaluating each intersection of the essential factors enables you to have discussions that can address finer details.
3. The matrices make it possible to look at specific combinations, determine the essential factors, and develop an effective strategy for solving the problem.

Matrix: _____

	Cause A	Cause B	Cause C	Cause D	Cause E	Cause F	Cause G	Cause H	Cause I	Cause J	Cause K
Defect A	○					△		○			
Defect B		◎	△		◎			○	○		
Defect C	△						○		○		
Defect D		◎	◎	○		◎	◎	◎		○	△
Defect E				◎	○				○		◎

Phenomenon ⟍ Cause / Process	Cause A	Cause B	Cause C	Cause D	Cause E	Cause F	Cause G	Cause H	Cause I	Cause J	Cause K
Process 1 — Element A$_1$		◎	◎						○		
Process 1 — Element A$_2$	◎	◎									◎
Process 1 — Element A$_3$		○	◎			◎		○			
Process 1 — Element A$_4$			○		◎			○	○	○	
Process 1 — Element A$_5$		○	○	○	◎	◎			○		
Process 2 — Element B$_1$		◎					○				
Process 2 — Element B$_2$		◎	○		◎		○				
Process 2 — Element B$_3$		◎					○				
Process 3 — Element C$_1$	○					◎					
Process 3 — Element C$_2$	○						◎				
Process 3 — Element C$_3$	○			◎			◎				
Process 3 — Element C$_4$				◎							○

◎ = strong relationship

○ = relationship

△ = possible relationship

Figure 23-1: **Conceptual Chart of a Matrix Diagram (T-type Matrix)**

How to Make a Matrix Diagram

Use the matrix diagram method to discuss the relationships among several phenomena and causes or processes. A T-type matrix is useful for discussing the relationships between phenomena, their causes, and the processes involved. Use the following procedure to produce a T-type matrix like the one shown in Figure 23-1.

STEP 1: Creating a format

Draw vertical and horizontal lines on graph paper. (See Figure 23-1 for the basic configuration.) Label the upper left rows "Phenomenon" or "Problem" and the lower left rows "Process." Label the columns "Cause." In the T-type matrix, you will be looking at causes in relationship to both phenomena and processes.

STEP 2: Sorting the phenomena

Sort the problems according to their subject matter. Fill in the phenomenon rows according to the seriousness and frequency of occurrence of the phenomena or events.

STEP 3: Sorting the causes

Sort the causes you believe are related to the problem. Write the causes in the cause columns.

STEP 4: Listing the processes

Fill in the processes or procedures related to the problem in the order in which they are performed.

STEP 5: Discussing phenomena and their causes

Discuss the relationship among phenomena and their causes. Make a mark indicating the strength of the relationship between a phenomenon and a cause where their row and column intersect. For example, use the ◎ mark to indicate a strong relationship, the ○ mark to indicate a relationship, and a △ mark to indicate a probable relationship. If the cause and the phenomenon are not related, leave the intersection of the row and column blank.

STEP 6: Discussing the cause and the process

Next discuss the relationship between the cause and the process. Where the rows and columns intersect, place a mark indicating the strength of their relationship.

STEP 7: Rechecking the relationship

Recheck the symbols at the intersections of each phenomenon with each cause factor. Next recheck the symbols at the intersection of each cause factor with each process item.

STEP 8: Evaluating the importance of the relationships

Assign point values for the relative strength of the relationships, such as ◎ = 3 points, ○ = 2 points, and Δ = 1 point. Total the points in each row of phenomena and processes and in each column of causes. Use these totals to evaluate quantitatively the importance of the many different problems associated with each phenomena, cause, and process.

Ways to Use Matrix Diagrams

Use the matrix diagram method if, after deciding on your theme, the number of problem phenomena is so great that you are not able to assign causes. The matrix diagram method helps you arrange information so that your discussion will not skip over important material. It also clarifies the degree of strength of the relationships.

Matrix diagrams are often used in the following applications:

1. To clarify the relationship between the functional quality that the user requires and the quality characteristics that should be built in during the manufacturing process. Matrix diagrams are used in quality tables and in quality deployment matrices.

2. To evaluate methods and measures relating to a particular item from many different perspectives. The diagram may combine such techniques as 4M analytical framework (men/women, machines, materials, methods), an evaluation of the importance, urgency, anticipated effectiveness, expenses, and object of each measure, as well as the 5W1H framework (what, why, when, who, where, and how) for making the measures you are implementing more specific (see Figure 23-2). These methods clarify the priority and the most important aspects of the measures that you are implementing. Systematic diagrams are often used in conjunction with matrix diagrams as a way of arriving at various means to reach a particular result. The matrix then helps evaluate the various means.

3. To sort out the relationships among three elements such as phenomena, causes, and measures to resolve the problem, or problematic factors, components, and processes. This process helps you isolate the essential points for solving the problem. The T-type matrix format is often used for working on this type of problem.

Figure 23-2 is an example of an L-type matrix. This example involves moving in and installing air conditioning equipment during the construction of a building. The L-type matrix diagram was used to study several problems in implementation and in the work steps. The date, time, and place from the 5W1H and the 4M are used in this matrix to extract the important points from the data.

Evaluating the points assigned to each item on a two-dimensional table enables you to understand where the problems are concentrated in various phases of the project:

- Preparatory step: lowering the load, assembly, restoration, moving to storage, and storage
- Moving step: temporary placement and installing the unit
- Elements: People, methods, and locations

This analysis enables you to make changes in details to eliminate repetitive manual operations, execute the implementation plan on schedule, and greatly reduce the time and expense of the move.

The T-type matrix diagram in Figure 23-3 was used to find problems in the process of making a small household vacuum cleaner (from component fabrication to final characteristics inspection) as part of an activity aimed at reducing vibration defects.

After using a relations diagram to generate and arrange the factors related to why vibration defects occur, construct a T-type matrix diagram to pinpoint the vibration factors, concentrating on:

- the relationship between the cause of the vibration and components (which components are vibration factors?) and
- the relationship between the cause of the vibration and the process (which processes are vibration factors?).

Operations Steps	Element	5W1H & 4M						Points
		Date	Place	Person	Machine or Tool	Material	Method	
Manufacturing	Manufacturing air conditioning equipment							—
Manufacturing	Manufacturing filter cartridges							—
Manufacturing	Transportation							—
Preparation	(1) Lowering the load and assembly	○	◎	○	◎			10
Preparation	(2) Preparing for operation	△	○	○		○	◎	10
Preparation	(3) Movement • storage		◎	○			○	7
Moving in	Stacking a load	○		○				4
Moving in	Transportation			○				2
Moving in	Guidance			△				1
Moving in	(4) Installing equipment			○	○	○	◎	9
Moving in	Sign			○				2
Moving in	Weight lifted							—
Installation	(5) Temporary location		◎	○		○	◎	10
Installation	Move			○			○	4
Installation	Installation	○		○				4
Points		7	11	21	5	6	13	

◎ = serious problem (3)   ○ = problem (2)   △ = potential problem (1)

*Toshio Higuchi and Tsutomu Kato, "Improvement Activities in the Work Place, " *Hinshitsu Kanri (Quality Control)*, 35 (May 1984 Special Issue): 117.

Figure 23-2: **L-type Matrix for Theme "Main Points for Installing Air Conditioning Equipment"***

Components / Defect	Balance	Difference in dimensions	Surface shaking	Shaking along axis	Deformation	Plate thickness	Degree of tightening	Mistake in installation	Degree of curvature	Weight	Variation	Equipment precision	Combination	Evaluation
Defective armature	●	○								○	○		○	●
Defective frame														
Defective casing			△	△						△				△
Defective screw or nut					△	△								
Defective washer				○	△				△	△			△	△
Defective fan	●	○	△	○	●	○	○	○	△	○	○		●	●

Phenomenon / Vibration defect factors / Process

Process	Balance	Difference in dimensions	Surface shaking	Shaking along axis	Deformation	Plate thickness	Degree of tightening	Mistake in installation	Degree of curvature	Weight	Variation	Equipment precision	Combination	Evaluation
Processing	△									△				△
Experiment														
Repair	△		○	△										○
Balance check	●									△		●		●
Apply pressure														
Combine													○	△
Motor tightness							△						○	△
Casing tightness							○	○				○	△	○
Washer tightness		○										○	○	○
Fan tightness	○	○					○						○	○
Normal operation														
Characteristics inspection												●		●

⇨ The fan and the armature are very likely causes of vibration.

● = strong relationship
○ = relationship
△ = weak relationship

⇨ Consider problems of automatic equipment such as torque adjustment of tightening machinery, capacity of balancing machinery, capacity of vibration determination equipment, mounting equipment, mounting capacity, etc.

*Noriyuki Oda, "Case Studies of Improvement Activities Which Apply the Seven New Tools of QC to Defective Processes," *Hinshitsu Kanri (Quality Control*, 36 (May 1985 Special Issue): 292.

Figure 23-3: **T-type Matrix for Theme "Small Vacuum Cleaner Vibration Defects"***

The analysis in this example shows that among components, fans and armatures are often significant sources of vibration defects. Problems in the precision of automatic machinery (sorters, bolt tighteners, etc.) used during the production process also can produce vibration defects. Now that the major factors have been determined, you can proceed with an improvement plan.

References

Higuchi, Toshio and Tsutomu Kato. "Improvement Activities in the Work Place." *Hinshitsu Kanri (Quality Control)*, 35 (May 1984 Special Issue): 117.

Nayatani, Yoshinobu, ed. "A Lecture on the New Seven Tools of QC." Japanese Standards Association, 1987.

Oda, Noriyuki. "Case Studies of Improvement Activities Which Apply the Seven New Tools of QC to Defective Processes." *Hinshitsu Kanri (Quality Control)*, 36 (May 1985 Special Issue): 292.

Arrow Diagrams

An arrow diagram* uses a network of arrows to represent the activities in a daily schedule. The order of the steps of a process and their relation to one another are represented by a network of connected arrows and points (see Figure 24-1).

Some types of daily plans can be designed and managed efficiently using arrow diagrams. Arrow diagrams have the following advantages over the Gantt charts often used to make daily schedules:

1. They make it easy to determine the effect a slowdown in one operation will have on related operations and on the entire schedule.

---

* Arrow diagrams are derived from the scheduling diagrams of the Program Evaluation and Review Technique (PERT) developed by the U.S. Navy in 1958.

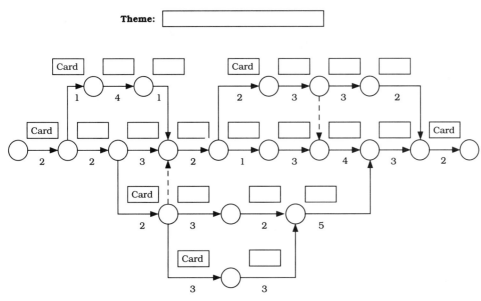

Figure 24-1: **Conceptual Chart of an Arrow Diagram**

2. They make it easy to determine which operations can be performed in parallel and which operations need to be speeded up to shorten the schedule.
3. They make it clear which operations should be managed most strictly to meet a final delivery date.
4. They enable you to make appropriate revisions to your plan without disrupting the entire schedule if an operation is unavoidably delayed and additional operations become necessary.

How to Make an Arrow Diagram

Arrow diagrams consist essentially of arrows and circles. Follow these rules when you draw an arrow diagram.

Graphic Symbols and Terminology

1. The operation, connection point, connection point number, and dummy symbols and their meanings are shown in Figure 24-2 and Table 24-1.

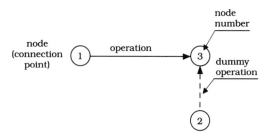

Figure 24-2: **Elements of an Arrow Diagram**

Element	Symbol	Meaning	Notes
Operation	⟶ (solid line with arrow)	Work, operations, and items that must be implemented to fulfill plan	Write time required next to operation; arrow length need not be proportional to time required
Node (connection point)	○ (circle mark)	Distinguishes preceding from subsequent operations	
Node number	(number inside the circle)	Shows the sequence of operations	Write a number in the circle for the sequence
Dummy operation	⤏ (broken line with arrow)	Shows sequential relationship for combining the relative timings of parallel operations	Time required not necessary

Table 24-1: **Arrow Diagram Symbols and Definitions**

2. Previous operations and subsequent operations: Where operation B cannot begin until operation A has ended, operation A is the previous operation for operation B and operation B is the subsequent operation for operation A. Figure 24-3 shows this relationship.

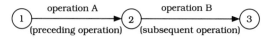

Figure 24-3: **Preceding Operations and Subsequent Operations**

3. Parallel operations: When operation A and operation B are proceeding during the same time period, they are operating in parallel. Operations A and B in Figure 24-4 are an example of parallel operations.

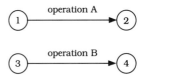

Figure 24-4: **Parallel Operations**

Basic Rules

1. A single pair of connection point numbers should indicate only one operation. This means that two connection points should be linked by only one arrow. To keep this rule, use a dummy, a broken-line arrow that indicates correlation among jobs, but no time relationship (see Figure 24-5).

- *Expressing two operations being performed in parallel:* Express parallel operations as shown in Figure 24-5(b). Do not use the format shown in Figure 24-5(a).

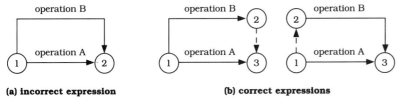

(a) incorrect expression   **(b) correct expressions**

Figure 24-5: **Displaying Parallel Operations**

- *Expressing parallel operations that also have relations of precedence:* For example, for operations A, B, C, and D in Figure 24-6, operation C is a subsequent operation for operations A and B. Operation D is a subsequent operation for operation B. Use a dummy to express this relationship, as shown in Figure 24-6.

2. Do not make a loop in related operations. For example, you should not make a loop such as the one involving operations B, C, and E shown in Figure 24-7. The sequence of operations cannot proceed in a cycle as shown in the figure.

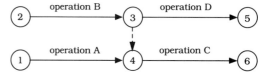

Figure 24-6: **Displaying Preceding, Subsequent, and Parallel Operations Using Dummy Operations**

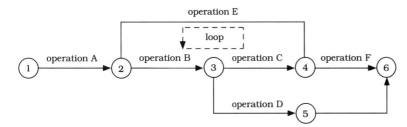

Figure 24-7: **Loop**

3. Do not use an unnecessary dummy operation. For example, in Figure 24-8(a), d_1, d_2, and d_3 are unnecessary dummy operations. You should draw a diagram resembling Figure 24-8(b).

(a) Example of unnecessary dummy operations

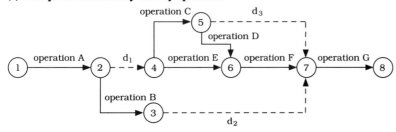

(b) This expression avoids unnecessary operations

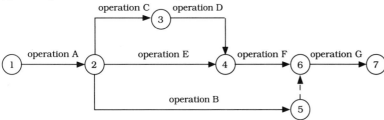

Figure 24-8: **Unnecessary Dummy Operations**

Steps for Making an Arrow Diagram

To execute a plan based on the theme selected, hold a group discussion to design the schedule. Use the following steps to create an arrow diagram as you develop this schedule.

STEP 1: Listing the operations needed

Make a straightforward list of the operations you will need to accomplish the theme.

STEP 2: Making operation cards

List all the operations required. Write each operation on a single card. These cards are called operation cards.

STEP 3: Arranging the operation cards

Spread out the cards on a large sheet of paper. Arrange them from the left to the right of the paper according to the relationships among preceding and subsequent operations. Eliminate unnecessary or redundant cards. If there has been an omission, write out a card and place it with the other operation cards.

STEP 4: Determining the position of operation cards

Place the series of operation cards that contains the most cards in the center, leaving spaces between the cards to draw in nodes (connection points). Place operation cards related to operations that can be carried out in parallel either above or below cards for operations that have the same timing.

STEP 5: Making an arrow diagram

After determining the positions of all the operation cards, paste or tape the cards in place. Draw arrows linking the nodes. Using a dummy if necessary, write in the node numbers in the order in which the operations are carried out.

STEP 6: Writing in the amount of time required

Determine the amount of time required to complete each operation and write it in under the arrow for that operation.

Ways to Use Arrow Diagrams

Use arrow diagrams when you know the causes of the problem and have devised a specific plan for solving it, but you are troubled by the complexities involved in actually implementing the plan. Arrow diagrams guide you to a dependable solution by scheduling the procedure for solving the problem.

Guidelines

1. Estimate the number of days required to complete each operation. Do not leave an additional margin for fear that a good link-up will not be made with the subsequent operation.

2. Find the longest path from the beginning to the end of the arrow diagram on the schedule (called the critical path). Note this path with a heavy or colored line to emphasize the critical points for daily management.

3. Make it clear which operations have a safety margin and which operations do not. Determine the effect a delay in a certain operation will have on the entire schedule.

4. Shorten the length of the entire schedule by reducing the number of days needed to complete the longest path (the critical path) on the schedule. Moreover, if you discover an operation that can proceed in parallel with another operation, place it in parallel with another operation on the schedule.

5. If you are unable to reduce the number of days needed to complete the critical path, change the operating conditions, contents, or position of that operation to shorten the length of the entire schedule.

6. Construct arrow diagrams according to the size, contents, management goals, and so on, of the subject. Use the time scale from Gantt charts to make the arrow diagram easier to understand.

7. If the path branches off to several different subsequent operations, depending on factors that cannot be determined at the planning stage, you will not be

able to make a definite schedule for the operation at that stage. In this situation, use a decision box (shown as a diamond shape in Figure 24-9) to represent the voluntary decision branching point.

Figure 24-10 shows an arrow diagram designed to facilitate precise scheduling to avoid delays in a plan and reduce waste and losses in a stainless steel pipe vinyl chloride lining process. It was developed through cooperation between the departments concerned.

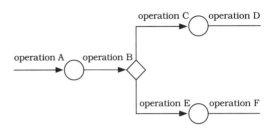

***Figure 24-9:* Decision Box**

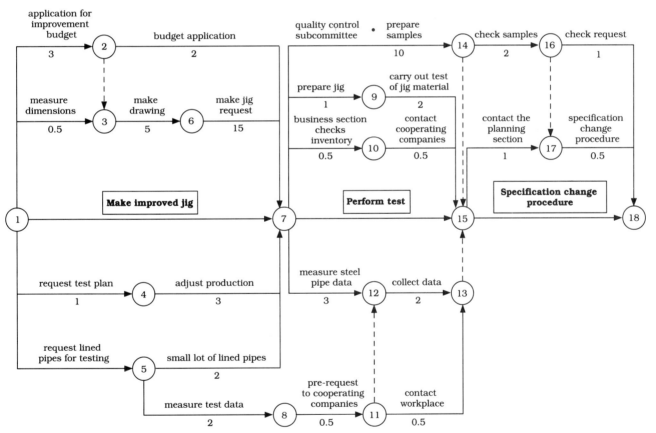

*Yutaka Yokoi, "Reducing Losses of Chloryl Vinyl Hot Water Pipes," *FQC*, 262 (August, 1984): 53.

Figure 24-10:* Arrow Diagram for Theme "Reducing Vinyl Chloride Lined Pipe Losses"

References

Futami, Ryoji. *Graphical Methods for TQC*. JUSE Press Ltd., 1985.

The Seven New QC Tools Research Group, ed. *The Seven New QC Tools Made Easy*. JUSE Press Ltd., 1984.

Yokoi, Yutaka. "Reducing Losses of Chloryl Vinyl Hot Water Pipes." *FQC*, 262 (August, 1984): 53.

Appendices

Number	Year	Theme	Slogan
1	1960	(None)	• Make Customers Happy by Eliminating Dispersion • Repair Defects — the Prodigal Son • Let's All Get Involved in QC Circles
2	1961	Quality Assurance	• Trust Begins with Quality Control in the Workplace • Let's Work Together to Develop Work Standards • Let's All Be Involved in Deming Circles • A Defect = Useless Sweat • Buy Quality • It's a Vice to Put Up with a Problem • Put Quality Above Fashion
3	1962	Buy Good Products Sell Good Products	• Correct Data Is Worth a Hundred Inspirations • Choose Quality When You Buy — You'll Never Regret It • Let's Use Quality to Make a Place for Ourselves in the World • Let's Join Together to Buy and Make Good Products • Ignoring Small Losses Creates Waste
4	1963	Let's Improve Quality	• Make Good Products People Will Want to Buy and Use • Quality Month Belongs to You and Me • Good Products Bring the People of the World Together • True Quality Gives You a Happy Life • Increase Product Lifetimes by Improving Quality
5	1964	Sell Quality and Buy Quality	• Quality Builds Happy Families and Prosperous Companies • Set Standards Using Data rather than Intuition • Quality Makes You Welcome throughout the World
6	1965	Improve Reliability	• Build Reliability with Your Hands and with Sincerity • When the Seller Has Confidence, the Buyer Has No Worries • Eliminate Waste and Irregularities through Planning and Management • No Irregularities — Every Part Is Reliable • Boost Reliability — Boost Confidence
7	1966	Quality Control Preserves Profitability Benefits of Quality Control to Consumers	• Boost Profitability and Reliability through QC • Quality Is a Blend of Attentiveness and Creativity • Reliability Is Lost One Defect at a Time • Quality Control Makes Consumers Dream Greater Dreams • Good Products Can Be Seen in the Faces of Customers
8	1967	Export Quality throughout the World Preserve Profitability through Quality Control	• Satisfy the World and Enrich Japan through QC • Build Quality that the Customer Will Want to Buy Again • Show Japan's Potential through Quality Control • QC Is Everyone's Efforts rather than One Person's Voice • Adhere to Standards and Eliminate Defects in Your Work
9	1968	Stay Competitive in the World Market through QC Live Wisely with Good Quality Products	• Use Quality Control to Ride Out Difficulties During Trade Liberalization • Data Shows How to Prevent Defects • Solve Problems in Your Circle and Create a Happy Workplace • Rely on QC to Stay Competitive in the World Market • Live Wisely with Good Quality Products

Appendix 1: **Quality Month Themes and Slogans**

Number	Year	Theme	Slogan
10	1969	Make the World Prosperous through Good Products Good Products Enrich Life	• Quality Control Builds Reliability and Profitability • Make Good Products That Meet Specifications • I Guarantee This Product I Made • Use Circles to Eliminate Losses and Irregularities in the Workplace • Quality Control with the Customer (the Next Process) in Mind
11	1970	Leap Ahead into the Seventies Put a Smile on the Customer's Face through Quality Control	• A New Era in Quality and Technology Begins • Our QC Derives from Practice rather than Theory • Our Workplace Does Not Make Defective Products • Small Circles, Big Activities • Quality Control with the Customer in Mind
12	1971	Enrich Society through Quality Control	• Quality Is the Key to a Wealthier Future • Trust Won through Quality Control Opens Up New Markets • You and I are Responsible for Assuring Quality • QC Unlocks Intelligence and Skills • Use QC to Open Up the World Market
13	1972	Comprehensive Quality Inspection in the Age of Internationalization	• Good Products Are Born of Creativity and Hard Work • Circles Build Personal and Social Harmony • Make Good Products That Consumers Want • Build on QC to Win the World's Confidence • Quality Starts from the Conscientiousness of Each Individual
14	1973	Build the Prosperity of Mankind through Quality	• Quality Depends on Human Harmony and Technology • Use QC Programs in which the Entire Work Force Participates to Send Good Products throughout the World • Create a Cheerful Society in which People Make and Use Quality Products • Send Good Quality, Affordable Products to Consumers • Build Quality to Create the Future
15	1974	Relying on Quality Control to Get Through a Turbulent Period Today's Consumers Make Wise Choices	• Don't Let Turbulent Times Affect Quality — Build for a Brighter Future • QC Creates a New Era in Resource Utilization • Use Quality Control to Eliminate Waste and Avoid Difficulties Caused by Irregularities • Manage Processes with Your Eyes and Mind on Quality • Consumers Wisely Choose Good Products
16	1975	Steady Growth through Quality Control Good Quality Builds a Good Society	• Use Quality Control to Utilize Important Resources Effectively • Build a Secure Tomorrow through Quality Control • Sincerity and Improved Technology Creates Good Products • QC is Everyone's Cooperation rather than One Person's Intelligence • Contribute to Society and to a Better Life through Quality Control
17	1976	Improve Organization through Quality Control Use Quality Control to Enrich Life	• Improve Quality to Strengthen the Organization • Create Good Products through Creativity and Hard Work • Win Trust through Quality Control to Build a Better Future • Make Promises You Can Keep — Quality Assurance • What Is Good Quality? Know It When You See It!

Number	Year	Theme	Slogan
18	1977	Quality Control Is the Foundation of Your Business Stimulate the Imagination to Create Breakthroughs	• Quality Control Builds the Foundation of Business • A Company Proud of Quality Has a Future • Gather Together Everyone's Small Insights to Make a Great Improvement • Workplace Circles Are Built on Human Harmony • Build Good Products the Customer Wants
19	1978	Stimulate the Imagination The entire work force can participate in Quality Control	• Everyone Should Think about and Play a Role in Carrying Out QC Activities • Build Quality by Enriching the Imagination • Tidying Up Data Distorts Reality • A Company that Relies on Quality for Its Growth Has a Future • Don't Keep Quiet about Defects
20	1979	Quality Control for the Eighties Build Japan's Future through Quality	• Quality Is a Bridge Between Business and Society • Efforts to Make High Quality Products Build the Future • "Just about right," "Maybe," and "Probably" Are Fatal • Our Circle Activities Support Quality • Quality Control Makes Effective Use of Limited Resources
21	1980	Challenging the Limits — Quality Control Choose the Real Thing over Imitations	• Don't Sacrifice Quality in Turbulent Times — Build for a Better Future • A New Era of Quality Control to Utilize Resources Effectively • Challenge What You See as Limits • Data Teaches You about Waste and Irregularities • Do Your "Individual Work" in Your Circle Instead of by Yourself
22	1981	Good Products Make the World Prosperous Use QC to Put Your Business on a Sound Footing	• Quality Builds Trust Between Business and Society • Quality Is Built in By Each Individual • QC Creates a Happy Workplace in which Everyone Plays a Role • Circles Make It Possible for Everyone to Participate in Management • Make Good Products that People Will Want to Buy and Use
23	1982	Make a Contribution to the World through Quality Control Make Better Products through Intelligence and Effort	• Companies that Promote TQC Have a Bright Future • Improvements Arise from Asking Why Five Times • Standardize the Trail Blazed by the Improvement Process • Promote TQC Circles in which Everyone Plays a Role • The Wisdom to Choose the Proper Degree of Quality
24	1983	Realize the Potential of the Company through TQC Quality Control — Doing What Should Be Done	• Quality Is the Face and the Heart of the Company • TQC Is the Wisdom of All, Not of One • Never Say that Any Improvement Is Final • Determine Standards Precisely and Observe Them Strictly • QC Circles Are Circles of Wisdom, of Human Harmony, and of the Workplace

Number	Year	Theme	Slogan
25	1984	Face the Challenges of the Future with TQC Determine the Facts to Do Your Work Properly	• Everyone Should Learn and Utilize QC Methods to Improve Quality • Reliability Is Built Up Over a Long Period through the Participation of All Personnel in Quality Control • A Small Clue Can Produce Excellent Results. Everyone Should Work to Improve the Workplace • After Finishing the Arduous Task, Standardize It • Build in Quality So People Will Want to Purchase the Product
26	1985	Spread QC To Invigorate the Company Go Around the PDCA Circle Properly to Enrich the Workplace	• Quality Is a Company's Public Image • Everyone Can Use QC Methods to Produce Excellent Results • Open Your Eyes — Potential Improvement Themes Are Everywhere • Good Results Are Built on Correct Fundamentals • Quality Control Gives Us Rich Life and Peace of Mind in Using Products
27	1986	Use TQC to Get Through Changes in the Business Environment Quality Comes First — This Is Fundamental	• TQC Involving All Employees Increases the Energy of Companies • Quality Is the Product of Many Correct Procedures • Standards Are Your Work Partner — Make Them, Observe Them, Modify Them • QC Circles Support Business when Everyone in the Company Has a Role • Focus the Attention of Society on Quality
28	1987	Quality Is a Common World Language Broaden QC — Put Customers First	• TQC Is the Combination of People, Wisdom, and Management Circles • Make Quality from the User's Point of View • Use Data to Assure Quality Based on the Facts • Maintain What Has Already Been Determined; Standardize New Levels of Quality • QC Circles in which All Employees Participate Increase the Energy of the Workplace

Year	Standardization and Quality Control Activities	Events in Society and Industry
1945	• Japanese Standards Association (JSA) founded	• End of World War II
1946	• Industrial Standards Committee founded, Japanese Standards (New JES) system established • Japan Science and Technology Federation founded	
1947	• International Standards Organization (ISO) founded	• Monopoly Prohibition Act, Minimum Labor Standards Act promulgated
1948	• Exchange of standards with foreign countries begins (JSA)	
1949	• First Quality Control Study Conference opens (JSA) • Industrial Standards Law goes into effect (sets Japanese Industrial Standard (JIS) mark system) • GHQ holds CCS lectures to teach business leaders about quality control	
1950	• Dr. Deming comes to Japan and gives seminars • Agriculture, Forestry, and Resources Standards Act (JAS marks) established	• Construction Standards Law promulgated • Foreign Investment Law promulgated
1951	• Japan Science and Technology Federation establishes the Deming Prize • Weights and Measures Law reforms the system of weights and measures — MKS unit system adopted • The First Quality Control Conference held	• The San Francisco Peace Treaty • Japan - U.S. Mutual Security Treaty signed
1952	• Name of Industrial Technology Agency changed to Agency of Industrial Science and Technology • Japanese Industrial Standards Study Association joins the International Standards Association (ISO)	
1953	• System established for training JIS inspectors in scientific quality control techniques • Quality control and standardization seminar begins (JSA) • Japanese Industrial Standards Study Committee joins the International Electrical Standards Conference (IEC) • Awards established: Outstanding Factory for Implementation of Industrial Standardization Award, the MITI Minister's Award, the Agency of Industrial Science and Technology Award, and the MITI Agency Head's Award	• Korean armistice signed • NHK begins television broadcasting
1954	• Transition from old JES, temporary JES, and new JES to JIS completed • Dr. Juran visits Japan and gives seminars	
1955	• Japan Productivity Center (JPC) founded	• Japan joins GATT
1956	• Japan begins shortwave broadcasting of "Quality Control Lectures" • Japan elected a member of the ISO (1957 to 1959)	• Japan joins the United Nations

Appendix 2: **Chronology of Standardization and Quality Control**

Year	Standardization and Quality Control Activities	Events in Society and Industry
1957	• Japan begins shortwave broadcasting of the educational program "Standardizing Inside the Company"	• The Kotake prosperity gives way to a long, lingering recession • The Law on Consulting Engineers promulgated
1958	• First National Standardization Conference held (JSA) • Changeover from SQC to TQC begins	• Law on the Inspection of Exports goes into force
1959	• Television educational programs on quality control and standardization begin • Japan Industrial Engineering Society founded	• Export volume returns to its prewar level (Iwato prosperity)
1960	• First Quality Control Month observed (JSA, Japan Science and Technology Federation)	
1961		• Japan Consumers' Association founded
1962	• Japan Science and Technology Federation promotes the formation of QC circles • Leader's Conference within the Quality Control Conference established • Electrical Products Regulatory Law goes into effect • Household Products Quality Marking Law goes into effect	
1963	• Top Executives Conference within the Quality Control Association established • QC Circle Center established within the Japan Science and Technology Federation	• Fundamental Law on Small and Medium Sized Enterprises goes into effect
1964	• Branch offices to support quality circle activities established in Kanto, Tokai, Kinki, and Hokuriku	• Tokai route of the Shinkansen (bullet train) completed • Tokyo Olympics held
1965	• First Quality Control Symposium held • 30th IEC Conference held in Tokyo	
1966	• Industrial Standardization Law Revised, application of the JIS mark system to processing technologies begins	• Unprecedented economic boom (Izanagi prosperity)
1967	• The First National Q-S Conference held (JSA)	• The Vietnam War intensifies
1968	• First training seminar on industrial standardization and quality control for developing countries held (Overseas Cooperation Agency, JSA)	• Japan's gross national product (GNP) is second among the free enterprise economies • Consumer Protection Law goes into effect • Noise Regulation Law and Air Pollution Prevention Law promulgated

Year	Standardization and Quality Control Activities	Events in Society and Industry
1969	• First International Quality Control Conference (ICQC) held in Tokyo	• Apollo 11 lands on the Moon
1970	• Japan Science and Technology Federation establishes the Japan Quality Control Award	• Expo '70 held in Osaka
1971	• Japan Quality Control Association founded • ISO standards adopts the international units system (SI) • The first QC circle seagoing university goes into operation (Japan Science and Technology Federation)	• Nixon ends gold-backed dollar • Transition to a variable market in foreign exchange rates
1972	• System developed for recognizing factories with outstanding quality control in business, industry, housing, and other fields	• okinawa returned to Japan • Consumer Product Safety Law goes into effect
1973	• Draft agreement to prevent the standards approval system of different countries from serving as a non-tariff trade barrier (GATT standard code)	• Vietnam War ends • Gas Removal Regulatory Law goes into effect • First oil shock
1974	• Ministry of Health and Welfare issues GMP Report, voluntary QC regulatory system for pharmaceutical manufacturing strengthened	• Inflationary surge
1975		• Sanyo Shinkansen line completed • Okinawa Aquarium opens
1976	• First East Asia QC Circle International Conference held in Seoul	• Viking 1 lands on Mars
1977	• Public agencies form Construction Q-S Round Table Discussion Group	• Recession due to high value of yen
1978	• Japan begins exchanging quality control technology with the People's Republic of China • First International QC Circle Conference held in Tokyo	• Narita Airport opens • Japan - China treaty of peace and friendship signed
1979	• GATT Tokyo round (multilateral trade negotiations) signed and submitted for ratification • Japan becomes a permanent member of the ISO	• Second oil shock • Tokyo summit
1980	• Industrial Standardization Law modified • Foreign factories given permission to use the JIS mark system • In Japan, an inspection system is introduced for JIS Marking approved factories	• Japan becomes world's top producer of automobiles and steel
1981	• New system implemented in which JIS marking approved factories become responsible for industry standardization and quality control	• Portopia '81 (Kobe) held • First flight of the space shuttle

Year	Standardization and Quality Control Activities	Events in Society and Industry
1982	• System for publication of inspection results of JIS marking approved factories begins	• Tohoku and Joetsu Shinkansen lines open
1983	• Forty-Eighth IEC Conference held in Tokyo	• Seikan tunnel completed
1984	• Seminar on JIS held in the USA	• Trade friction worsens
1985	• Thirteenth ISO Conference held in Tokyo	• Tsukuba '85 Science Exposition held

About the Editors

Tetsuichi Asaka, born in 1914, graduated in 1939 from the School of Science, Department of Mathematics, of Tokyo University. He became instructor at Tokyo University School of Engineering in 1946 and Professor in 1958. Currently he is Professor Emeritus at Tokyo University.

Kazuo Ozeki was born in 1930. On graduating from the School of Engineering, Department of Statistical Engineering, Tokyo University, in 1953, he joined Nippon Seiko. He is currently the director of the Human Development Department at Nippon Seiko.

Index

Other Books and AVs on Quality

Productivity Press publishes and distributes materials on continuous improvement in productivity, quality, customer service, and the creative involvement of all employees. Many of our products are direct source materials from Japan that have been translated into English for the first time and are available exclusively from Productivity. Supplemental products and services include newsletters, conferences, seminars, in-house training and consulting, audio-visual training programs, and industrial study missions. Call 1-800-274-9911 for our free book catalog.

Quality Function Deployment
Integrating Customer Requirements into Product Design

edited by Yoji Akao

More and more, companies are using quality function deployment, or QFD, to identify their customers' requirements, translate them into quantified quality characteristics and then build them into their products and services. This casebook introduces the concept of quality deployment as it has been applied in a variety of industries in Japan. The materials include numerous case studies illustrating QFD applications. Written by the creator of QFD, this book provides direct source material on Quality Function Deployment, one of the essential tools for world class manufacturing. It is a design approach based on the idea that quality is determined by the customer. Through methodology and case studies the book offers insight into how Japanese companies identify customer requirements and describes how to translate customer requirements into qualified quality characteristics, and how to build them into products and services.
ISBN 0-915299-41-0 / 400 pages / $ 75.00 / Order code QFD-BK

Managerial Engineering
Techniques for Improving Quality and Productivity in the Workplace (rev.)

by Ryuji Fukuda

A proven path to managerial success, based on reliable methods developed by one of Japan's leading productivity experts and winner of the coveted Deming Prize for quality. Dr. W. Edwards Deming, world-famous consultant on quality, says that the book "provides an excellent and clear description of the devotion and methods of Japanese management to continual improvement of quality." (CEDAC training programs also available.)
ISBN 0-915299-09-7 / 208 pages / $39.95 / Order code ME-BK

CEDAC
A Tool for Continuous Systematic Improvement

by Ryuji Fukuda

CEDAC, or Cause and Effect Diagram with the Addition of Cards, is a modification of the "fishbone diagram," one of the standard QC tools. One of the most powerful, yet simple problem-solving methods to come out of Japan (Fukuda won a Deming Prize for developing it), CEDAC actually encompasses a whole cluster of tools for continuous systematic improvement. They include window analysis (for identifying problems), the CEDAC diagram (for analyzing problems and developing standards), and window development (for ensuring adherence to standards). Here is Fukuda's manual for the in-house support of improvement activities using CEDAC. It provides step by step directions for setting up and using CEDAC. With a text that's concise, clear, and to the point, nearly 50 illustrations and sample forms suitable for transparencies, and a removable CEDAC wall chart, the manual is an ideal training aid.
ISBN 0-915299-26-7 / 144 pages / $49.95 / Order code CEDAC-BK

Productivity Press, Inc., Dept. BK, P.O. Box 3007, Cambridge, MA 02140 1-800-274-9911

TQC Solutions
A 14-Step Process

edited by JUSE Problem Solving Research Group

Foreword by Dr. H. James Harrington

Here's a clear-cut, thoroughly explained process for putting the tools of quality control to work in your company. With a strong emphasis on the use of quality control in problem solving, this book was originally written as a handbook for the Union of Japanese Scientists and Engineers' (JUSE) renowned Quality Control seminar. Filled with practical, highly useful information, it shows you not only *how* to use the 7 QC tools, the 7 "new" QC tools, and basic statistical tools, but also suggests *when* to use them. The use of charts and matrices in problem solving is carefully examined and illustrated with examples of various problems and their solutions.
ISBN 0-915299-79-8 / 448 pages, 2 volumes / $120.00 / Order TQCS-BK

TQC for Accounting
A New Role in Companywide Improvement

by Takashi Kanatsu

TQC for accounting means more than streamlining office procedures or upgrading financial analyses. It requires, instead, a linking of the basics of marketing with the fundamentals of accounting through the medium of TQC. This book is a guide for top and middle managers who wish to turn their companies around by re-designing the roles played by the accounting, sales, and marketing departments. The book's format offers detailed examinations of accounting TQC in relation to a company's business plan, accounting department, and specific statistical methods. Its use will help to create the "awareness revolution" that is imperative in turning around a factory or any type of company.
ISBN 0-915299-73-9 / 256 pages / $45.00 / Order code TQCA-BK

TQC Wisdom of Japan
Managing for Total Quality Control

by Hajime Karatsu, translated by David J. Lu

As productivity goes up, the cost of quality comes down. And as quality improves, the cost to produce comes down. Karatsu, winner of a Deming Prize who has been involved with the quality movement in Japan since its inception, discusses the purpose and techniques of Total Quality Control (TQC), how it differs from QC, and why it is so effective. There is no better introduction to TQC than this book; essential reading for all American managers.
ISBN 0-915299-18-6 / 152 pages / $34.95 / Order code WISD-BK

Measuring, Managing, and Maximizing Performance

by Will Kaydos

You do not need to be an exceptionally skilled technician or inspirational leader to improve your company's quality and productivity. In non-technical, jargon-free, practical terms this book details the entire process of improving performance, from "why" and "how" the improvement process works to "what" must be done to begin and to sustain continuous improvement of performance. Special emphasis is given to the role that performance measurement plays in identifying problems and opportunities.
ISBN 0-915299-98-4 / 304 pages / $34.95 / Order MMMP-BK

Productivity Press, Inc., Dept. BK, P.O. Box 3007, Cambridge, MA 02140 1-800-274-9911

20 Keys to Workplace Improvement

by Iwao Kobayashi

This easy-to-read introduction to the "20 keys" system presents an integrated approach to assessing and improving your company's competitive level. The book focuses on systematic improvement through five levels of achievement in such primary areas as industrial housekeeping, small group activities, quick changeover techniques, equipment maintenance, and computerization. A scoring guide is included, along with information to help plan a strategy for your company's world class improvement effort.
ISBN 0-915299-61-5 / 264 pages / $34.95 / Order code 20KEYS-BK

Management for Quality Improvement
The 7 New QC Tools

edited by Shigeru Mizuno

Building on the traditional seven QC tools, these new tools were developed specifically for managers. They help in planning, troubleshooting, and communicating with maximum effectiveness at every stage of a quality improvement program. Just recently made available in the U.S., they are certain to advance quality improvement efforts for anyone involved in project management, quality assurance, MIS, or TQC.
ISBN 0-915299-29-1 / 324 pages / $59.95 / Order code 7QC-BK

Poka-Yoke
Improving Product Quality by Preventing Defects

compiled by Nikkan Kogyo Shimbun, Ltd./Factory Magazine (ed.)

preface by Shigeo Shingo

If your goal is 100% zero defects, here is the book for you — a completely illustrated guide to poka-yoke (mistake-proofing) for supervisors and shop-floor workers. Many poka-yoke devices come from line workers and are implemented with the help of engineering staff. The result is better product quality — and greater participation by workers in efforts to improve your processes, your products, and your company as a whole.
ISBN 0-915299-31-3 / 288 pages / $59.95 / Order code IPOKA-BK

Achieving Total Quality Management
A Program for Action

by Michel Perigord

This is an outstanding book on total quality management (TQM) a compact guide to the concepts, methods, and techniques involved in achieving total quality. It shows you how to make TQM a company-wide strategy, not just in technical areas, but in marketing and administration as well. Written in an accessible, instructive style by a top European quality expert, it is methodical, logical, and thorough. An historical outline and discussion of the quality-price relationship, is followed by an investigation of the five quality imperatives (conformity, prevention, excellence, measurement, and responsibility). Major methods and tools for total quality are spelled out and implementation strategies are reviewed.
ISBN 0-915299-60-7 / 384 pages / $45.00 / Order Code ACHTQM-BK

Productivity Press, Inc., Dept. BK, P.O. Box 3007, Cambridge, MA 02140 1-800-274-9911

The Quality and Productivity Equation
American Corporate Strategies for the 1990s
edited by Ross E. Robson

How well will your business succeed in the next decade? What challenges are in store, and how are you planning to meet them? Here's what over thirty of America's most forward-thinking business and academic leaders (including John Diebold, Malcolm Forbes, Donald Ephlin, Alan Magazine, and Wickham Skinner) are already thinking about and doing. Based on presentations made at Utah State University's College of Business "Partners in Business" seminars for 1989. Take advantage of their expertise to shape your own strategy.
ISBN 0-915299-71-2 / 558 pages / $29.95 / Order code QPE-BK

Competing Through Productivity and Quality
edited by Y.K. Shetty and Vernon M. Buehler

Fifty authorities from American industry, labor, and higher education share their most up-to-date strategies and policies for productivity and quality improvement. Inspiring, insightful, and practical guidance from such people as David Halberstam, Shigeo Shingo, C. Jackson Grayson, Lynn Williams, and John Young. This book provides the information necessary to ensure the long-term economic health of the U.S.
ISBN 0-915299-43-7 / 576 pages / $39.95 / Order code COMP-BK

Zero Quality Control
Source Inspection and the Poka-yoke System
by Shigeo Shingo, translated by Andrew P. Dillon

A remarkable combination of source inspection (to detect errors before they become defects) and mistake-proofing devices (to weed out defects before they can be passed down the production line) eliminates the need for statistical quality control. Shingo shows how this proven system for reducing defects to zero turns out the highest quality products in the shortest period of time. With over 100 specific examples illustrated. (Audiovisual training program also available.)
ISBN 0-915299-07-0 / 328 pages / $70.00 / Order code ZQC-BK

The Poka-Yoke System (AV)
by Shigeo Shingo, translated by Andrew P. Dillon

Shingo shows how to implement Zero Quality Control (ZQC) on the production line with a combination of source inspection and mistake-proofing devices in this two-part program. Part I explains the theory and concepts and Part II shows practical applications. Package includes facilitator's guides with worksheets, and is available in either slide or video format (please specify when ordering). Each part is approximately 25 minutes long.
235 Slides / ISBN 0-915299-13-5 / $749.00 / Order code S6-BK
2 Videos / ISBN 0-915299-28-3 / $749.00 / Order code V6-BK

Productivity Press, Inc., Dept. BK, P.O. Box 3007, Cambridge, MA 02140 1-800-274-9911

COMPLETE LIST OF TITLES FROM PRODUCTIVITY PRESS

Akao, Yoji (ed.). **Quality Function Deployment: Integrating Customer Requirements into Product Design**
ISBN 0-915299-41-0 / 1990 / 387 pages / $ 75.00 / order code QFD

Akiyama, Kaneo. Function Analysis: **Systematic Improvement of Quality and Performance**
ISBN 0-915299-81-X / 1991 / 288 pages / $59.95 / order code FA

Asaka, Tetsuichi and Kazuo Ozeki (eds.). **Handbook of Quality Tools: The Japanese Approach**
ISBN 0-915299-45-3 / 1990 / 336 pages / $59.95 / order code HQT

Belohlav, James A. **Championship Management: An Action Model for High Performance**
ISBN 0-915299-76-3 / 1990 / 265 pages / $29.95 / order code CHAMPS

Birkholz, Charles and Jim Villella. **The Battle to Stay Competitive: Changing the Traditional Workplace**
ISBN 0-915-299-96-8 / 1991 / 110 pages / $9.95 /order code BATTLE

Christopher, William F. **Productivity Measurement Handbook**
ISBN 0-915299-05-4 / 1985 / 680 pages / $137.95 / order code PMH

D'Egidio, Franco. **The Service Era: Leadership in a Global Environment**
ISBN 0-915299-68-2 / 1990 / 165 pages / $29.95 / order code SERA

Ford, Henry. **Today and Tomorrow**
ISBN 0-915299-36-4 / 1988 / 286 pages / $24.95 / order code FORD

Fukuda, Ryuji. **CEDAC: A Tool for Continuous Systematic Improvement**
ISBN 0-915299-26-7 / 1990 / 144 pages / $49.95 / order code CEDAC

Fukuda, Ryuji. **Managerial Engineering: Techniques for Improving Quality and Productivity in the Workplace** (rev.)
ISBN 0-915299-09-7 / 1986 / 208 pages / $39.95 / order code ME

Gotoh, Fumio. **Equipment Planning for TPM: Maintenance Prevention Design**
ISBN 0-915299-77-1 / 1991 / 272 pages / $75.00 / order code ETPM

Grief, Michel. **The Visual Factory: Building Participation Through Shared Information**
ISBN 0-915299-67-4 / 1991 / 320 pages / $49.95 / order code VFAC

Hatakeyama, Yoshio. **Manager Revolution! A Guide to Survival in Today's Changing Workplace**
ISBN 0-915299-10-0 / 1986 / 208 pages / $24.95 / order code MREV

Hirano, Hiroyuki. **JIT Factory Revolution: A Pictorial Guide to Factory Design of the Future**
ISBN 0-915299-44-5 / 1989 / 227 pages / $49.95 / order code JITFAC

Hirano, Hiroyuki. **JIT Implementation Manual: The Complete Guide to Just-In-Time Manufacturing**
ISBN 0-915299-66-6 / 1990 / 1006 pages / $2500.00 / order code HIRANO

Horovitz, Jacques. **Winning Ways: Achieving Zero-Defect Service**
ISBN 0-915299-78-X / 1990 / 165 pages / $24.95 / order code WWAYS

Ishiwata, Junichi. **I.E. for the Shop Floor 1: Productivity through Process Analysis**
ISBN 0-915299-82-8 / 1991 / 208 pages / $39.95 / order code SHOPF1

Japan Human Relations Association (ed.). **The Idea Book: Improvement Through TEI (Total Employee Involvement)**
ISBN 0-915299-22-4 / 1988 / 232 pages / $49.95 / order code IDEA

Productivity Press, Inc., Dept. BK, P.O. Box 3007, Cambridge, MA 02140 1-800-274-9911

Japan Human Relations Association (ed.). **The Service Industry Idea Book: Employee Involvement in Retail and Office Improvement**
ISBN 0-915299-65-8 / 1990 / 294 pages / $49.95 / order code SIDEA

Japan Management Association (ed.). **Kanban and Just-In-Time at Toyota: Management Begins at the Workplace** (rev.), Translated by David J. Lu
ISBN 0-915299-48-8 / 1989 / 224 pages / $36.50 / order code KAN

Japan Management Association and Constance E. Dyer. **The Canon Production System: Creative Involvement of the Total Workforce**
ISBN 0-915299-06-2 / 1987 / 251 pages / $36.95 / order code CAN

Jones, Karen (ed.). **The Best of TEI: Current Perspectives on Total Employee Involvement**
ISBN 0-915299-63-1 / 1989 / 502 pages / $175.00 / order code TEI

JUSE. **TQC Solutions: The 14-Step Process**
ISBN 0-915299-79-8 / 1991 / 416 pages / 2 volumes / $120.00 / order code TQCS

Kanatsu, Takashi. **TQC for Accounting: A New Role in Companywide Improvement**
ISBN 0-915299-73-9 / 1991 / 244 pages / $45.00 / order code TQCA

Karatsu, Hajime. **Tough Words For American Industry**
ISBN 0-915299-25-9 / 1988 / 178 pages / $24.95 / order code TOUGH

Karatsu, Hajime. **TQC Wisdom of Japan: Managing for Total Quality Control**, Translated by David J. Lu
ISBN 0-915299-18-6 / 1988 / 136 pages / $34.95 / order code WISD

Kato, Kenichiro. **I.E. for the Shop FLoor 2: Productivity through Motion Study**
ISBN 1-56327-000-5 / 1991 / 224 pages / $39.95 / order code SHOPF2

Kaydos, Will. **Measuring, Managing, and Maximizing Performance**
ISBN 0-915299-98-4 / 1991 / 208 pages / $34.95 / order code MMMP

Kobayashi, Iwao. **20 Keys to Workplace Improvement**
ISBN 0-915299-61-5 / 1990 / 264 pages / $34.95 / order code 20KEYS

Lu, David J. **Inside Corporate Japan: The Art of Fumble-Free Management**
ISBN 0-915299-16-X / 1987 / 278 pages / $24.95 / order code ICJ

Maskell, Brain H. **Performance Measurement for World Class Manufacturing: A Model for American Companies**
ISBN 0-915299-99-2 / 1991 / 448 pages / $45.00 / order code PERFM

Merli, Giorgio. **Total Manufacturing Management: Production Organization for the 1990s**
ISBN 0-915299-58-5 / 1990 / 304 pages / $39.95 / order code TMM

Mizuno, Shigeru (ed.). **Management for Quality Improvement: The 7 New QC Tools**
ISBN 0-915299-29-1 / 1988 / 324 pages / $59.95 / order code 7QC

Monden, Yasuhiro and Michiharu Sakurai (eds.). **Japanese Management Accounting: A World Class Approach to Profit Management**
ISBN 0-915299-50-X / 1990 / 568 pages / $59.95 / order code JMACT

Nachi-Fujikoshi (ed.). **Training for TPM: A Manufacturing Success Story**
ISBN 0-915299-34-8 / 1990 / 272 pages / $59.95 / order code CTPM

Nakajima, Seiichi. **Introduction to TPM: Total Productive Maintenance**
ISBN 0-915299-23-2 / 1988 / 149 pages / $39.95 / order code ITPM

Nakajima, Seiichi. **TPM Development Program: Implementing Total Productive Maintenance**
ISBN 0-915299-37-2 / 1989 / 428 pages / $85.00 / order code DTPM

Productivity Press, Inc., Dept. BK, P.O. Box 3007, Cambridge, MA 02140 1-800-274-9911

Nikkan Kogyo Shimbun, Ltd./Factory Magazine (ed.). **Poka-yoke: Improving Product Quality by Preventing Defects**
ISBN 0-915299-31-3 / 1989 / 288 pages / $59.95 / order code IPOKA

NKS/Esme McTighe (ed.). **Factory Management Notebook Series: Mixed Model Production**
ISBN 0-915299-97-6 / 1991 / 184 pages / $175.00 / order code N1-MM

NKS/Esme McTighe (ed.). **Factory Management Notebook Series: Visual Control Systems**
ISBN 0-915299-54-2 / 1991 / 194 pages / $175.00 / order code N1-VCS

NKS/Esme McTighe (ed.). **Factory Management Notebook Series: Autonomation/ Automation**
ISBN 0-56327-002-1 / 1991 / 200 pages / $175.00 / order code N1-AA

Ohno, Taiichi. **Toyota Production System: Beyond Large-scale Production**
ISBN 0-915299-14-3 / 1988 / 162 pages / $39.95 / order code OTPS

Ohno, Taiichi. **Workplace Management**
ISBN 0-915299-19-4 / 1988 / 165 pages / $34.95 / order code WPM

Ohno, Taiichi and Setsuo Mito. **Just-In-Time for Today and Tomorrow**
ISBN 0-915299-20-8 / 1988 / 208 pages / $34.95 / order code OMJIT

Perigord, Michel. **Achieving Total Quality Management: A Program for Action**
ISBN 0-915299-60-7 / 1991 / 384 pages / $45.00 / order code ACHTQM

Psarouthakis, John. **Better Makes Us Best**
ISBN 0-915299-56-9 / 1989 / 112 pages / $16.95 / order code BMUB

Robinson, Alan. **Continuous Improvement in Operations: A Systematic Approach to Waste Reduction**
ISBN 0-915299-51-8 / 1991 / 416 pages / $34.95 / order code ROB2-C

Robson, Ross (ed.). **The Quality and Productivity Equation: American Corporate Strategies for the 1990s**
ISBN 0-915299-71-2 / 1990 / 558 pages / $29.95 / order code QPE

Shetty, Y.K and Vernon M. Buehler (eds.). **Competing Through Productivity and Quality**
ISBN 0-915299-43-7 / 1989 / 576 pages / $39.95 / order code COMP

Shingo, Shigeo. **Non-Stock Production: The Shingo System for Continuous Improvement**
ISBN 0-915299-30-5 / 1988 / 480 pages / $75.00 / order code NON

Shingo, Shigeo. **A Revolution In Manufacturing: The SMED System**, Translated by Andrew P. Dillon
ISBN 0-915299-03-8 / 1985 / 383 pages / $70.00 / order code SMED

Shingo, Shigeo. **The Sayings of Shigeo Shingo: Key Strategies for Plant Improvement**, Translated by Andrew P. Dillon
ISBN 0-915299-15-1 / 1987 / 208 pages / $39.95 / order code SAY

Shingo, Shigeo. **A Study of the Toyota Production System from an Industrial Engineering Viewpoint** (rev.)
ISBN 0-915299-17-8 / 1989 / 293 pages / $39.95 / order code STREV

Shingo, Shigeo. **Zero Quality Control: Source Inspection and the Poka-yoke System**, Translated by Andrew P. Dillon
ISBN 0-915299-07-0 / 1986 / 328 pages / $70.00 / order code ZQC

Shinohara, Isao (ed.). **New Production System: JIT Crossing Industry Boundaries**
ISBN 0-915299-21-6 / 1988 / 224 pages / $34.95 / order code NPS

Productivity Press, Inc., Dept. BK, P.O. Box 3007, Cambridge, MA 02140 1-800-274-9911

Sugiyama, Tomo. **The Improvement Book: Creating the Problem-Free Workplace**
ISBN 0-915299-47-X / 1989 / 236 pages / $49.95 / order code IB

Suzue, Toshio and Akira Kohdate. **Variety Reduction Program (VRP): A Production Strategy for Product Diversification**
ISBN 0-915299-32-1 / 1990 / 164 pages / $59.95 / order code VRP

Tateisi, Kazuma. **The Eternal Venture Spirit: An Executive's Practical Philosophy**
ISBN 0-915299-55-0 / 1989 / 208 pages/ $19.95 / order code EVS

Yasuda, Yuzo. **40 Years, 20 Million Ideas: The Toyota Suggestion System**
ISBN 0-915299-74-7 / 1991 / 210 pages / $39.95 / order code 4020

Audio-Visual Programs

Japan Management Association. **Total Productive Maintenance: Maximizing Productivity and Quality**
ISBN 0-915299-46-1 / 167 slides / 1989 / $749.00 / order code STPM
ISBN 0-915299-49-6 / 2 videos / 1989 / $749.00 / order code VTPM

Shingo, Shigeo. **The SMED System**, Translated by Andrew P. Dillon
ISBN 0-915299-11-9 / 181 slides / 1986 / $749.00 / order code S5
ISBN 0-915299-27-5 / 2 videos / 1987 / $749.00 / order code V5

Shingo, Shigeo. **The Poka-yoke System**, Translated by Andrew P. Dillon
ISBN 0-915299-13-5 / 235 slides / 1987 / $749.00 / order code S6
ISBN 0-915299-28-3 / 2 videos / 1987 / $749.00 / order code V6

Returns of AV programs willl be accepted for incorrect or damaged shipments only.

TO ORDER: Write, phone, or fax Productivity Press, Dept. BK, P.O. Box 3007, Cambridge, MA 02140, phone 1-800-274-9911, fax 617-864-6286. Send check or charge to your credit card (American
Express, Visa, MasterCard accepted).

U.S. ORDERS: Add $5 shipping for first book, $2 each additional for UPS surface delivery. CT residents add 8% and MA residents 5% sales tax. For each AV program that you order, add $5 for programs with 1 or 2 tapes, and $12 for programs with 3 or more tapes.

INTERNATIONAL ORDERS: Write, phone, or fax for quote and indicate shipping method desired. Pre-payment in U.S. dollars must accompany your order (checks must be drawn on U.S. banks). When quote is returned with payment, your order will be shipped promptly by the method requested.

NOTE: Prices subject to change without notice.